Marisol

Foreword

Marisol (1930-2016) remains one of the most radical and visionary artists of her generation. Born María Sol Escobar, in Paris to Venezuelan parents, she moved to New York at age 20, where she would live and work for much of her life. In the early 1960s, she made a splash on the international art scene with her carved and painted wooden sculptures of life-sized human figures, often combined with found objects and plaster casts of parts of her own body in large tableaux merging Pop and folk art. Her art references early Mesoamerican and South American cultures as well as the contemporary American juggernaut of consumerism and celebrity culture. Frequently revolving around her self-portrait, Marisol's universe is at once unsettling and colourful, dark and humorous. Her works are loaded with existential questions and powerful political statements about entrenched gender roles and equality.

Marisol quickly became a star on the New York avant-garde art scene. She was a close friend of Andy Warhol who featured her in some of his early experimental films. In 1957, the renowned gallerist Leo Castelli organised Marisol's first one-woman show in New York, and awareness of her work continued to grow. In 1968, she represented Venezuela at the Venice Biennale, and she was one of only four women among the 149 artists selected for that year's Documenta in Kassel, Germany.

Despite her fame in the 1960s, especially in the US, Marisol fell out of favour with critics and the public in the 1970s when she abandoned Pop for more overtly political art. Undaunted, she continued her work in sculpture, while exploring other media, including drawing, printmaking and photography. She also designed sets and costumes for dance

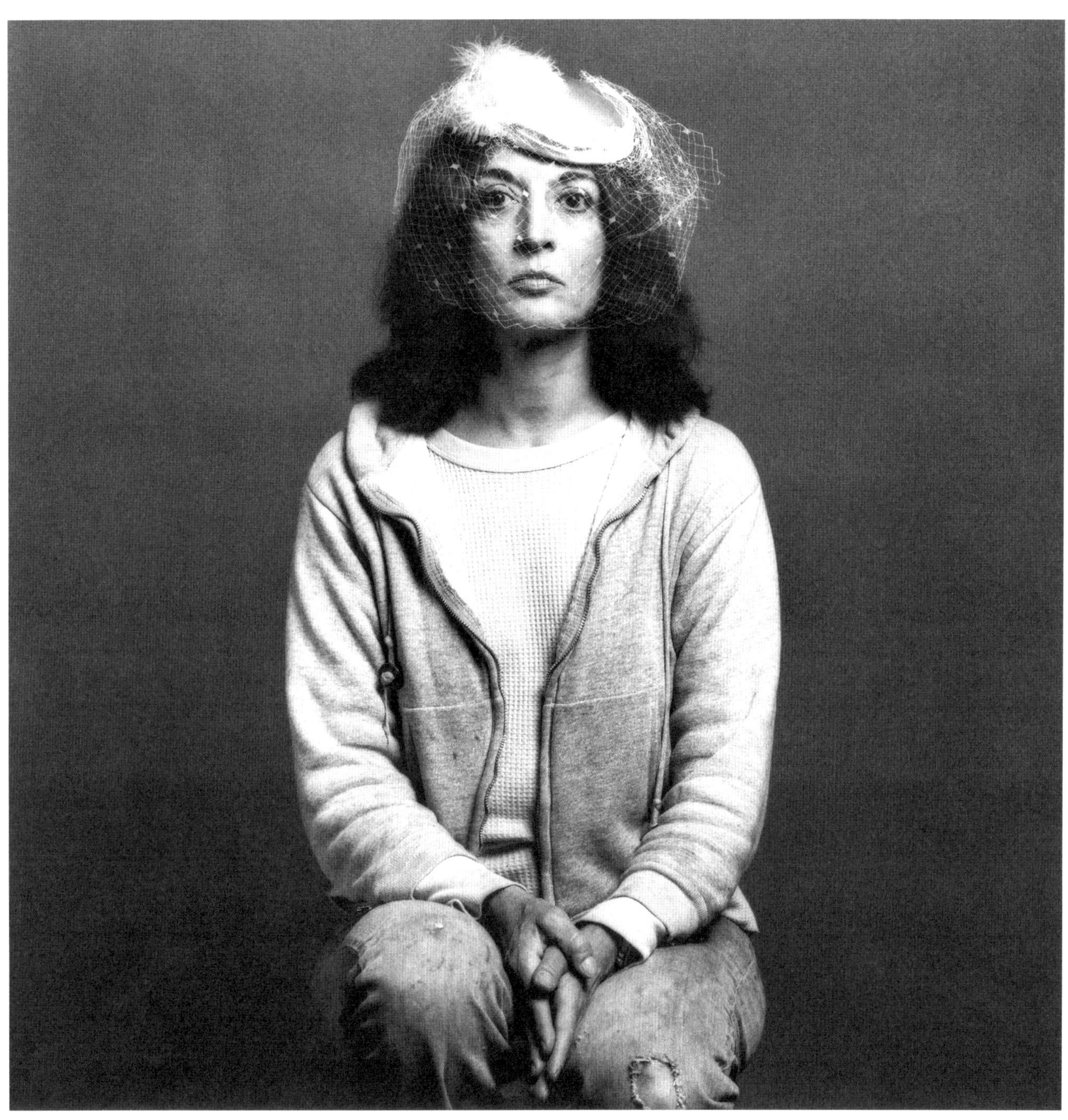

Robert Mapplethorpe: *Marisol*, 1979
Gelatin silver print, 35.08 x 35.08 cm
Collection Buffalo AKG Art Museum
Bequest of Marisol, 2016 (2022:6)

performances by Martha Graham and others, and created public monuments to historical figures, many of them in Venezuela. In her late work, Marisol used nearly every medium available to explore themes important to her – from the experiences of women and immigrants to social injustice and the human relationship to nature.

At the time of her death in 2016, she had been all but forgotten and written out of art history. From a European perspective, she remains virtually unknown. Just two of her works are in European museum collections, and she has never before been the subject of a major exhibition in Europe. Only now is Marisol's art enjoying a richly deserved comeback.

This exhibition presents more than 100 works spanning all periods and media, showcasing the full range of Marisol's art. In addition to her iconic works of the 1960s, the exhibition also highlights lesser-known aspects of her practice for the first time in Europe. A special focus is given to Marisol's wide-ranging works on paper. Throughout her career, she made drawings and prints that preserve the enigmatic intimacy of her sculptures while allowing for a broader investigation of the female body and experience.

Surveying her work in all its variety across five decades, from the 1950s to the late 1990s, this exhibition and catalogue open up a new understanding of Marisol's work, helping to reinstate her as a singular figure in the history of modern art.

Poul Erik Tøjner
Director

Kirsten Degel
Curator

Lenders
Buffalo AKG Art Museum
Art Institute of Chicago
Cisneros Fontanals Art Foundation, Miami
Colorado Springs Fine Arts Center at Colorado College
Crystal Bridges Museum of American Art, Bentonville, Arkansas
Institute of Contemporary Art, Boston
Museum Boijmans Van Beuningen, Rotterdam
Museum Ludwig, Cologne
Private collection, courtesy of Craig Starr Gallery, New York
Susan G. and Richard M. Rieser, Jr., Palm Beach, Florida
Betsy and Andy Rosenfield
Richard and Carole Cocks Art Museum at Miami University, Oxford, Ohio
The Fralin Museum of Art at the University of Virginia
The Museum of Modern Art, New York
The Andy Warhol Museum, Pittsburgh
Mimi Trujillo

Acknowledgments

This exhibition has been organised in close partnership with the Marisol Estate at the Buffalo AKG Art Museum. In 2016 Marisol bequeathed the Buffalo AKG (then called the Albright-Knox Art Gallery) her full artistic estate, including more than 100 sculptures, over 600 works on paper and thousands of photographs, as well as the artist's archive and library. As a result, Buffalo AKG holds the most important collection of Marisol's work anywhere in the world.

In 2018, the Louisiana began a dialogue with the Buffalo AKG about organising a Marisol exhibition in Europe to follow the major North American retrospective of 2023-2025 curated by Cathleen Chaffee, the Buffalo AKG's Charles Balbach Chief Curator. That ambition has now been realised. We are deeply thankful to the Buffalo AKG Art Museum for a productive partnership. It has been a great privilege to have had nearly unlimited access to the museum's collection, as well as to the extensive documentary and photographic materials in Marisol's archive.

Our warmest thanks to Cathleen Chaffee for her collegial support and scholarly generosity. She has shared with us the deep insights gained through nine years of researching and stewarding the artist's estate. Her contribution was vital to every stage of this exhibition's preparation. Likewise, we thank all our colleagues at Buffalo AKG who, in their various roles, have accommodated our many requests and supported this exhibition with practical and academic assistance.

Exceptional loans from private collections and other institutions have further enriched this exhibition. We are profoundly grateful for the trust and support the lenders have shown. Without their generosity, this exhibition would not have achieved its full scope and quality.

We extend our sincere thanks to our partner institution, Kunsthaus Zürich. We are very happy that the first major Marisol exhibition in Europe also will be shown at a distinguished museum in Switzerland. Our heartfelt thanks to the museum's director Ann Demeester and her team for sharing our belief in the importance of this project and for their commitment to supporting a production of this scale. We are also grateful to our co-curator, Sandra Gianfreda of Kunsthaus Zürich, whose dedication and expertise have greatly contributed to shaping the exhibition's content and curatorial approach.

We would like to thank the Bank Austria Kunstforum Wien, especially its director Ingried Brugger and curator Lisa Ortner-Kreil, for their joint initiative to bring Marisol to Europe, as well as for their collegial cooperation and long-standing enthusiasm for the project.

Thanks to the authors of this catalogue – Cathleen Chaffee, Nicole Rudick, David J. Getsy and Delia Solomons – whose contributions add new layers of interpretation to Marisol's work.

Out thanks to the entire Louisiana team, as well as to exhibition designer Gudrun Krabbe for giving the exhibition its final form.

Finally, we are immensely grateful to the C.L. David Foundation and Collection, whose financial support has once again made it possible for the Louisiana to realise an exhibition of this scope and importance.

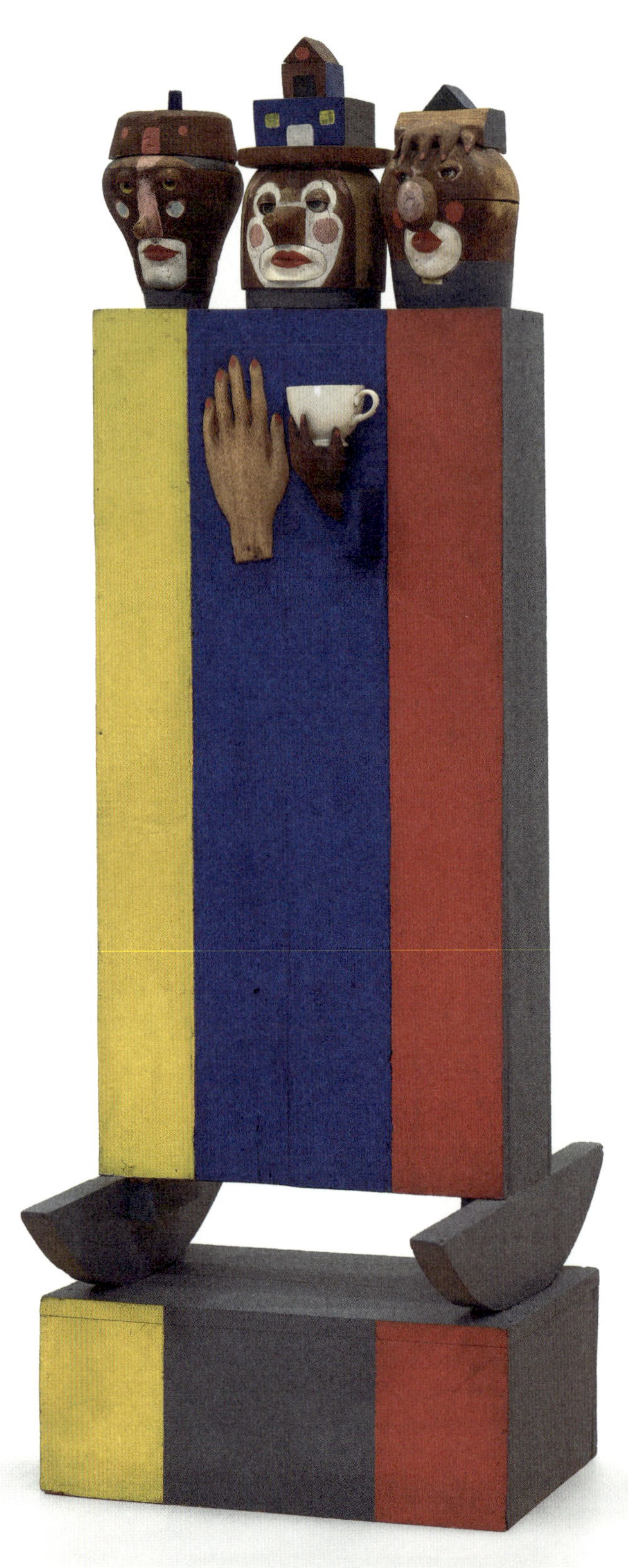

10. *Tea for Three*, 1960 (detail opposite)

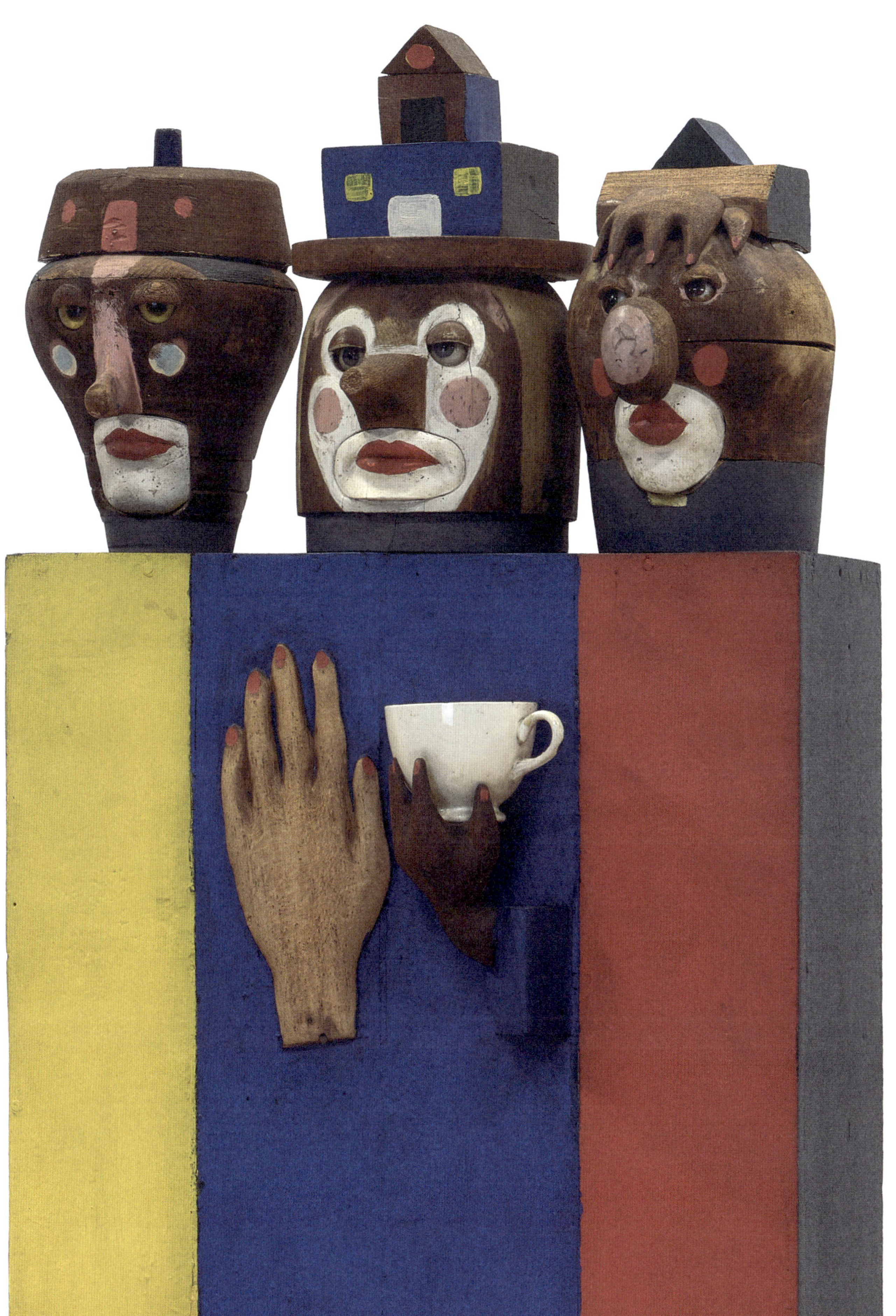

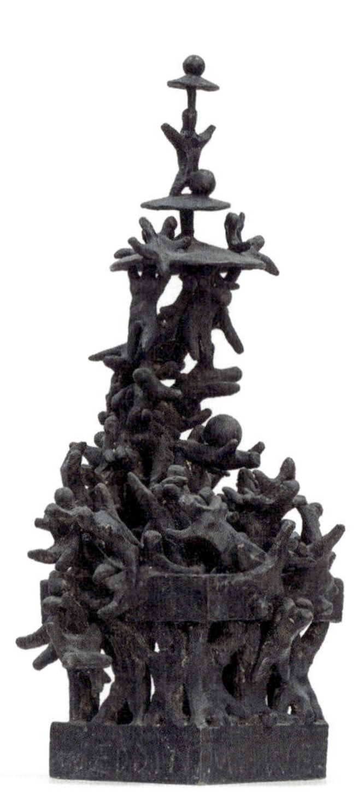

9. *My Wedding Cake*, 1959

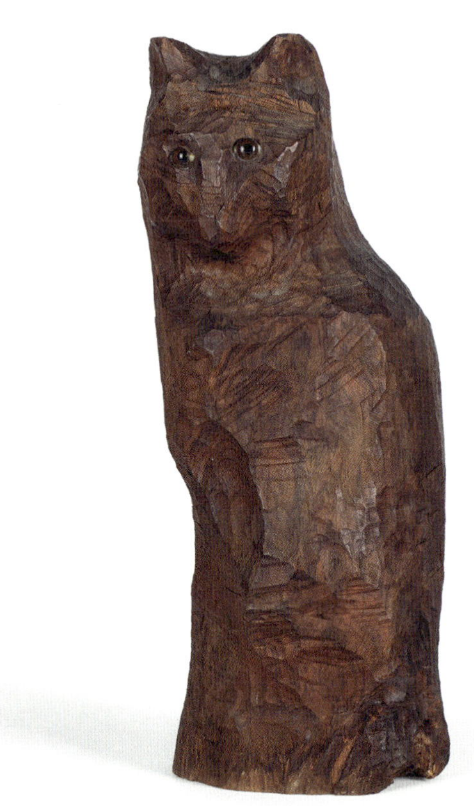

5. Untitled (Cat), 1957

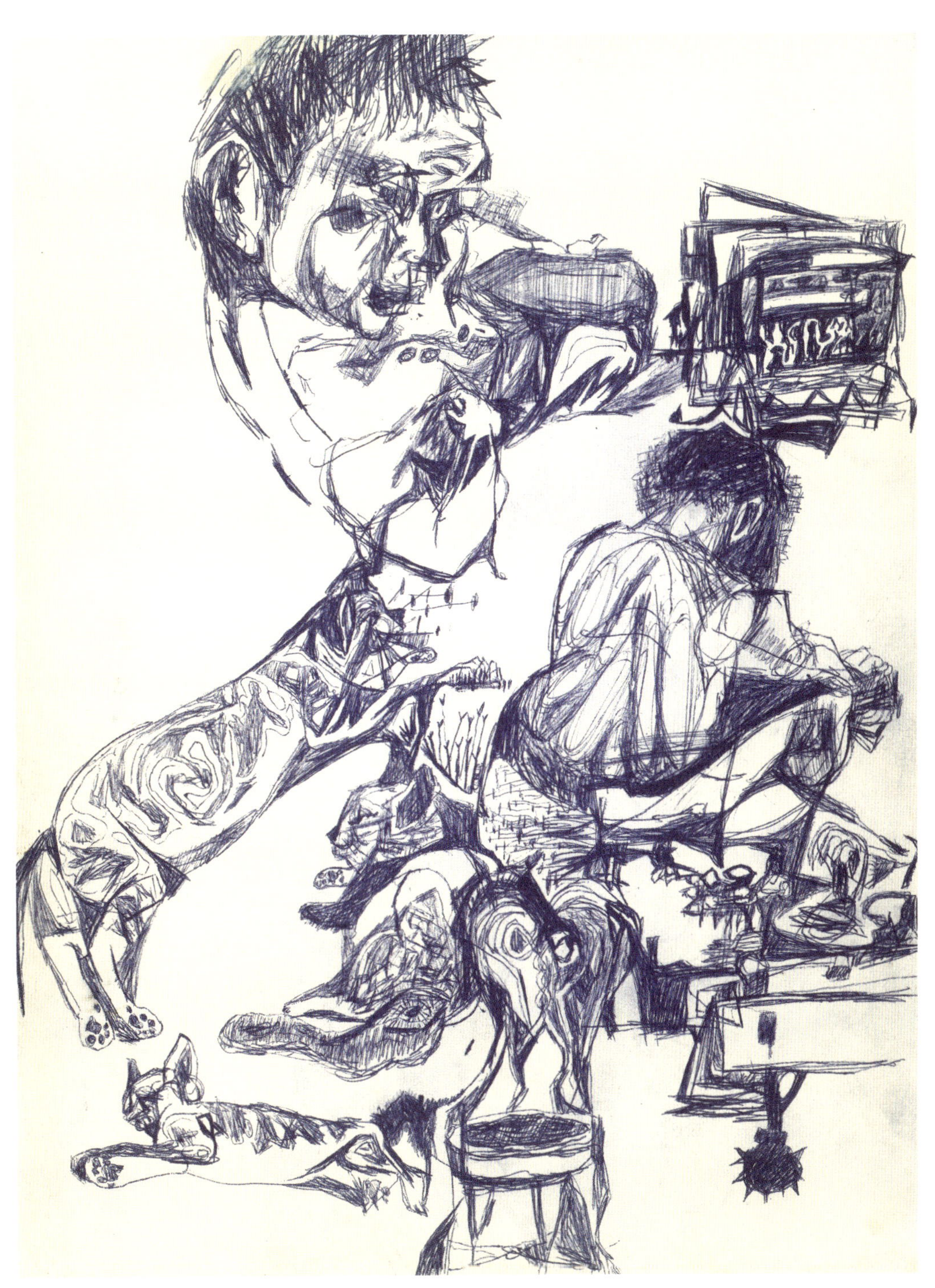

1. Untitled, c. 1954-58

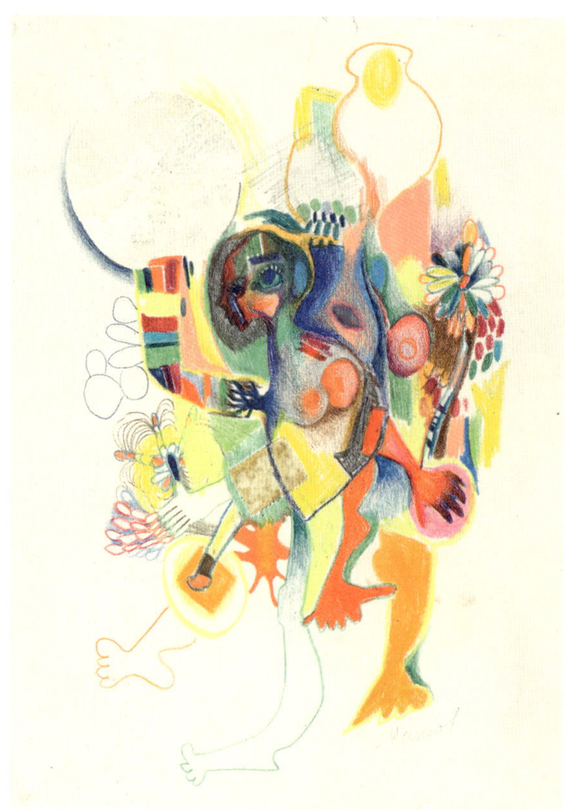

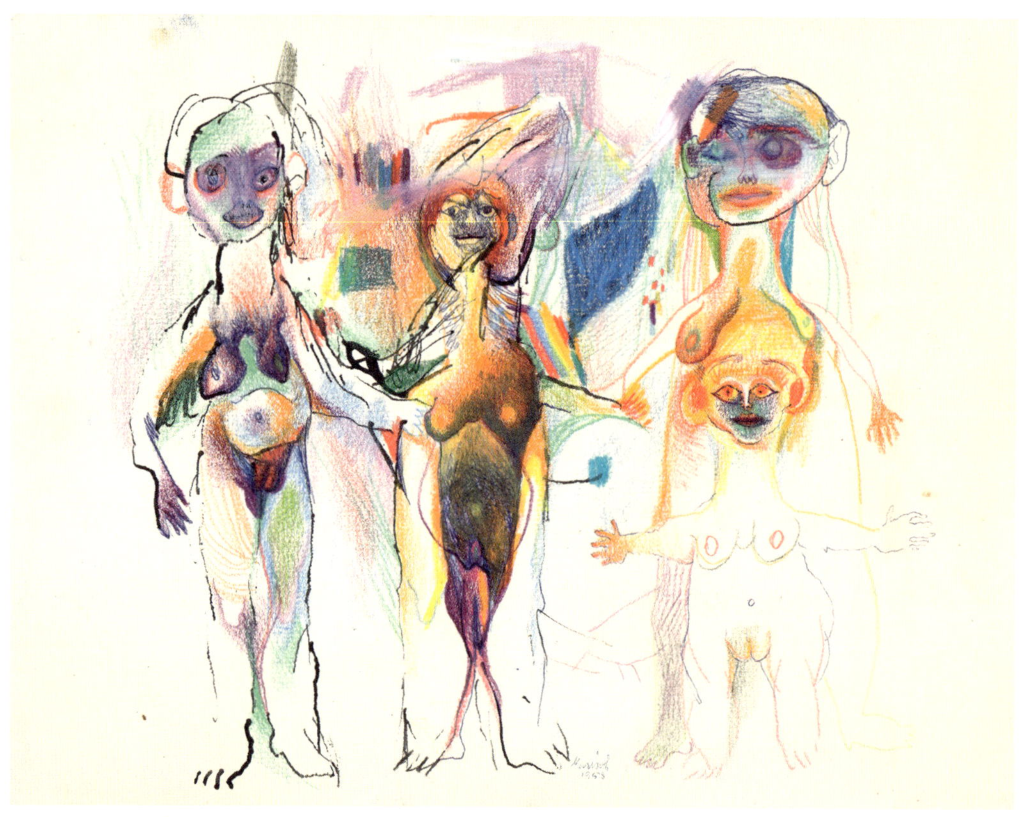

4. Untitled, c. 1957

6. Untitled, 1958

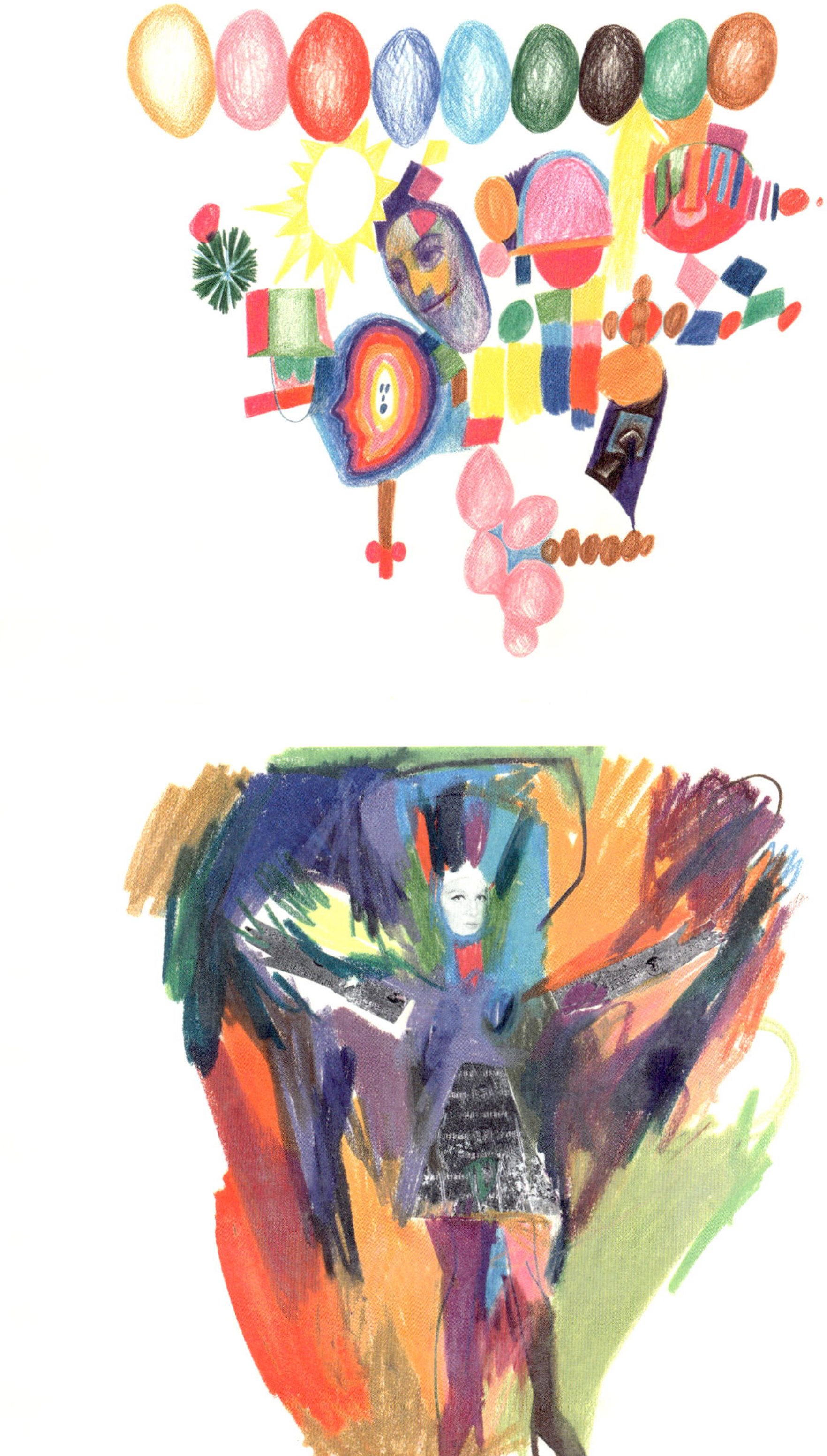

7. Untitled page from a sketchbook, c. 1958–60

8. Untitled page from a sketchbook, c. 1958–60

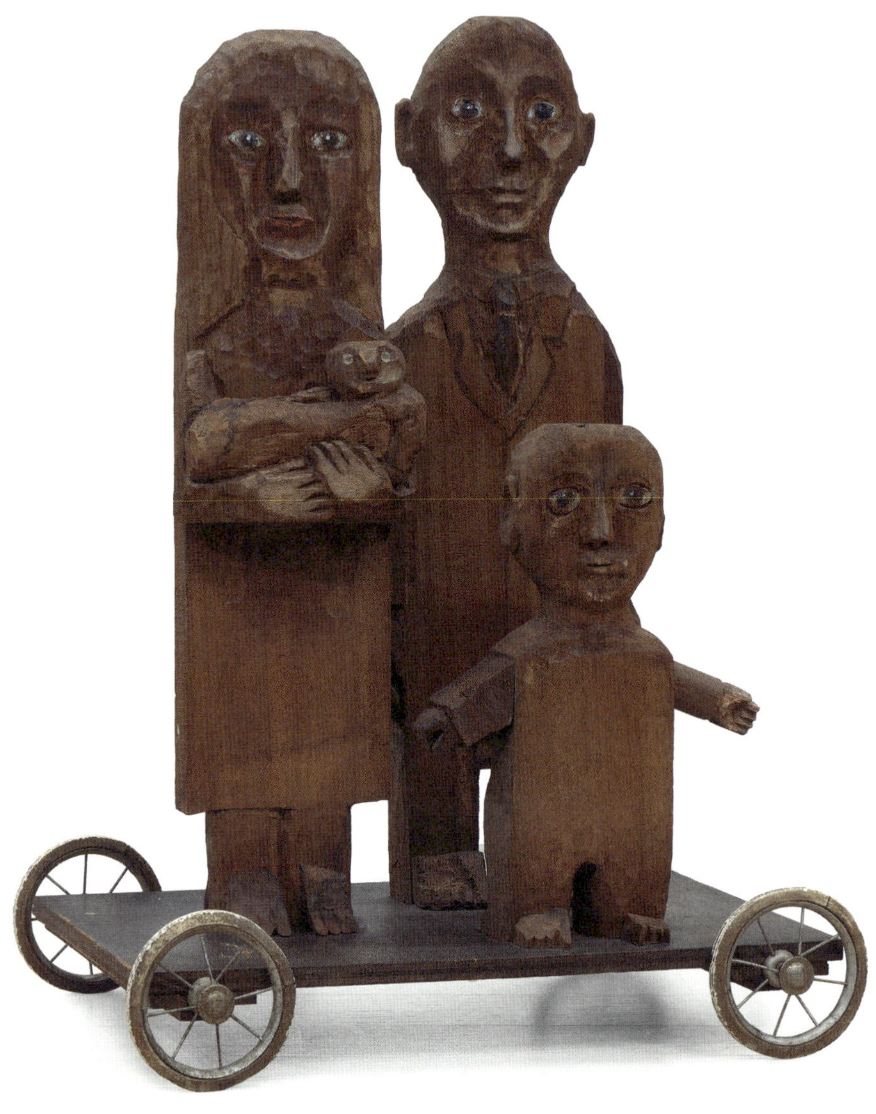

2. *The Hungarians*, 1955

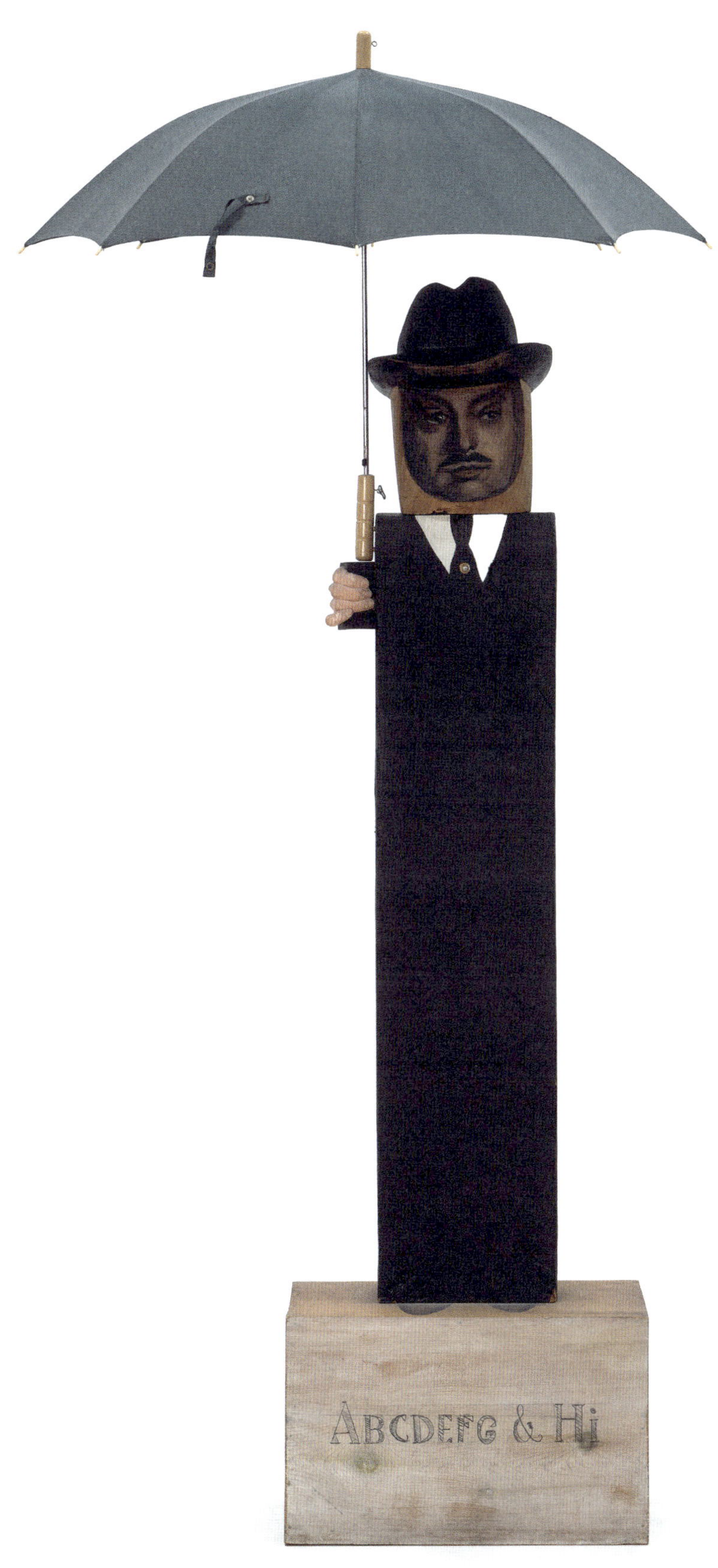

15. *ABCDEFG & Hi*, 1961-62

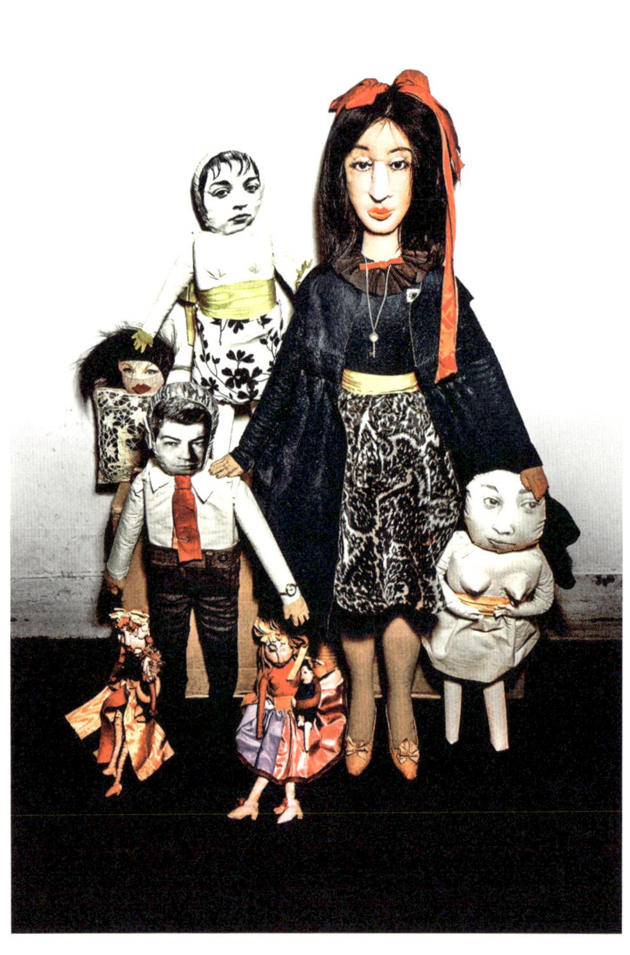

Dolls made by the artist, c. 1955-63

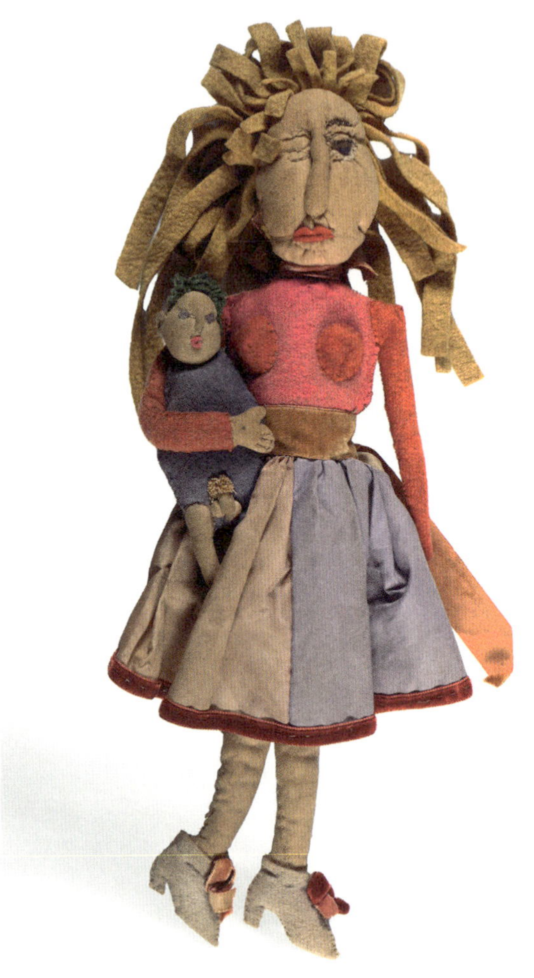

3. Untitled (Doll), c. 1955-63

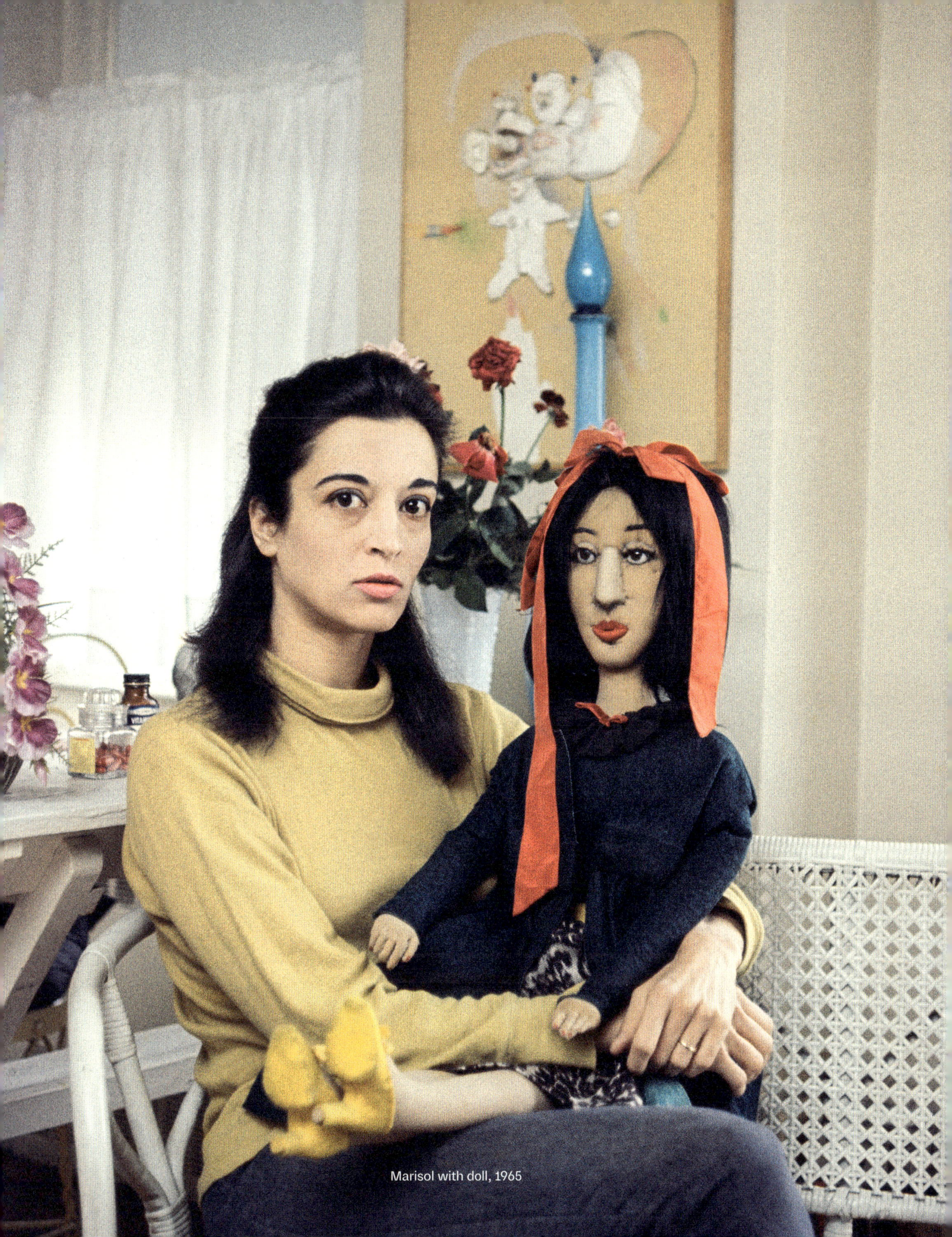

Marisol with doll, 1965

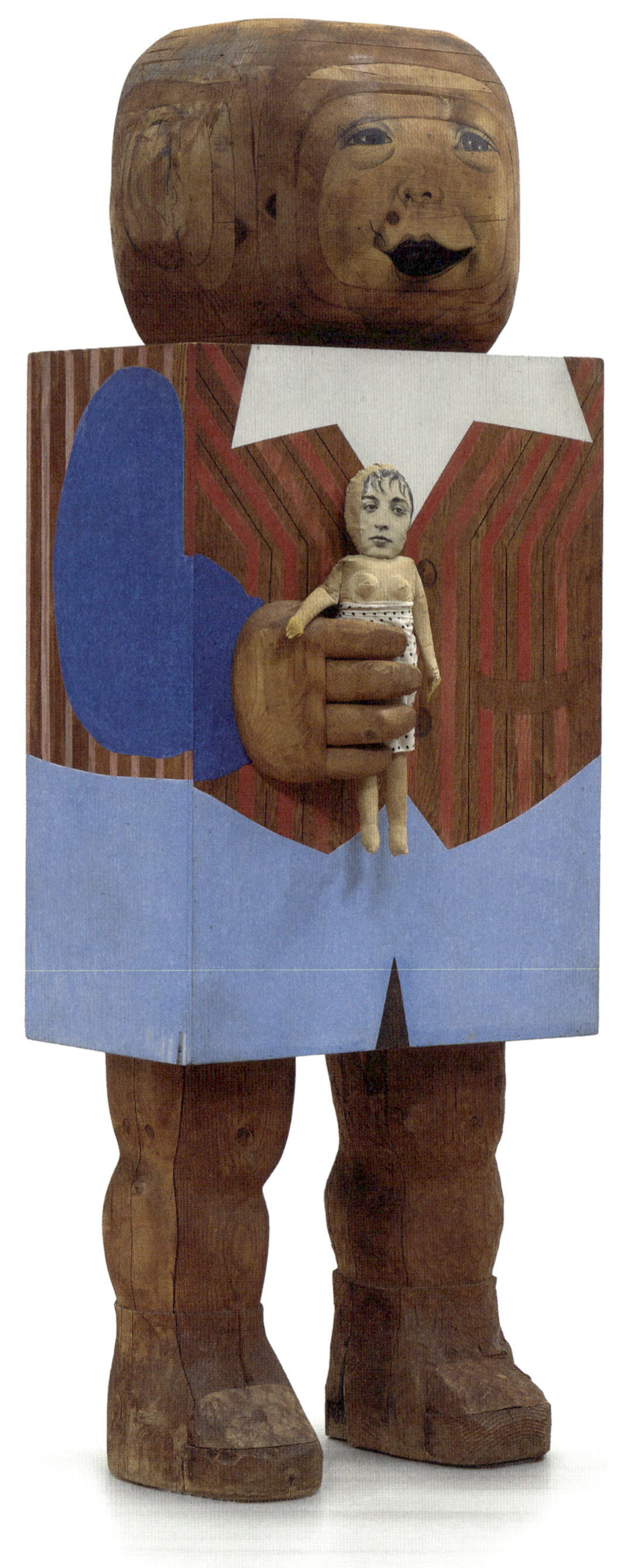

18. *Baby Boy*, 1962–63

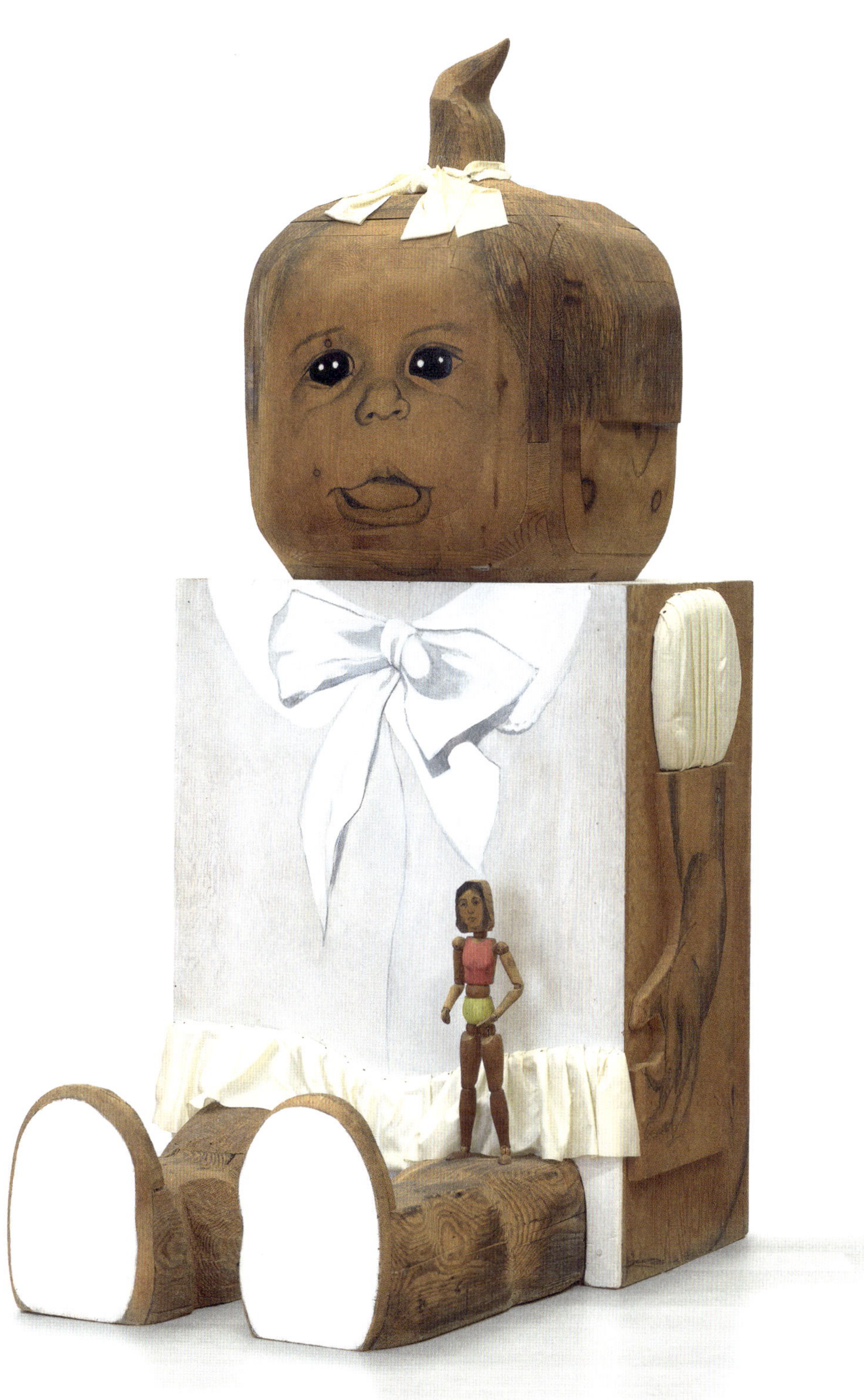

19. *Baby Girl*, 1963

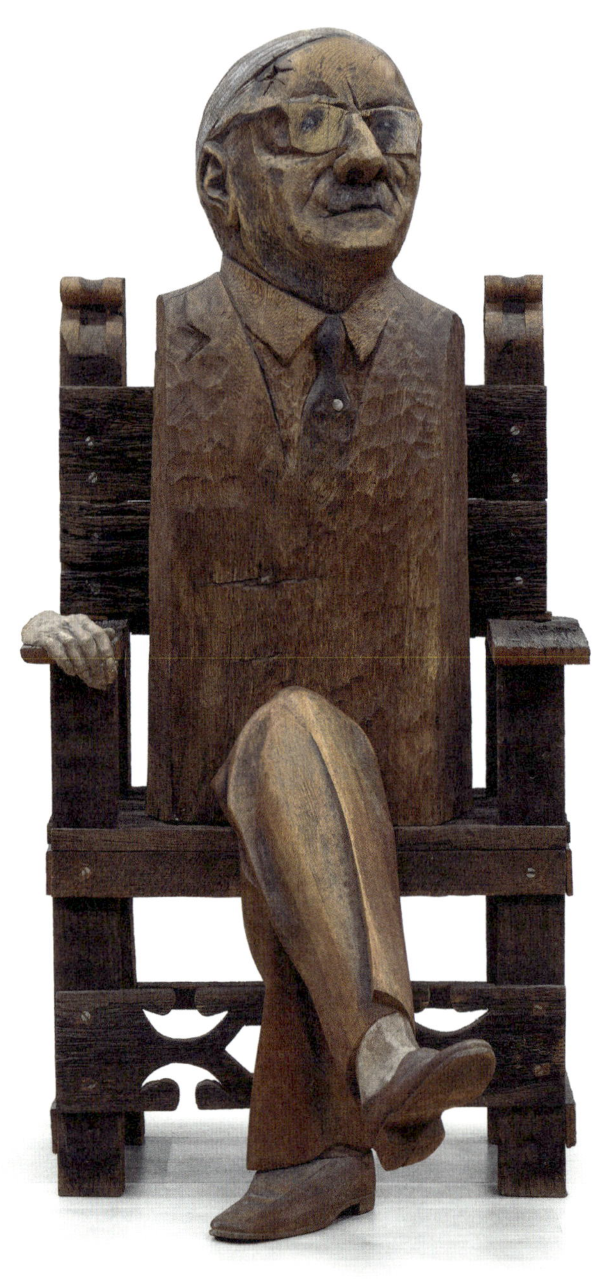

87. *My Father*, 1977

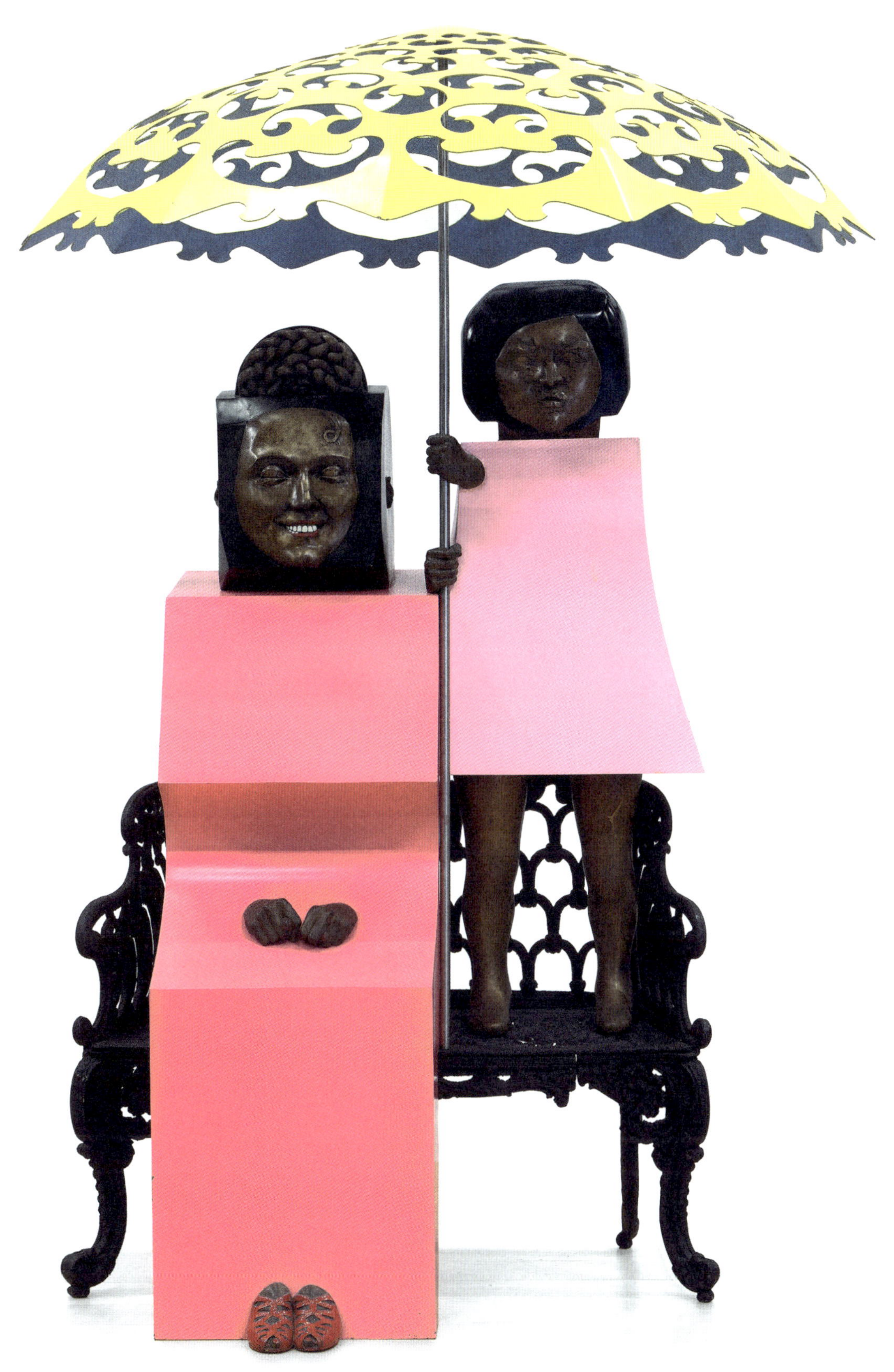

35. *Mi Mama y Yo*, 1968

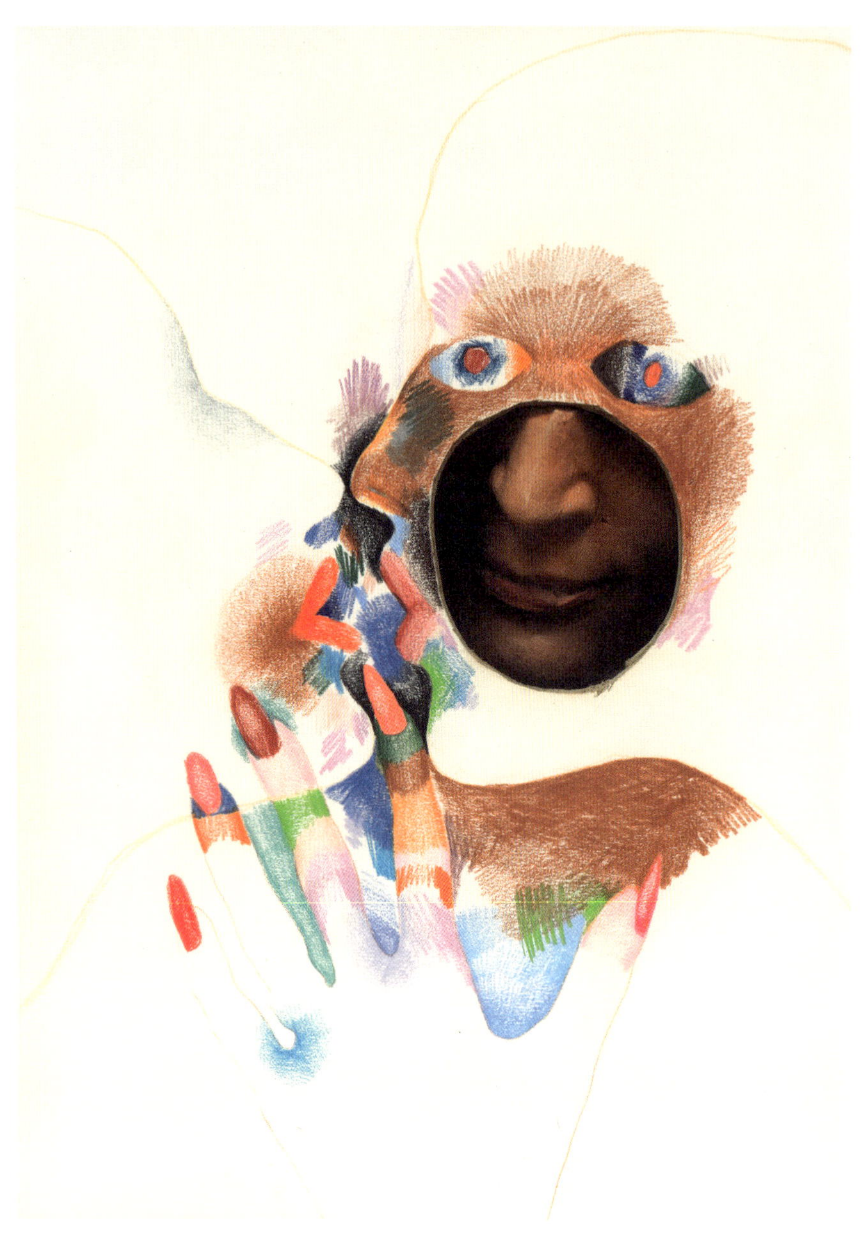

12. *Face Behind a Mask*, 1961

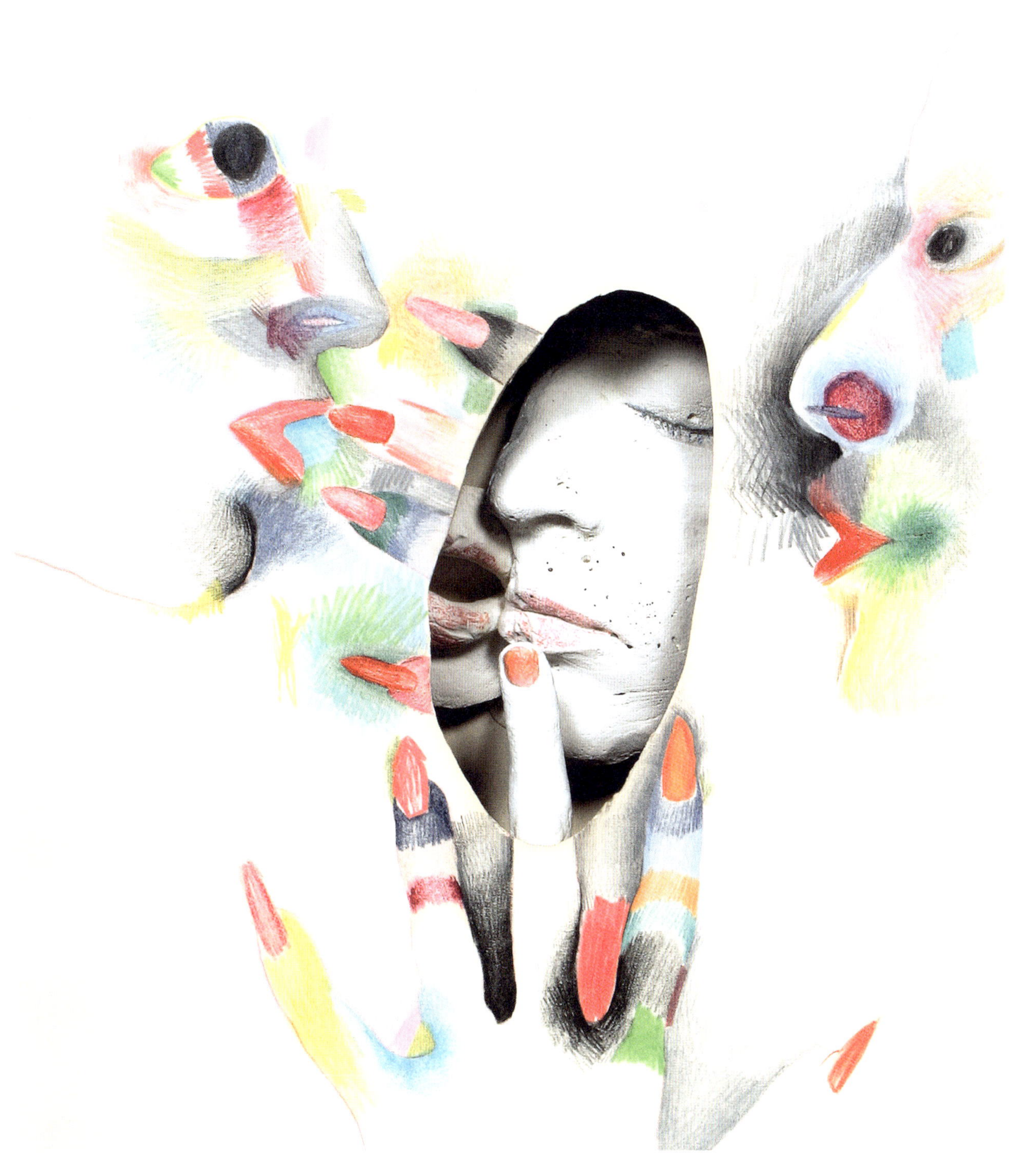

14. *Portrait of Betty*, 1961

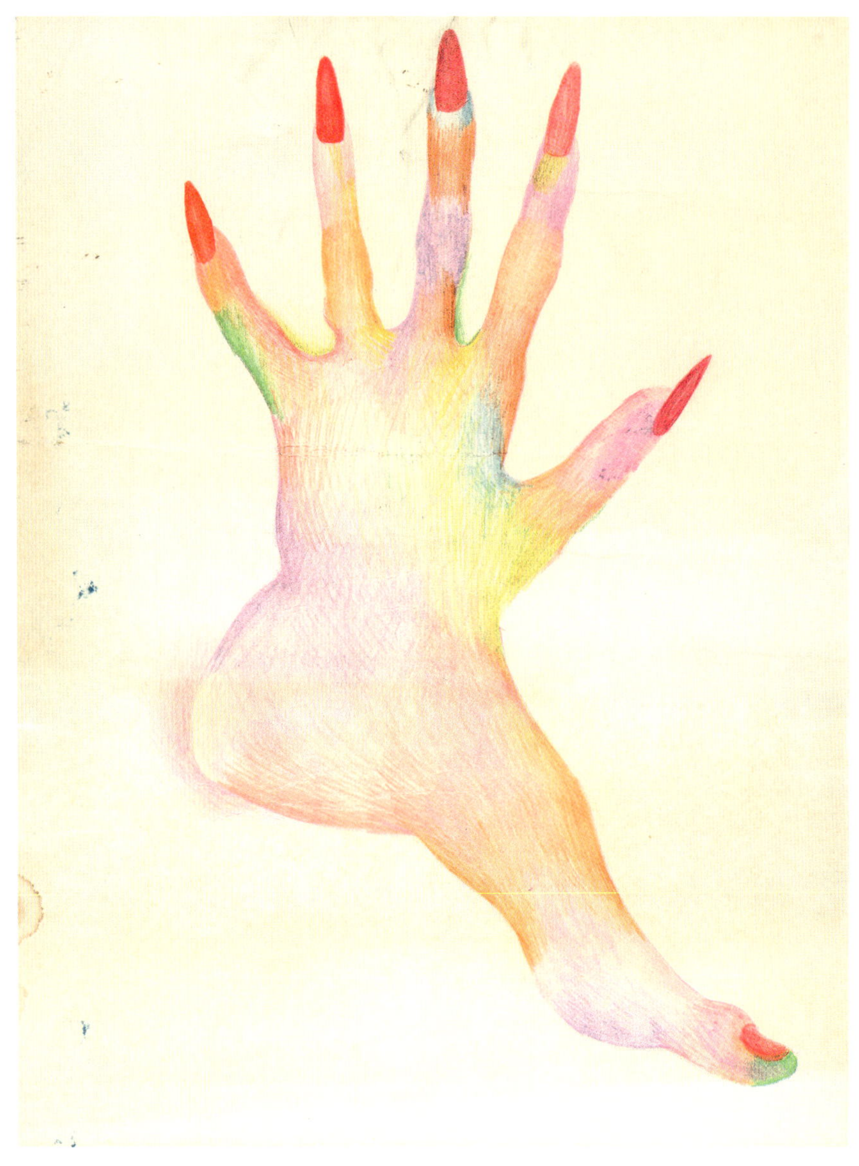

37. Untitled, c. 1969-72

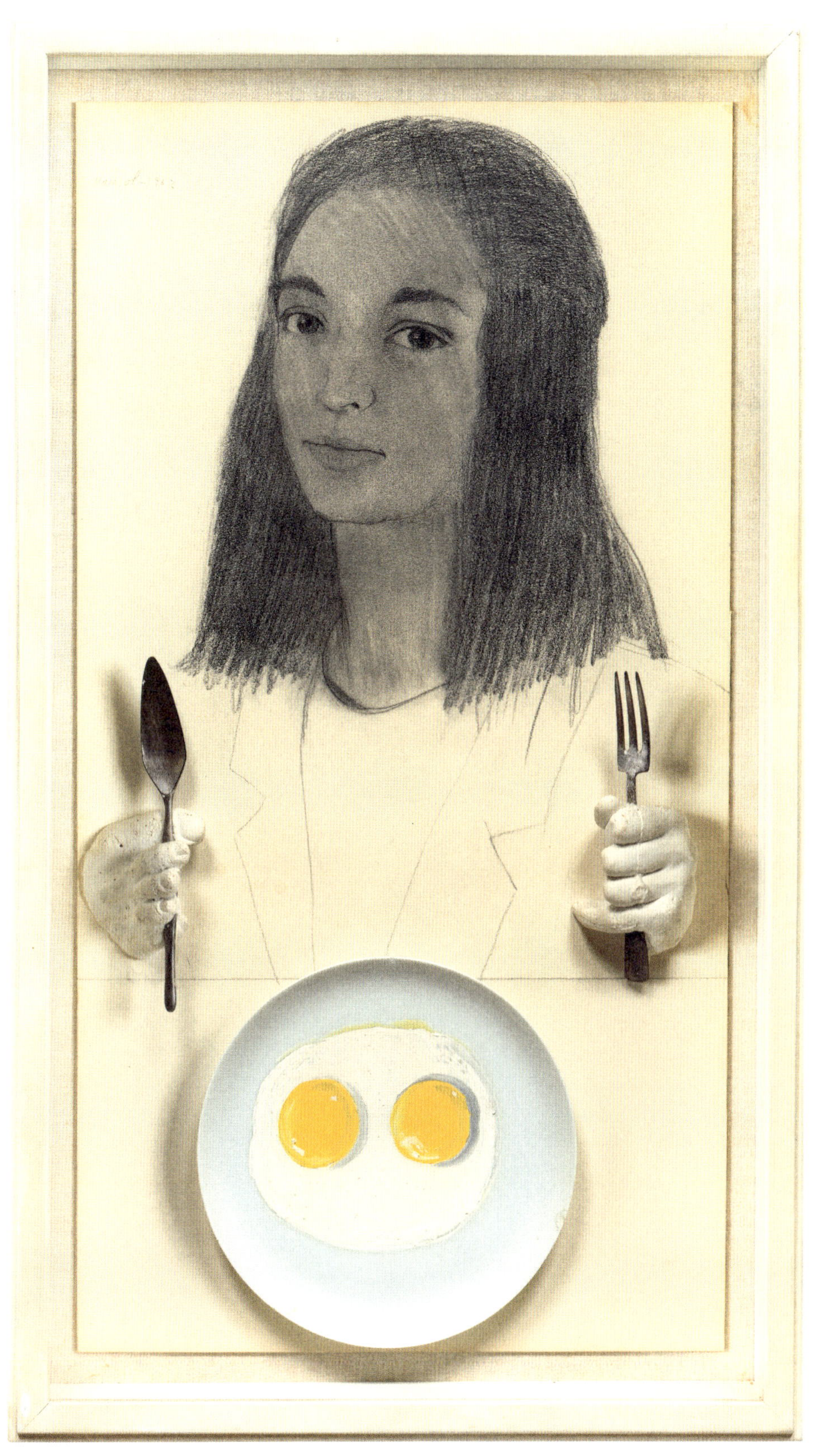

17. *Self-Portrait*, 1962

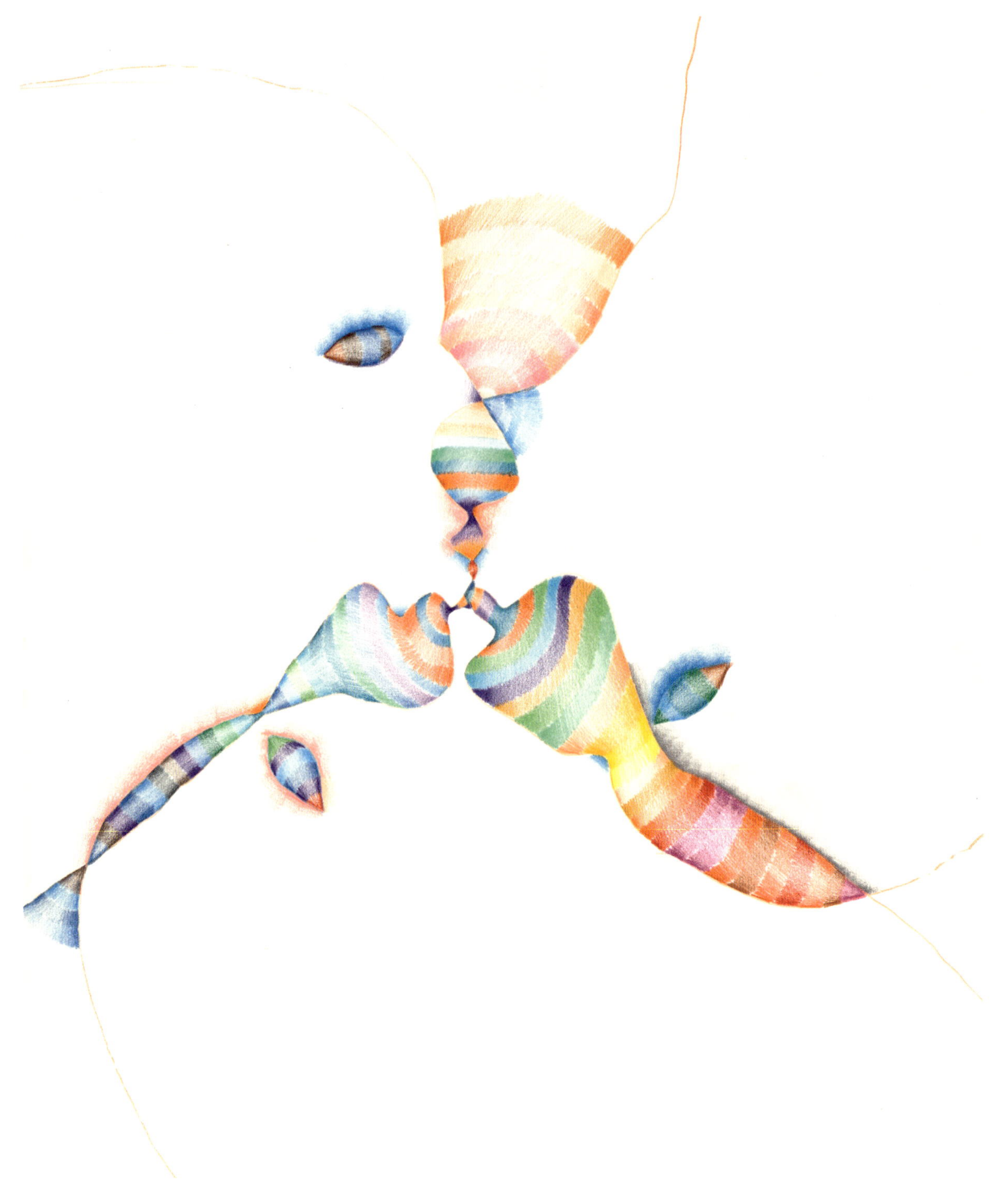

27. Untitled, c. 1966

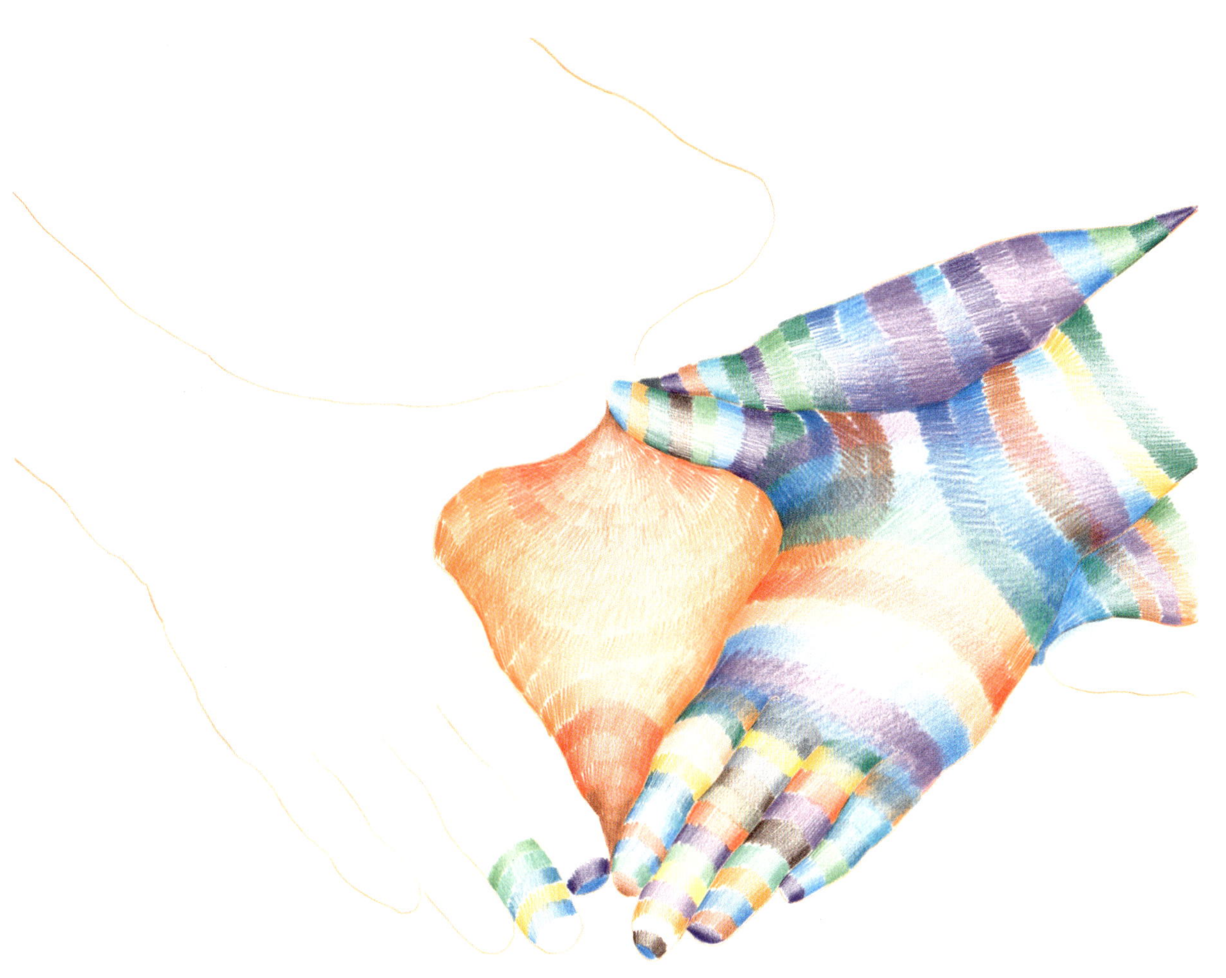

36. Untitled, c. 1969

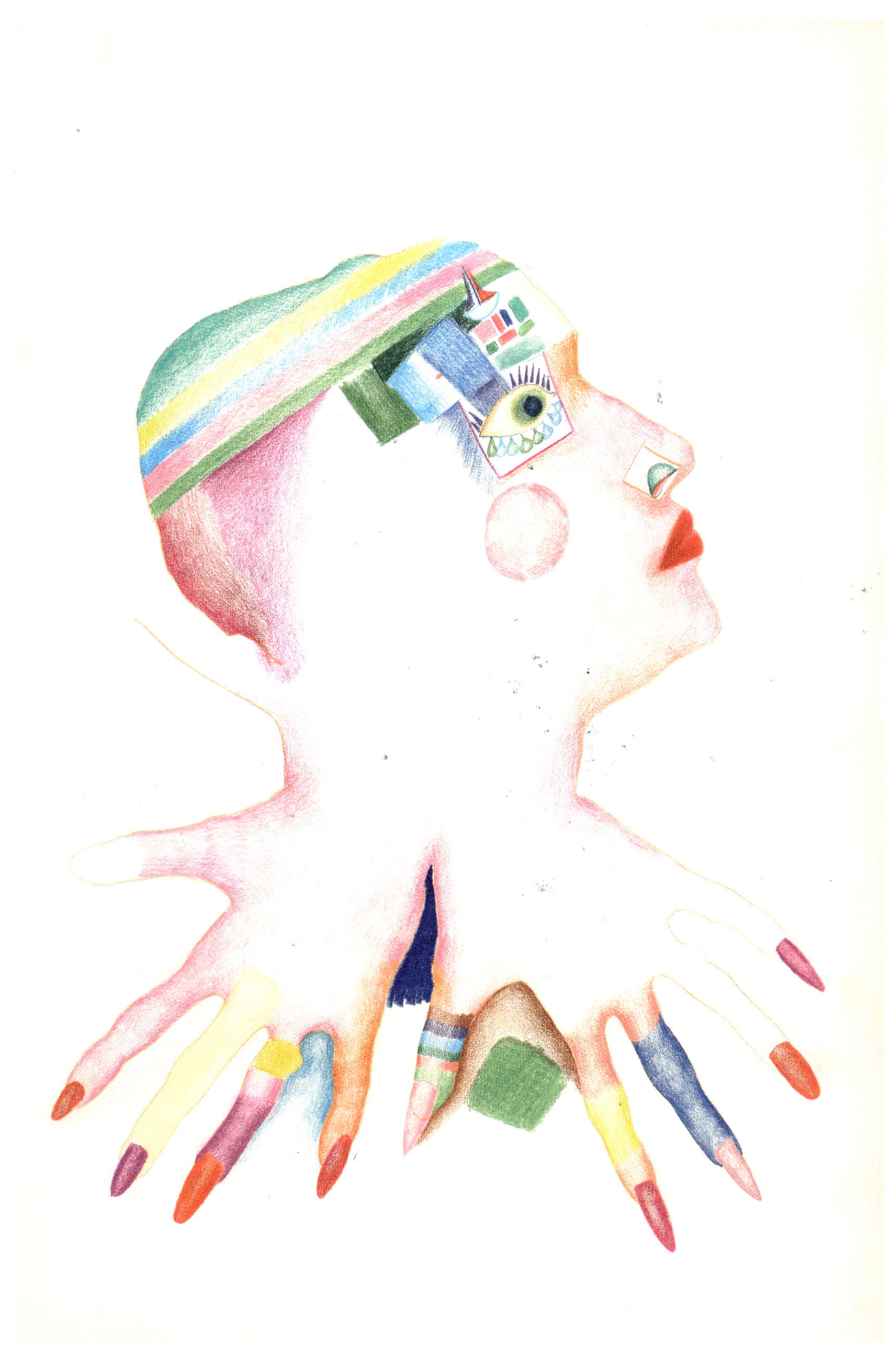

11. Untitled, c. 1960-65

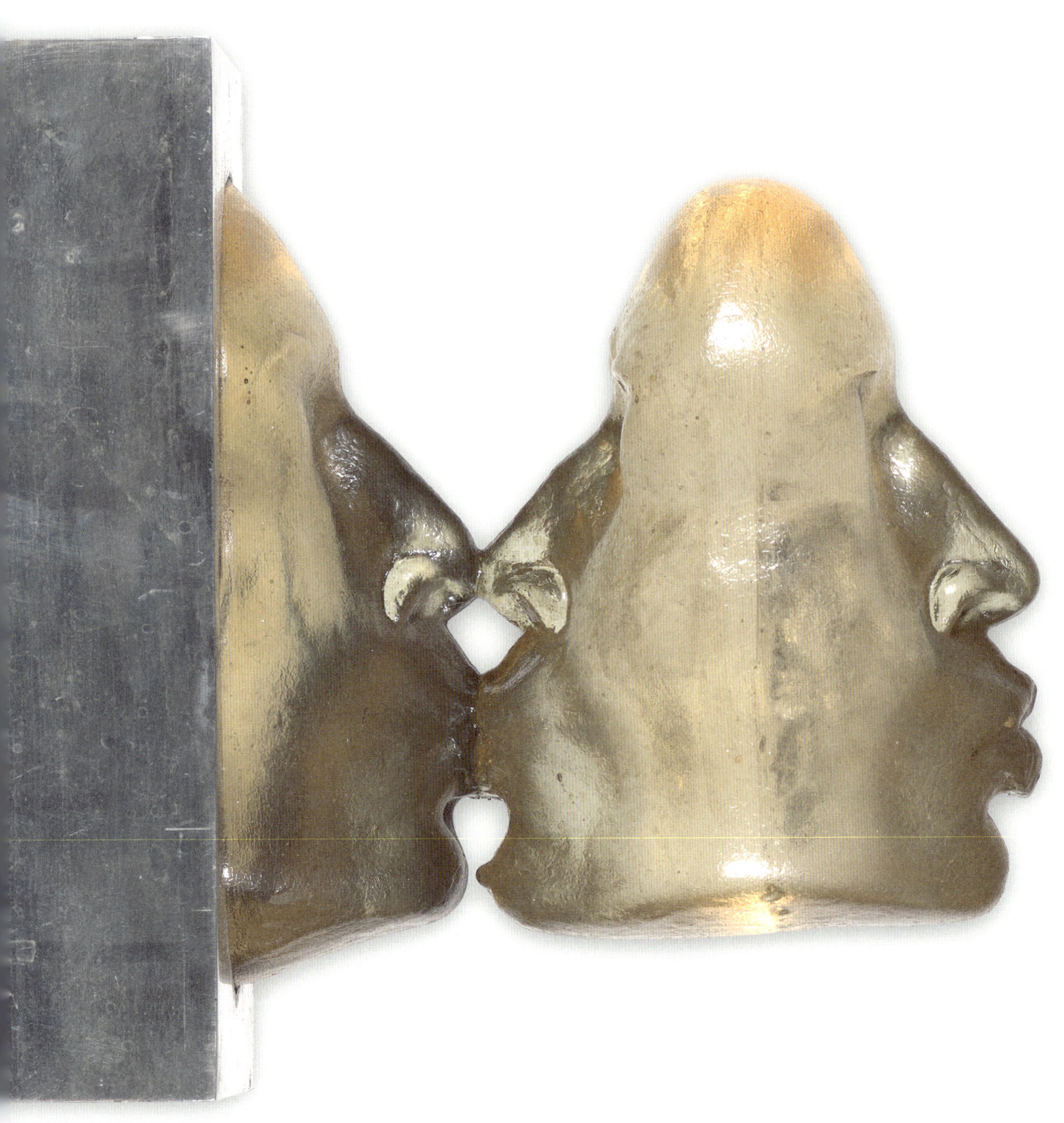

28. *Kiss*, 1966

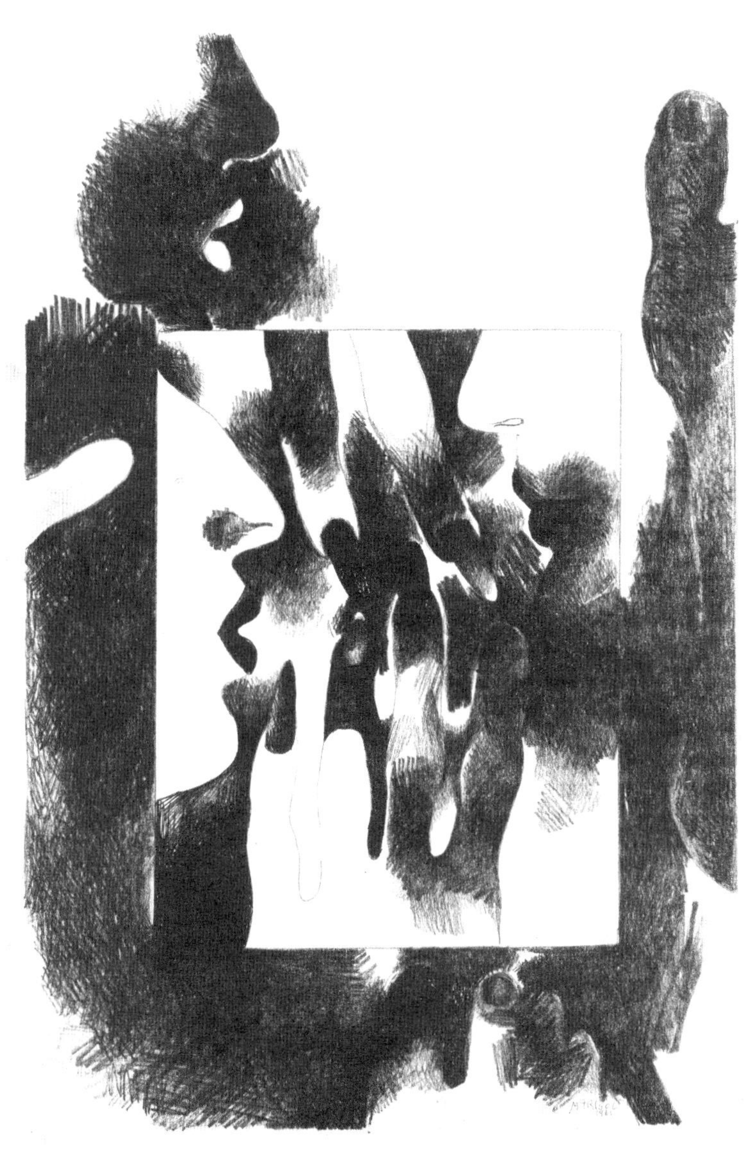

13. *Fingers and Faces*, 1961

Marisol in Pieces: An Introduction

Cathleen Chaffee

By the time she began gaining notoriety as an artist in 1957, Marisol (1930-2016) had already lived several lives.[1] Born María Sol Escobar to a peripatetic Venezuelan family then living in Paris, Marisol spent her early childhood between the French capital and travel destinations around Europe. When she was five, her family moved back to Caracas, Venezuela where Marisol spent her middle childhood. There, she was exposed to the local cultural scene through her mother, a patron of artists including the visionary painter, Armando Reverón. She recalled in the 1960s, "I always liked art before I thought it was art. I was always drawing, ever since I can remember."[2]

In 1941, her mother died by suicide and Marisol stopped speaking. She would later say: "I really didn't talk for years except for what was absolutely necessary in school and in the street."[3] Then, in 1946, her father moved the family to Los Angeles, where, as a high schooler, Marisol took evening classes at the Otis Art Institute and the Jepson Art Institute. After graduating high school in 1949, she spent a year in Paris, attending the Académie Julian and the École des Beaux-Arts. While following copy-based training at such schools in Paris may have been the typical formation for an aspiring artist earlier in the 20th century, Marisol abhorred repetition and seemed attuned to the art world shifting under her young feet. She moved to New York City in 1950 at the age of 20.

There, she continued taking art classes and planned to attend university although ultimately she never did so. She would later say that the museums and libraries of New York furnished her art education.

1. Untitled, c. 1954-58

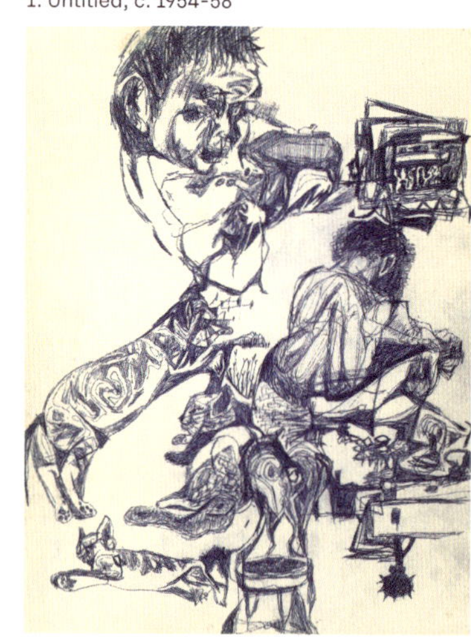

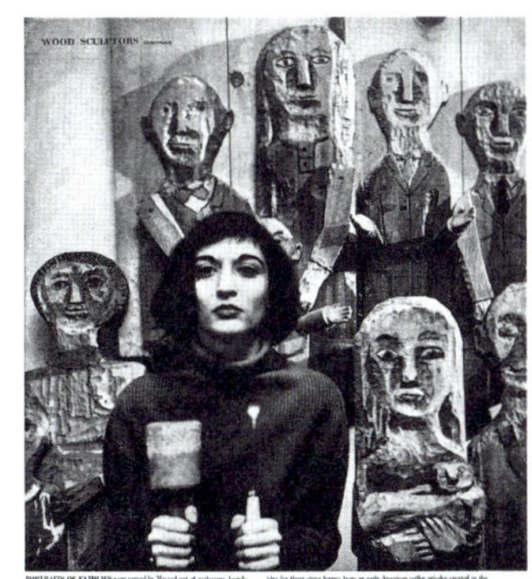

LATIN BEAUTY'S HOST OF STERN PEOPLE, STARING PETS

LIFE 14 JULY 1958

Marisol featured in the article "Latin Beauty's Host of Stern People, Staring Pets", *Life* magazine 45, no. 2, 14 July, 1958. Marisol Papers, Buffalo AKG Art Museum

Her first few years were spent studying art and getting high while living communally with friends immersed in the city's Beat-era bohemia. By the mid-1950s, she was hanging out with the Abstract Expressionist circle of painters at the Cedar Tavern. Her earliest mature works are from this period, as she began experimenting widely with materials, including wood relief, plaster casting, terracotta, bronze and stone. These works – which reference Pre-Columbian sculpture, Auguste Rodin and frequently depict family groups as well as exaggeratedly erotic constructions – drew the attention of new gallerist Leo Castelli, who, in 1957, included her in a group show with Jasper Johns and Robert Rauschenberg followed by a solo exhibition later the same year.

The parameters of Pop art were only just being delineated in the United States, and she was featured in a number of articles that rather tried to locate her as part of a revival of craft or carving. She left the city just as this media attention was taking off. "I got so scared after I had my first show that I went to Europe and disappeared", she would later say of her 18-month hiatus abroad.[4] She travelled first to Paris and then settled in Rome where, exhibiting signs of a breakdown, she struggled with the disparities between the images of her that circulated in the media, the judgement of others and her own self-identity. "You start getting publicity, and then all of a sudden you lose everything you have", she said.[5]

Between representation and self-representation

During this period, Marisol tried to learn to be comfortable with solitude, and while continuing to sculpt, would often seek to ground herself by tracing her body, hands and head on paper. Soon after her return to New York in 1960, she translated the fragmented selves of these drawings into a new medium as she began using plaster to make indexical casts of her face, hands, buttocks and other body parts, a practice that she would continue for the rest of her life. She added these casts to new larger-scale figurative sculptures such as *Tea for Three* (cat. 10, p. 6) which use remarkably spare means: often rectangular wood boxes adorned with just enough carved, cast, found or photographic elements to coalesce a form that can be read as human. Paradoxically, these restrained efforts at figuration created a uniquely engaged viewer, an underrecognised key to the runaway success of such works. Indeed, viewing Marisol's sculptures is seldom passive; from the moment we lay eyes on one, looking becomes a deeply pleasurable experience of co-creation: even unintentionally, we are imaginatively bridging the gaps between recognisable fragments, one missing arm or torso at a time.

Although she claimed to cast her own body out of convenience – telling reporters she was the one reliably available to serve as her own model – the actual effect of her own proliferating body fragments belies this pithy assertion.[6] If Jasper Johns's plaster casts were largely anonymised, wherever you look in Marisol's work, there is a trace that seems to imply the artist could not be contained: it is Marisol's hand holding an umbrella above a trim portrait of a male New York jeweller (cat. 15, p. 13); her hands are surrogates for those of her lost mother's in a filial portrait (cat. 35, p. 19 and this spread); her outstretched finger becomes a bird's perch on an oblivious society type (cat. 26, p. 37).

35. *Mi Mama y Yo*, 1968

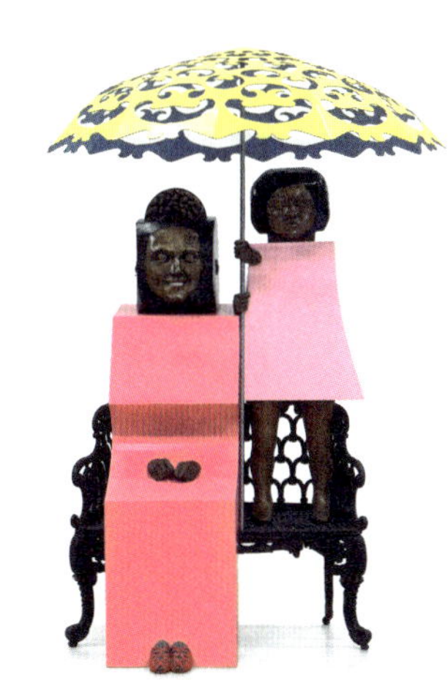

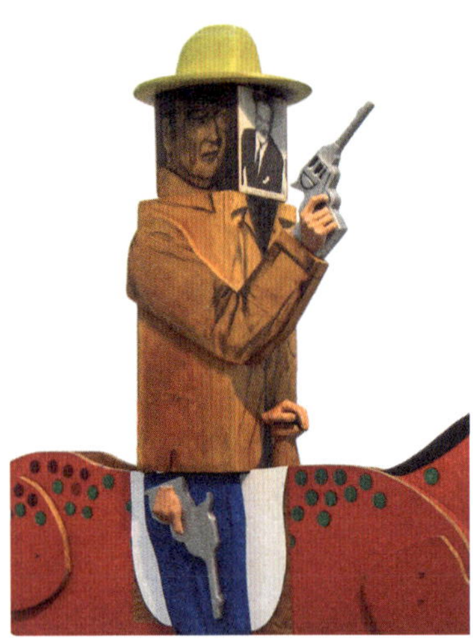

21. *John Wayne*, 1963 (detail)

And her many small-scale cast artworks, including sculptures of hands and feet, masks made from her face, and weapons cast to fit her fists, fragmented her further between representation and self-representation, space and time. Marisol noted: "Sometimes I feel as though I'm being blown away [...]. When I do a portrait, but really do myself in the portrait, or use my own hands or shoes, it brings me back to reality."[7] Indeed, these dispersed pieces of the artist across the field of her work suggest Marisol's understanding of identity as episodic rather than continuous; self-continuity across a lifetime can be compared to a story we have simply learned to tell ourselves.

After a decade celebrating the relative romanticism of Abstract Expressionist painters, critics effusively praised Marisol for approaching portraiture in a unique and satirical way and she became a celebrity. While she may be best known for her pop culture subjects from this period – including depictions of icons such as the Kennedy family, Andy Warhol and John Wayne (cat. 21, pp. 42-43 and this spread) – her most incisive sculptures of the 1960s tackled women's roles in society, norms of gender and sexuality in the midcentury, self-identity, Cold War politics and the immigrant experience. By the end of the decade, according to one critic, she had "been written about more than any living artist in women's magazines as well as art journals."[8]

Mimicry and empathy

In 1968, Marisol represented Venezuela at the Venice Biennale and in a subsequent exhibition in Rotterdam at the Museum Boijmans Van Beuningen; she was also one of only four women among the 149 artists selected for that year's Documenta exhibition in Kassel, Germany. Despite her success, she grew frustrated with the brutal police response to Vietnam War protests in the United States and spent much of the second half of 1968 travelling in India, Nepal, Cambodia, Sri Lanka and Thailand. In 1969, she intensively trained to scuba dive in Tahiti. In new works made after these experiences, she explored human-animal interdependence as well as connections between the American military-industrial complex and the life of the oceans.[9] These sculptures include her chimeralike *The Fishman* (1973, cat. 58, p. 75 and this spread) and sculptures of barracuda and needlefish, which she connected to missiles and other modern forms of weaponry.

58. *The Fishman*, 1973

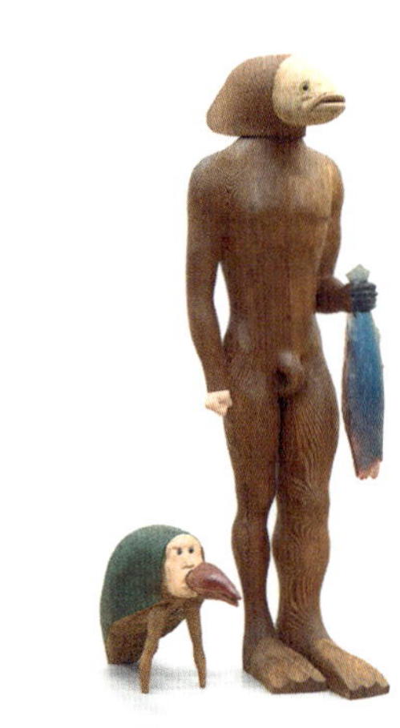

As she later told an interviewer, "I have always had a special communication with the world of animals. I wish humans were like that."[10] In seeking to understand the life of underwater creatures through her remarkable sculptures, Marisol combined aspects of the evolutionary mimicry so common in the animal kingdom with a deeply sympathetic human approach. One of the most direct ways to understand another is to try to see from their perspective and feel what it is like to *be* them: to "walk in their shoes", swim in their water. In casts she appended to these deeply strange aquatic sculptures, Marisol studiously puckered and contorted her face to appear like the fish with which she was absorbed.

She dove long enough to witness significant damage to the coral reefs that had inspired her and wrote of her dismay at rapid changes affecting the ecosystem.[11] This was a key reason she would later stop

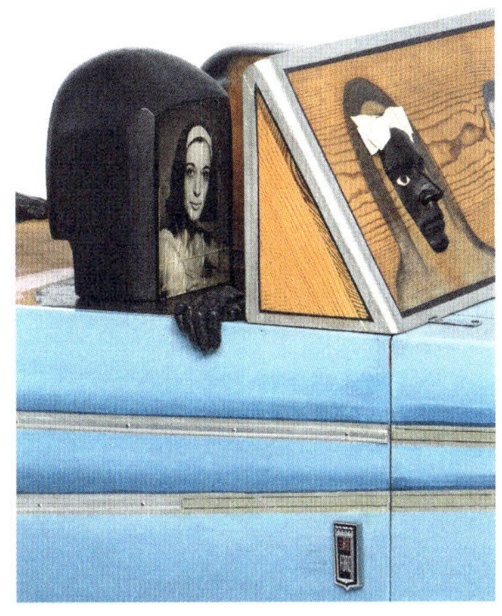

22. *The Car*, 1964 (detail)

diving. At a time in the 21st century when we ignore at our peril the interconnectedness of life above and below the oceans, Marisol's wholehearted foregrounding of and even self-identification with threatened marine species in her sculptures of this period feel prescient and inescapably relevant.

The fish sculptures offer a doorway into Marisol's extensive, if less obvious, use of mimicry and empathy as tools throughout her career; they should be seen as belonging to a larger series of works in which she deployed her body fragments to both satirise human weakness and also sympathise with others. In addition to casting her face to depict a territorial fish, she was also a possibly white-society woman (cat. 26, p. 37), a jazz musician (cat. 20, pp. 54-55), a bride and a bridegroom (*The Wedding,* 1962-63, p. 67), although she was none of these things in life. That she also used a painted cast of her face to express a certain level of identification with an objectified Native American in her self-portrait as a cigar-store Indian is more difficult to accept from a contemporary perspective (*Indian*, 1969). As is her use of black-tinted casts of her own face and arm to depict two Black female passengers in *The Car* (cat. 22, pp. 38-39 and this spread), a witty sculpture of a half-scale Ford containing four Black and white adults and an apparently white child out for a drive together, at a time, as Sid Sachs has pointed out, "when miscegenation was still illegal in a quarter of the states".[12]

In that work, Marisol fully owns the artifice of her representation by choosing to colour the cast of her face peering through the car's window black, while replacing the head on view on the other side of the "glass" with an unaltered studio photograph of her own light-skinned face. *The Car* and *Indian* may be seen as belonging to a much larger series of works in which Marisol's frustration with social injustice led her to foreground and figure the disenfranchisement of others. Indeed, they moot the constructed nature of boundaries between us and hold space to think through the artifice of such naturalised forms of racism. These sculptures in particular are also, however, examples of redface and blackface, and difficult illustrations of the ways a critique of objectification or segregation can easily, in the realm of figuration, reinstate that objectification. Such works, in which Marisol used her own face to channel the experience of historically marginalised others, are object lessons in the real limits of well-intentioned liberal empathy.

New approaches

In 1975, Marisol debuted new and often anxiety-provoking face casts and large-scale drawings that resonated with many topics being debated within the feminist movement, including gender and eroticism, pregnancy, abortion, the objectification of women's bodies and interpersonal violence (cat. 74, p. 90 and this spread). In some works, Marisol parodically devalued the gendered signs that society takes as legible and stable and seemed to deliberately chip away at perceptions of a stable and binary system of gender. Her drawings often featured body tracings as well as fragments of text sourced from personal confessions and overheard conversations. Her sculptural wall hangings feature face casts hung with Coke bottles, beer cans and other objects whose imprints can be read on the damaged faces above (cats. 63-67, 70-76, pp. 90-91).

74. *M. Marisol*, 1975

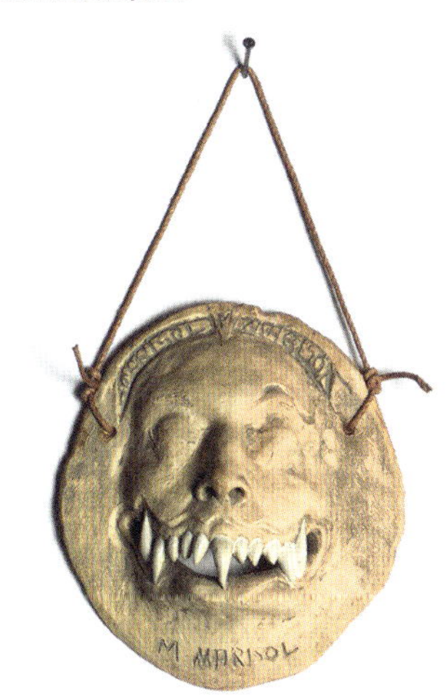

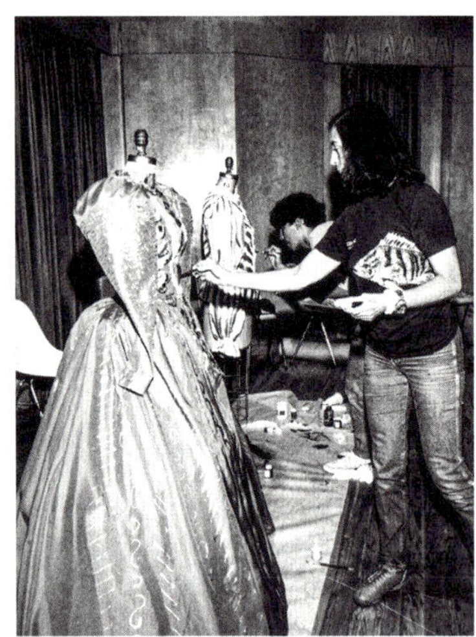

Marisol preparing costumes for *Las Paredes Oyen*, c. 1985
Marisol Papers, Buffalo AKG Art Museum

In the late 1970s she largely stopped casting her own face and embarked on a new series, this time figuring creatives such as Marcel Duchamp, Martha Graham, William Burroughs, Georgia O'Keeffe (cat. 89, p. 109) and Virgil Thomson, who played a significant role in her own development as an artist and were then late in their own lives. Most were based on Marisol's own photographs of the subjects and her time spent with them. This was also when she began creating more public monuments depicting historical figures, including many for sites in Venezuela. From the 1970s to the 1990s, Marisol was often visible in New York theatre settings as she was invited to collaborate on designing sets and costumes for some of the most prominent dance companies of the later 20th century, including Louis Falco and the Martha Graham Dance Company (cat. 41, p. 81).

The Forgotten Star of Pop Art

Marisol's last major body of work, the one that occupied her from the 1980s until her death, earnestly attempted to shine a light on disenfranchisement in the postcolonial era. Some works focus on individuals in former colonies suffering from scarce resources, including India, Bangladesh and Cuba, while others are preoccupied by the legacies of violence against Native Americans in the United States (*Woman with Child and Two Lambs*, 1995). In her last decade, Marisol experienced memory loss and was diagnosed with Alzheimer's disease. While her production decreased dramatically during these years, she continued to work nearly until her death in 2016.

Although Marisol's 1960s sculptures have often remained on view in North American museums, most frequently in dialogue with Pop art, as fashions changed and her work became more overtly political in the 1970s she fell largely out of favour critically and commercially. "Marisol: The Forgotten Star of Pop Art" announced her obituary in the *Guardian* in 2016.[13] Today, a significant portion of Marisol's creative achievement remains unknown even to specialists, including, for example, her extraordinarily varied drawing practice and her engagement with the world of performance and public art. In comparison with other artists who also worked in a Pop vein in the 1960s and attained celebrity as that movement ascended, she has been the subject of surprisingly little scholarly research.[14] Incredibly, the current exhibition represents the artist's first solo exhibition in Europe since 1968.

In her iconic lecture and subsequent book, *The Body in Pieces: The Fragment as a Metaphor of Modernity*, art historian Linda Nochlin wrote of Modernism's dawn amid the violence of the French Revolution as a period "marked by the will toward totalization" yet metaphorised by fragments, in which "the coherence of the body is totally shattered".[15] Many of Marisol's often-disquieting later works help one read her best-known earlier sculptures in a new light, and with a new understanding that her unique contributions to modern sculpture included a hard-won approach to representing individuals as porous containers of fragmentary and shifting, rather than fixed and resolved, identities.

Those areas of her practice that largely failed to resonate with audiences in their time are also those engaged with particularly relevant concerns today. These include works that consider the intelligence of animals and allude to environmental precarity, express feminist anger

Woman with Child and Two Lambs, 1995
Wood, paint and charcoal, 203.2 x 91.4 x 31.1 cm. Collection Buffalo AKG Art Museum. Bequest of Marisol, 2016 (2021:53a-d)

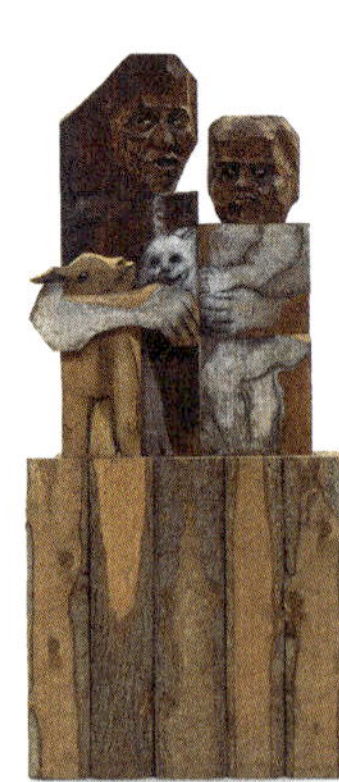

CATHLEEN CHAFFEE is Charles Balbach Chief Curator at the Buffalo AKG Art Museum, where she also oversees work on the estate of Marisol and curated the exhibition *Marisol: A Retrospective*, the major North American retrospective exhibition in 2023-2025. She has recently organised exhibitions with artists including Stanley Whitney, Eric N. Mack, Tony Conrad, Clyfford Still and Mark Bradford. Chaffee holds a PhD from the Institute of Fine Arts at New York University. She previously held curatorial positions at the Yale University Art Gallery, the Museum of Modern Art, New York and the Cleveland Museum of Art.

and testify to sexual violence, connect with the immigrant experience, figure postcolonial disenfranchisement and destabilise norms of gender and sexuality. Throughout her entire career, Marisol created works that obstinately fail to resolve lightly or clearly, that inhabit non-binary spaces, that are – in a word – ambiguous; as such, her corpus may help us practice seeing, and seeing through, the entrenched contemporary craving for reductionism.

1. Portions of this text have been adapted by the author from her essay "Hereafter, Marisol" in her catalogue for *Marisol: A Retrospective* (Buffalo AKG Art Museum and DelMonico Books, 2023).
2. "A Conversation with Marisol and Red Grooms", 1965, p. 10, John Bernard Myers papers, Archives of American Art, Smithsonian Institution, Washington, DC.
3. Jeff Goldberg, "Pop Artist Marisol – 20 Years After Her First Fame – Recalls Her Life and Loves", *People*, 24 March 1975, p. 40.
4. "A Conversation with Marisol and Red Grooms" (see note 2 above), pp. 18-19.
5. Ibid.
6. "Marisol", *Wet Magazine* (February 1979).
7. For example, see Grace Glueck, "It's Not Pop, It's Not Op – It's Marisol", *New York Times Magazine*, (7 March 1965), p. 34; Charlotte Willard, "Eye to I", *Art in America 54* (March-April 1966): p. 52; Lawrence Campbell, "The Creative Eye of the Artist Marisol", *Cosmopolitan* (June 1964), p. 62.
8. Jacqueline Barnitz, "The Marisol Mask", *Artes Hispanicas* 1 (Autumn 1967): p. 41.
9. See on this subject, Julia Vázquez, "Marisol Underwater, 1970-1973" in *Marisol: A Retrospective* (Buffalo AKG Art Museum and DelMonico Books, 2023).
10. Transcript of an interview by Ana María Escallón, Marisol Papers, Buffalo AKG Art Museum. A revised version of this interview was published in Ana María Escallón, *Marisol* (Brenau University Galleries and Art Museum of the Americas, 1999).
11. August/September 1976 notebook, 1.8-1.13, Marisol Papers, Buffalo AKG Art Museum.
12. Sid Sachs, "Beyond the Surface: Women and Pop Art 1958-1968" in *Seductive Subversion: Women Pop Artists 1958-1968* (University of the Arts and Abbeville Press, 2010), p. 36.
13. Jason Farago, "Marisol: The Forgotten Star of Pop Art", *Guardian* (3 May 2016).
14. Rare exceptions include Cécile Whiting, "Figuring Marisol's Femininities", *RACAR: Revue d'Art Canadienne* 18, nos. 1-2 (1991): pp. 73-90; Delia Solomons, "Marisol's Antimonument: Masculinity, Pan-Americanism, and Other Imaginaries", *The Art Bulletin* 102, no. 3 (2020): pp. 104-129; and the substantial new research presented in *Marisol: Sculptures and Works on Paper,* ed. Marina Pacini (Memphis Brooks Museum of Art, 2014) and *Marisol: A Retrospective*, ed. Cathleen Chaffee (Buffalo AKG Art Museum and DelMonico Books, 2023). As Sid Sachs summarised: "Lauded by less-important critics, she was virtually ignored by Greenberg, Rosenberg, Lippard, Alloway, Judd, Sandler, Barr, and Geldzahler. Critical language was often used to deny Marisol acceptance as a Pop artist; either she was too involved with pathos or a folk artist. When considered in the literature at all, articles on Marisol tended to be prosaically descriptive, anecdotal, and less supportive." Sid Sachs, "Beyond the Surface: Women and Pop Art 1958-1968" in *Seductive Subversion: Women Pop Artists 1958-1968* (University of the Arts and Abbeville Press, 2010), p. 36.
15. Linda Nochlin, *The Body in Pieces: The Fragment as a Metaphor of Modernity* (Thames and Hudson, 1994), pp. 53, 19.

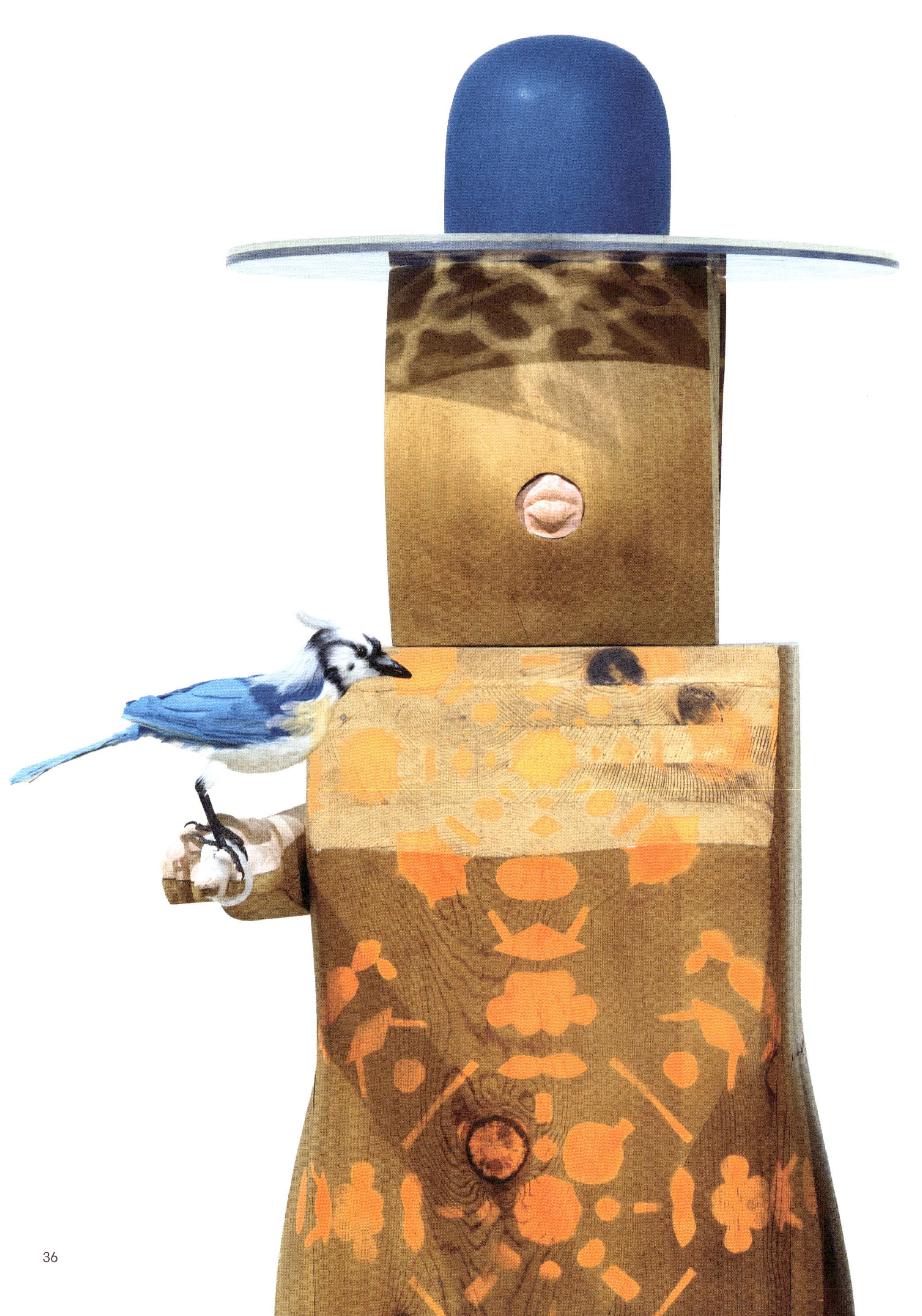

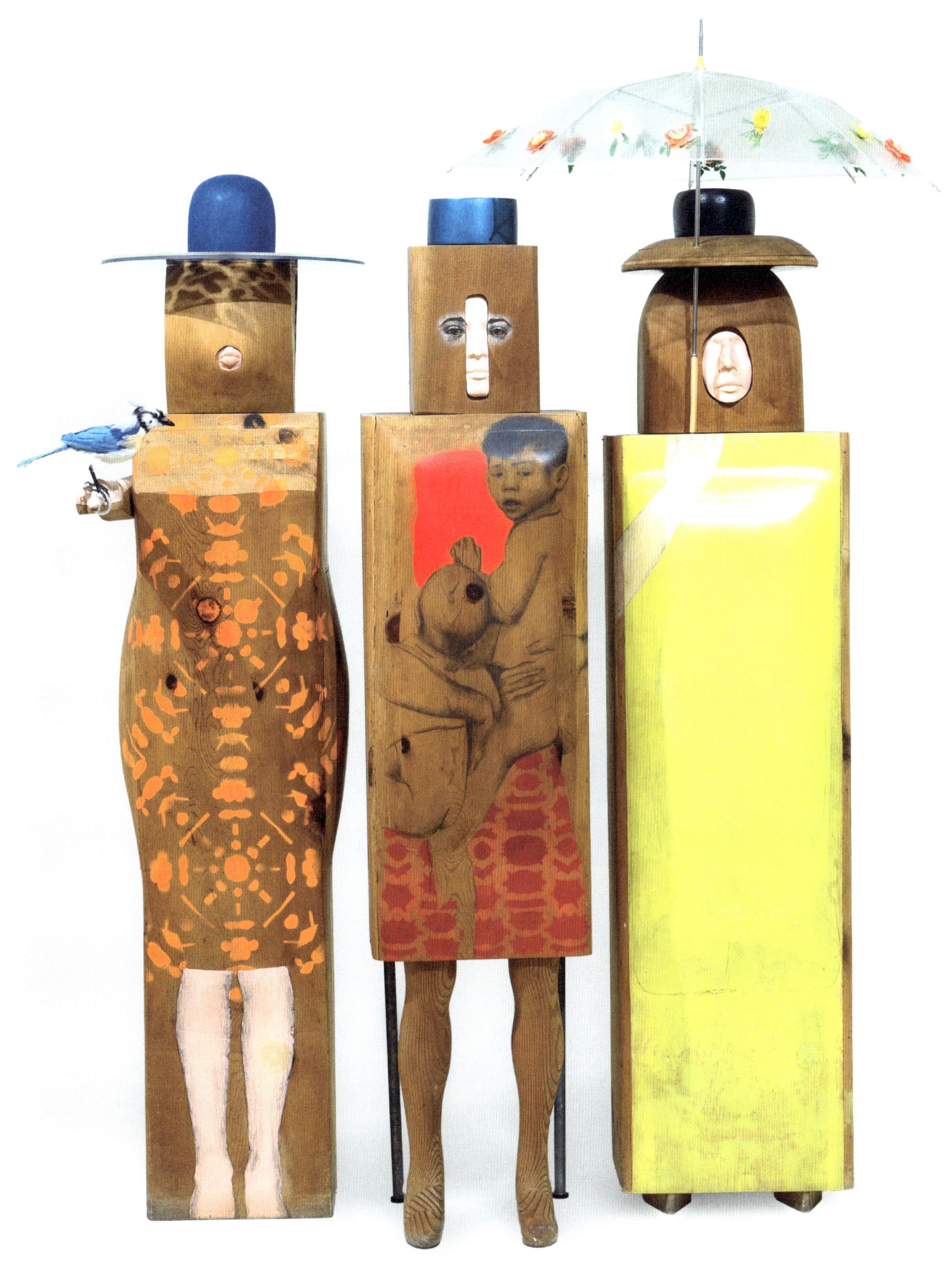

26. *Three Women with Umbrella*, 1965-66 (detail opposite)

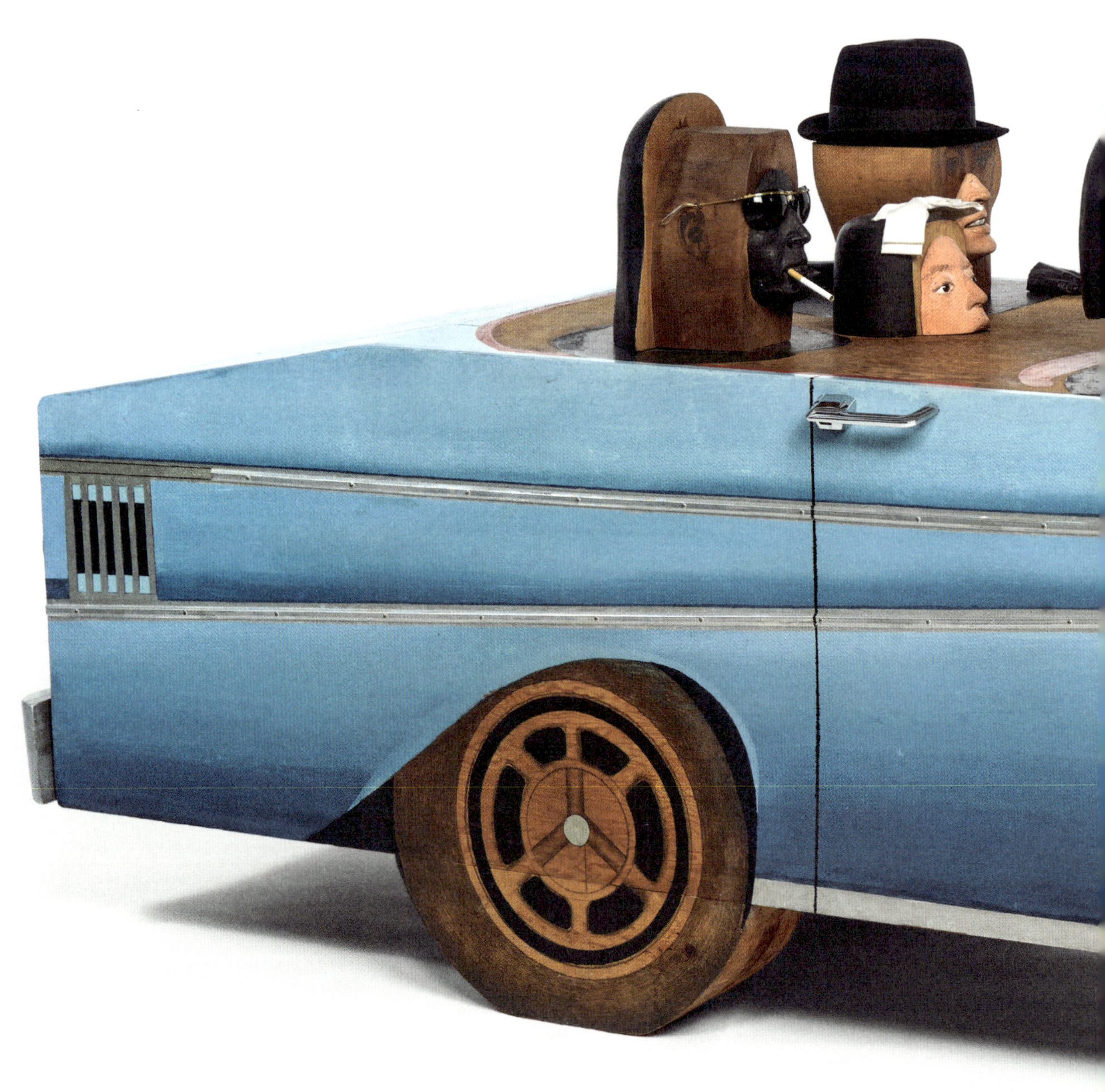

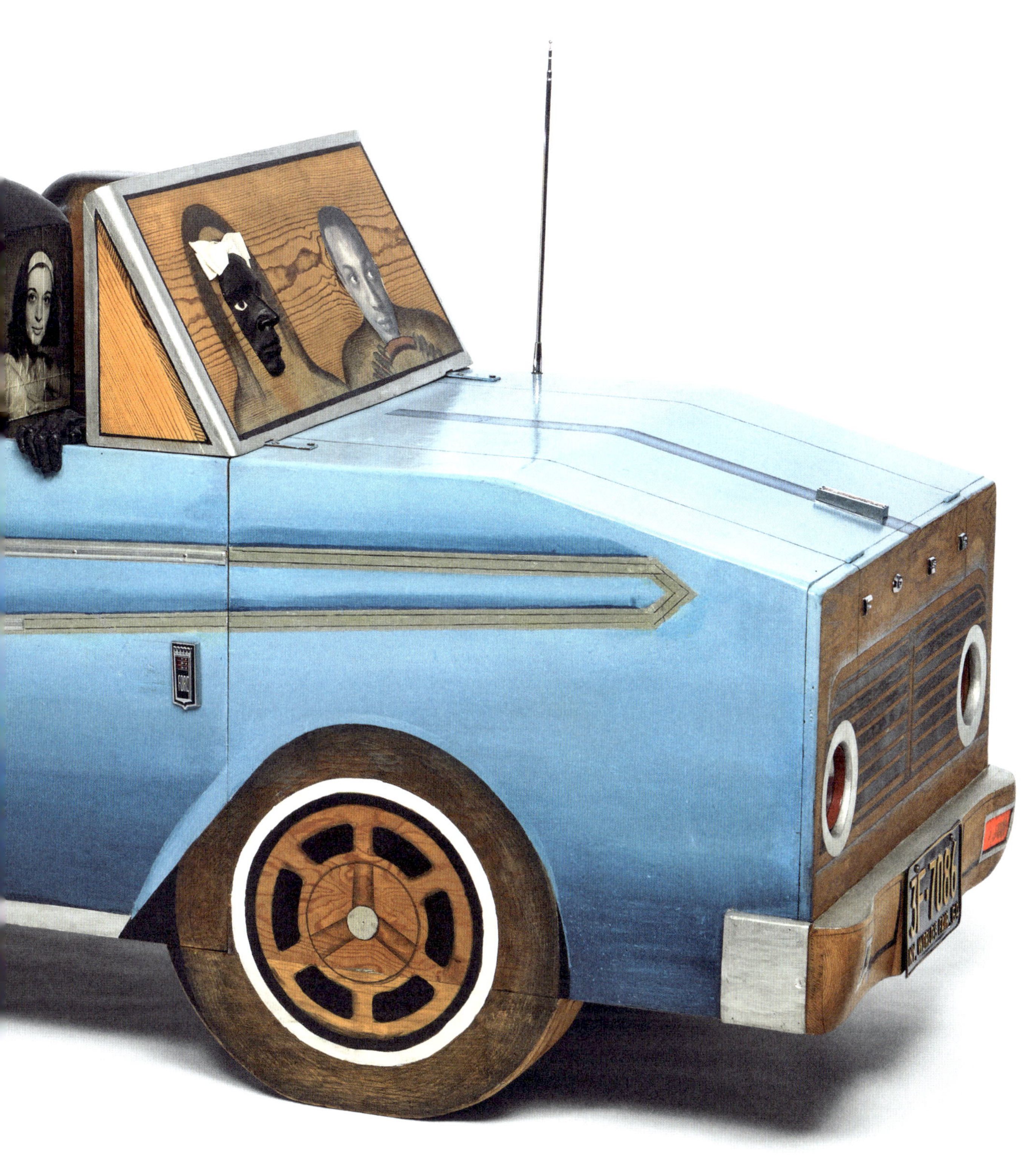

22. *The Car*, 1964

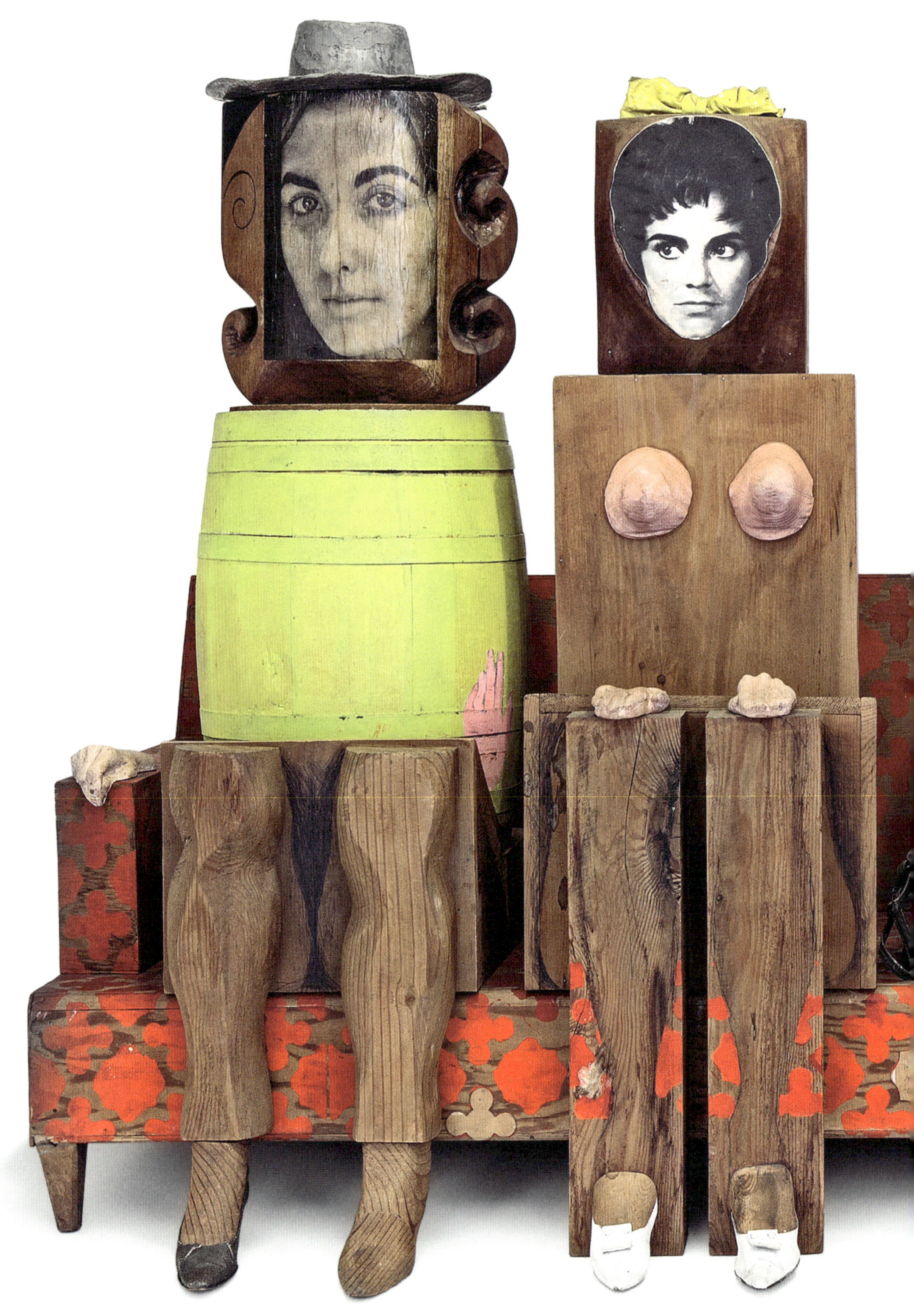

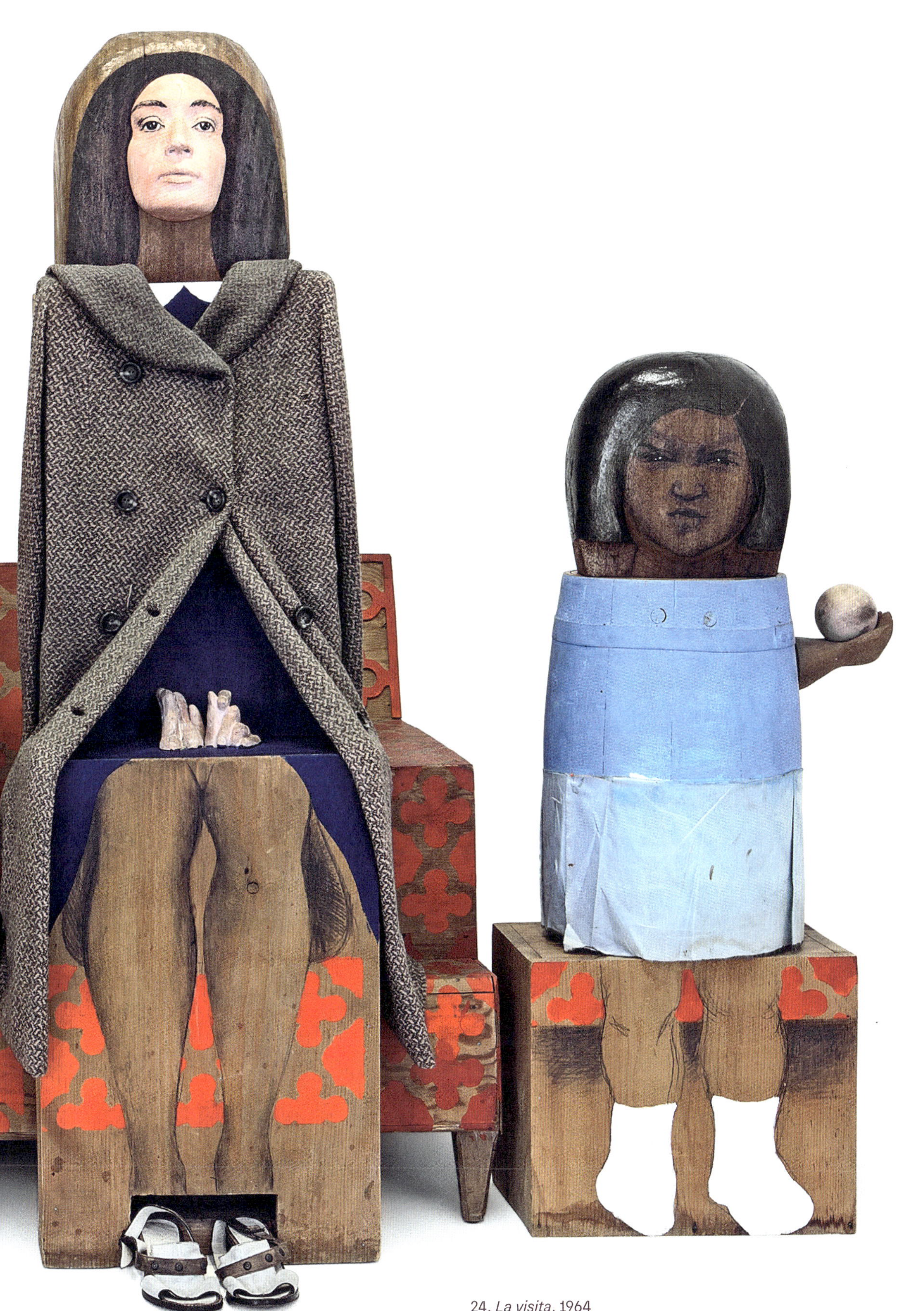

24. *La visita*, 1964

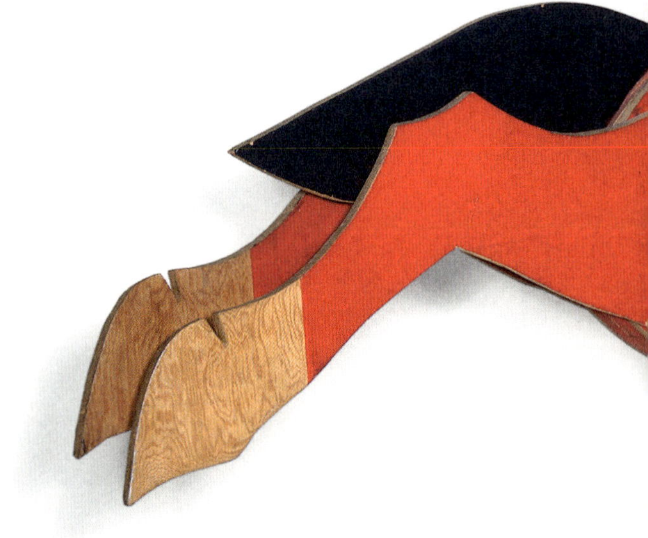

21. *John Wayne*, 1963

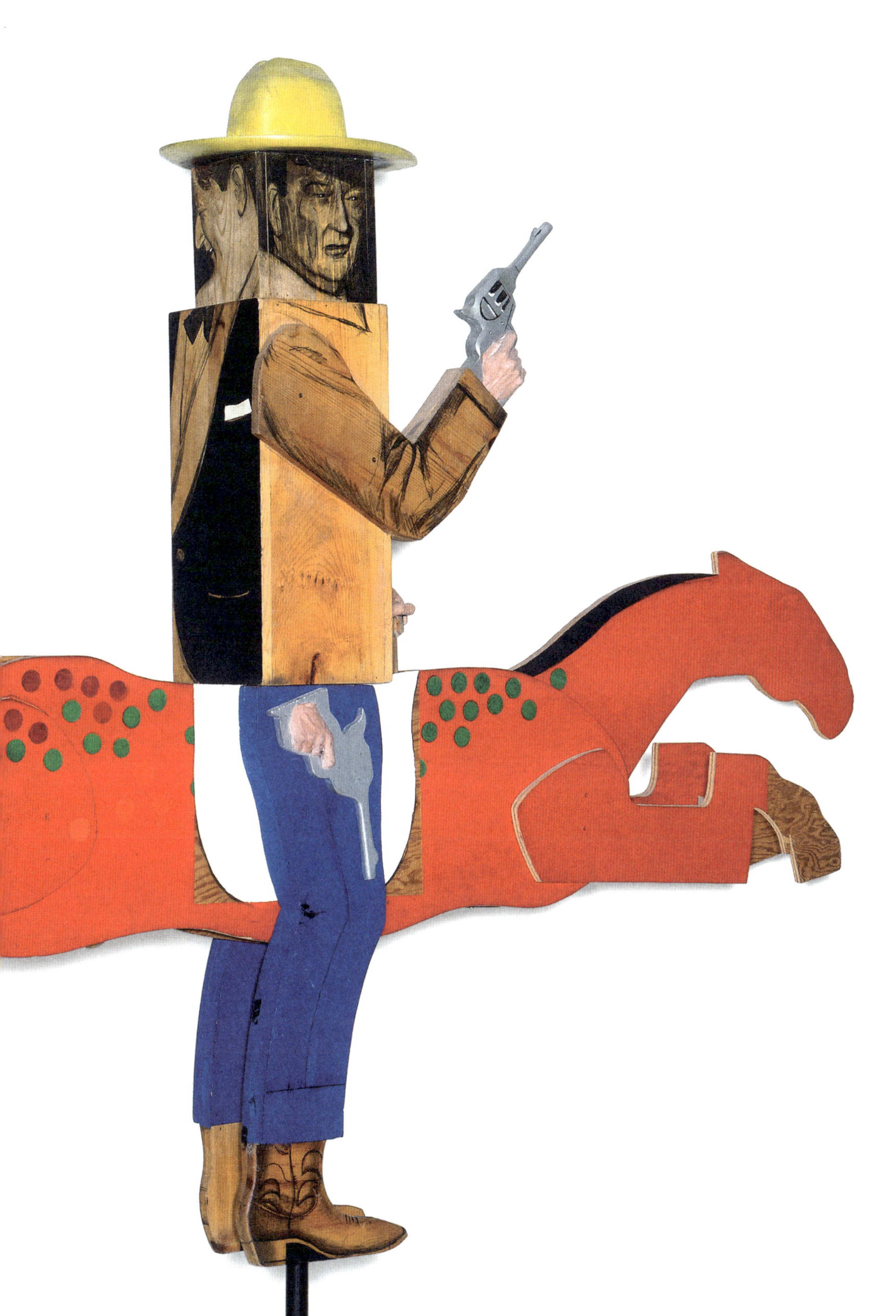

16. *The Bathers,* 1961-62

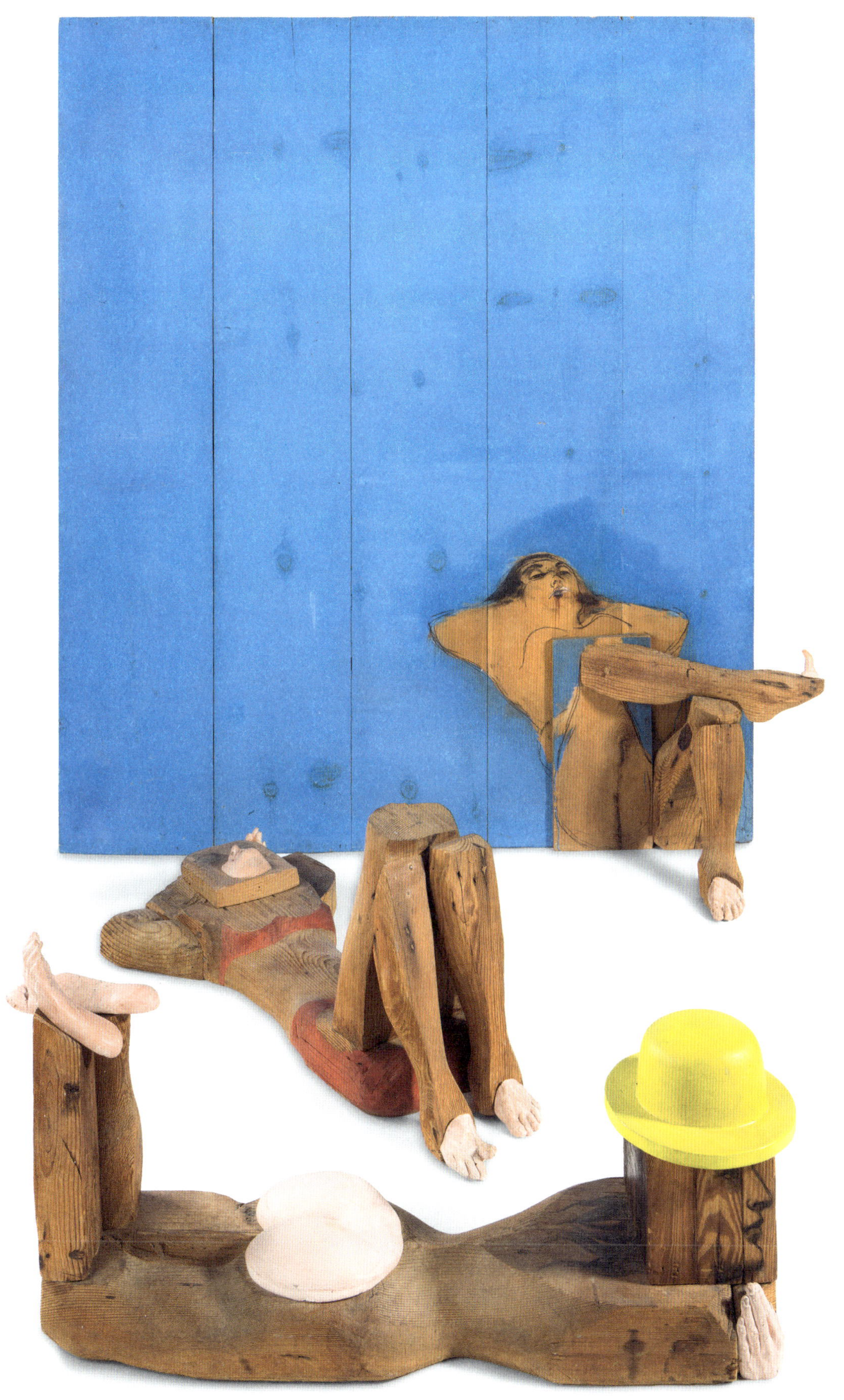

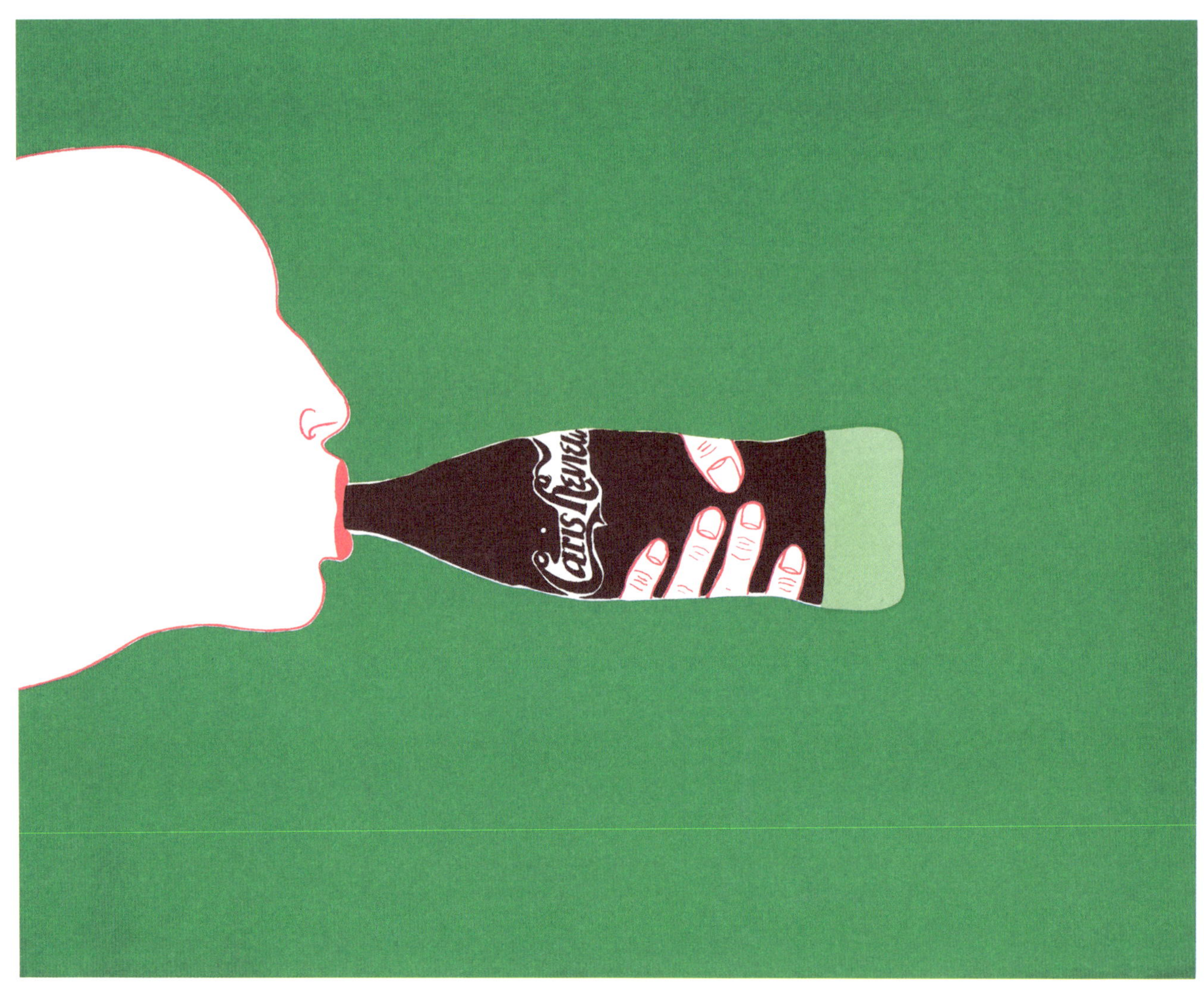

30. *Paris Review*, 1967

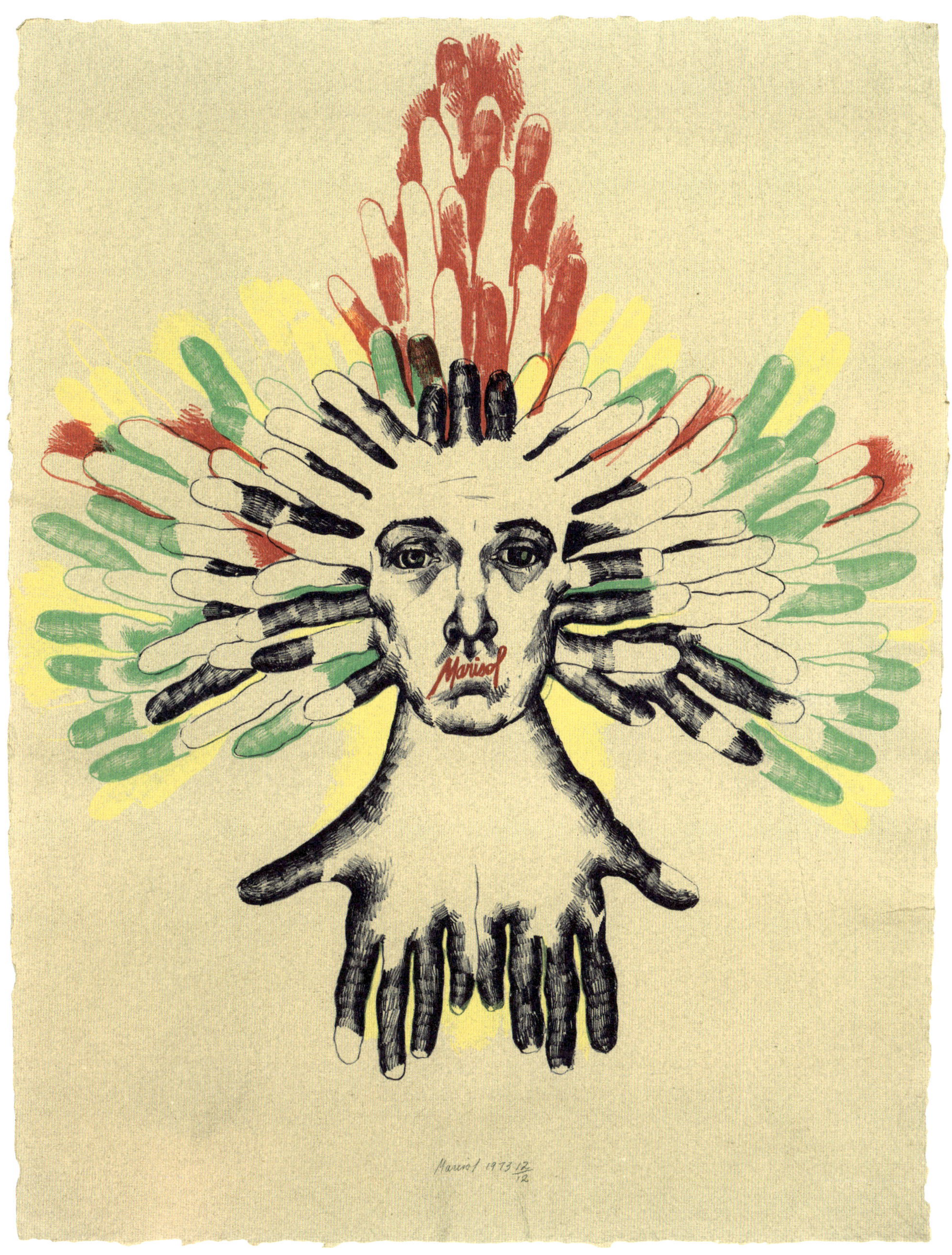

57. *Cultural Head,* 1973

Women of Pop

Nicole Rudick

In a 1973 article for *Ms. Magazine*, the art critic Lucy Lippard opined that had Pop art been dominated by women from the start, "the movement might never have gotten out of the kitchen".[1] Pop was considered a "breakthrough", Lippard writes, because it was men, not women, who showed an interest in the domestic sphere, producing work that dwelled in many realms that were not their own: cans of soup, tubes of lipstick, romance comics, household appliances and women's bodies. The earliest American exhibitions of Pop featured no women at all. In 1962, *International Exhibition of the New Realists* at Sidney Janis, in New York, cast a wide net, featuring 29 male artists from five countries. On the West Coast, *New Painting of Common Objects* at the Pasadena Art Museum marked the first museum survey of American Pop but included only eight artists. The next year, *Six Painters and the Object* at the Guggenheim Museum, in New York, and *The Popular Image* at the Washington Gallery of Modern Art, in Washington, DC, showed a combined 17 artists, several of whom appeared in both exhibitions, narrowing the scope of who was Pop even further.

Before 1962, Pop was known in Europe and America as New Realism, Popular Realism, Factualism and Neo-Dada. On 13 December 1962, the Museum of Modern Art, New York, held a symposium on this developing form, effectively introducing the term 'Pop art' to American audiences. Peter Selz, the museum's Curator of Painting and Sculpture Exhibitions and the evening's moderator, later wrote that they chose 'Pop art' because it better described the phenomenon by homing in on its relationship to mass culture.[2] Though the panelists were not uniformly

Installation view of the exhibition *Marisol*, Stable Gallery, New York, 1964. Photo: John D. Schiff. Marisol Papers, Buffalo AKG Art Museum

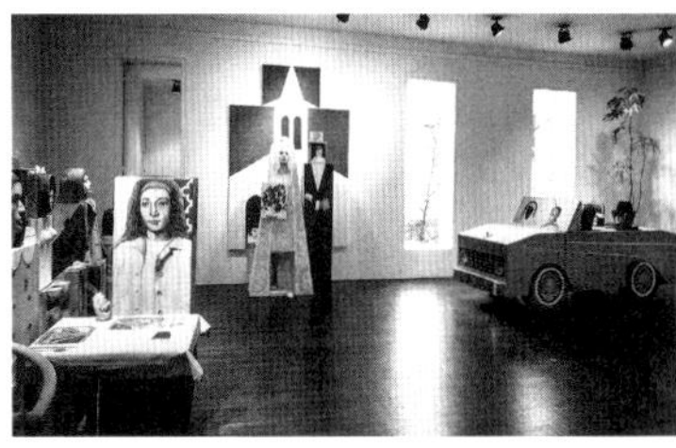

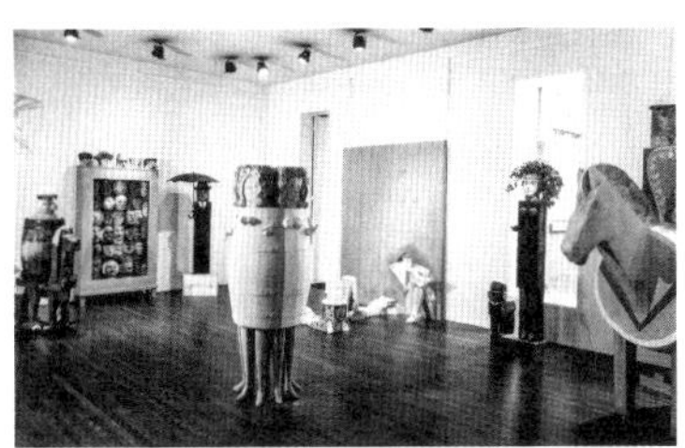

Installation view of *An Exhibition of New Work by Marisol*, Sidney Janis Gallery, New York, 1966. Photo: John D. Schiff. Marisol Papers, Buffalo AKG Art Museum

convinced of Pop's worthiness – at issue were its debt to Dada, whether it transformed or merely transposed its imagery and the strength or weakness of its processes and styles – they recognised its fundamental engagement with object, image and environment. The curatorial focus of the three early surveys shared this basic definition: art of "the daily object" or "the factual object", art whose "subject matter consists of pre-existing conventional signs and common images".[3]

It would not have been a challenge to find work by women that fit the bill. An international roster of women working in a Pop idiom included Marisol Escobar, Niki de Saint Phalle, Dorothy Iannone, Kiki Kogelnik, Rosalyn Drexler, Yayoi Kusama, Idelle Weber, Pauline Boty, Evelyne Axell, Nicola L., Marjorie Strider, Corita Kent, Joyce Wieland, Chryssa, Jann Haworth and Mara McAfee – each of whom used the language or materials (or both) of mass media and manufactured objects to examine modern society. In the catalogue for the Sidney Janis show, John Ashbery wrote of the artists' urge to make sense of "the unmanageable vastness of our experience [...] that of man on one side and a colourful indifferent universe on the other".[4] As second-wave feminism made clear by the end of the decade (and as the explosion of feminist art in the 1970s would attest), the personal was political. Who better than women, then, to dilate on this strange imbalance, this "struggle to determine the real nature of reality"[5]?

Human interest values

Pop is a troublesome category: it was not a movement with a founding group, manifesto or ideological alliances, and the artists who were then or have come to be associated with it made art too diverse to fit under a single umbrella. Even at the time, the sense of which work properly constituted Pop was unsettled. Jasper Johns denied being a Pop artist in an *Art News* interview in 1964. "Once a term is set, everybody tries to relate anybody they can to it", he said. "Labeling is a popular way of dealing with things."[6] Writing that same year, art historian Carl Belz identified in the American iteration "the chance assemblage of materials and a sensitivity to the expressive quality of natural and man-made object".[7] Of the American women associated with Pop, perhaps none were as prominent in the early 1960s as Marisol. In 1957, Leo Castelli put her in a show alongside Johns and Robert Rauschenberg (both of whom appeared in *Six Painters and the Object*), and the critic Irving Sandler judged her smash solo exhibition at the Stable Gallery in May 1962 "one of the most remarkable shows to be seen this season".[8] Later that year, a special issue of *Life* magazine included Marisol in its list of "One Hundred of the Most Important Young Men and Women in the US" (she and Chryssa were two of only nine women).[9] Marisol's eloquent sculptural portraits and tableaux made from wood and found objects depict a variety of modern and popular subjects. But in her 1966 study of Pop, Lippard swept Marisol's work out of contention, arguing that she "rarely, if ever, uses commercial motifs" and deeming it rather dismissively "a sophisticated and theatrical folk art justifiably reflecting her own beautiful face".[10] Lippard confined Pop to the "New York five" – all white American men – whose work was tough, detached and unconcerned with the "'human interest' values"[11] she saw in Marisol's art.

Installation view of the exhibition *Marisol*, Stable Gallery, New York, 1962. Photo: Geoffrey Clements Marisol Papers, Buffalo AKG Art Museum

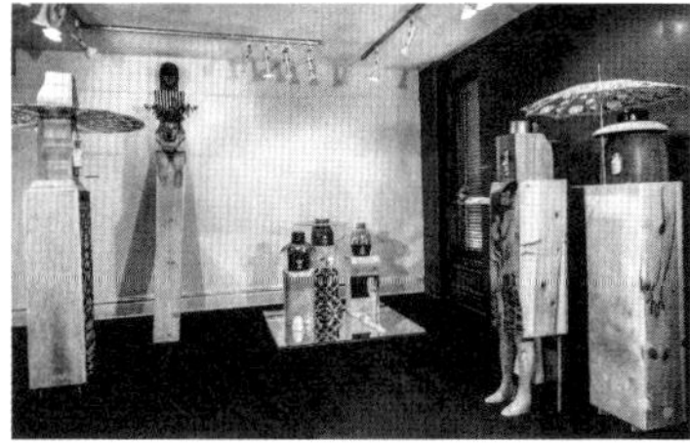

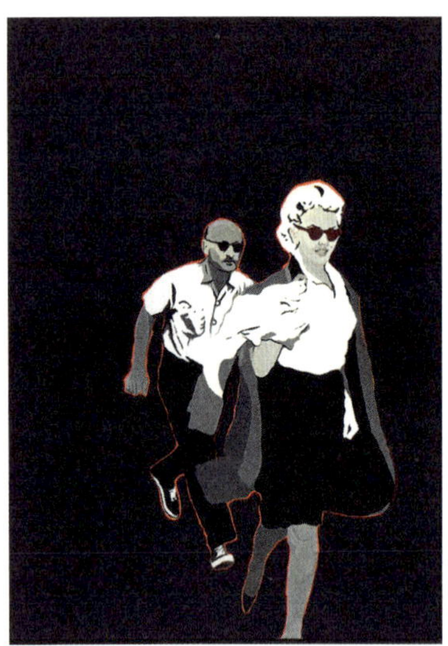

Rosalyn Drexler: *Marilyn Pursued by Death*, 1963. Acrylic and silver gelatin photograph on canvas, 126.7 × 101.6 cm. Whitney Museum of American Art

Pop is frequently noted for its detachment and impersonal approach to popular culture.[12] But for women artists, cultural representations of women are not secondhand sources in the way that, say, a beer can or a hamburger might be. Identity is complicated by the way women in general are presented in media, and much of the work by women in this decade reclaims or reorients common symbols. One of the most famous women in the world at this moment was Marilyn Monroe, whose face and body endure as a vessel for endless cultural meaning. In Rosalyn Drexler's *Marilyn Pursued by Death* (1963), Monroe strides across an isolating black canvas while a man rushes up menacingly behind her. Though he looks intently at Monroe, she appears to look out at the viewer with a smile as her left foot steps off the edge of the canvas; her body, perspectively larger, overlaps his. These oppositions give Monroe the advantage of evasion and escape. The British painter Pauline Boty also brought Monroe into her art. *Epitaph to Something's Gotta Give* (1962) references Monroe's last, unfinished film and is based on a photograph of the actress swimming in the nude. In the painting, Boty tightens the view around Marilyn's smiling face, cropping out her celebrated body, and frames it with bursts of bright colour. As an epitaph, Boty's painting restores Marilyn to life, not as an object but as a luminous subject.

Female consciousness

Many of the women who worked in Pop's idiom brought to their art a distinctly female consciousness. Their work contains narratives about women's lives and socio-political concerns at a time when art was still dominated by men (both in the gallery and on the critic's page) and when narrative, according to Clement Greenberg, was the domain of literature, not visual art. Some of these women fought battles on multiple fronts, most widely fending off intrusive, dismissive commentary about their physical appearances. For instance, in 1962 *Scene* magazine pronounced, "Actresses often have tiny brains. Painters often have large beards. Imagine a brainy actress who is also a painter and a blonde and you have PAULINE BOTY."[13] In a conversation with French *Vogue* in 1965, Niki de Saint Phalle was asked by her male interviewer, "Listen, Niki, if you have so much contempt for men, why sport such extraordinary costumes, so provocative, so feminine – man-catching clothes, it seems to me...?"[14] Marisol was a frequent target: critics wrote about her "impressively celebratable face"[15] and her "chic, bones-and-hollows face" and "faraway, whispery voice, toneless as a sleepwalker's".[16] She was described as "a black-haired, wide-eyed unmarried woman of 33"[17] by *Time*, a "Latin Beauty"[18] by *Life*, and a "sensual señorita"[19] by *Playboy*.

The use of materials traditionally associated with "women's crafts" was another area of tension. Women didn't receive the same reception as men who chose similar materials and processes. Yayoi Kusama exhibited her first soft sculpture, *Accumulation No. 1*, in a group exhibition at Green Gallery in June 1962. Among other work on view was Claes Oldenburg's papier-maché sculpture *Men's Jacket with Shirt and Tie* (1961). Up to that point, Oldenburg constructed his sculptures by soaking muslin in plaster, shaping it over a wire frame, and painting it. In September of that year, he exhibited his first soft sculptures in a solo

Yayoi Kusama: *Accumulation*, c. 1963. Sewn and stuffed fabric, wood chair frame and paint, 87.2 × 98.9 × 92.2 cm. Whitney Museum of American Art

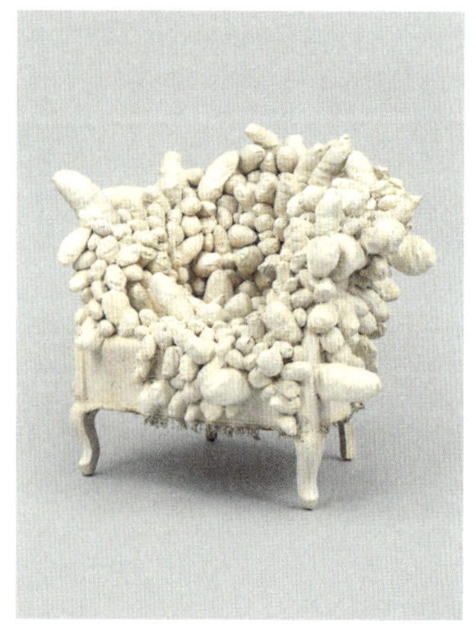

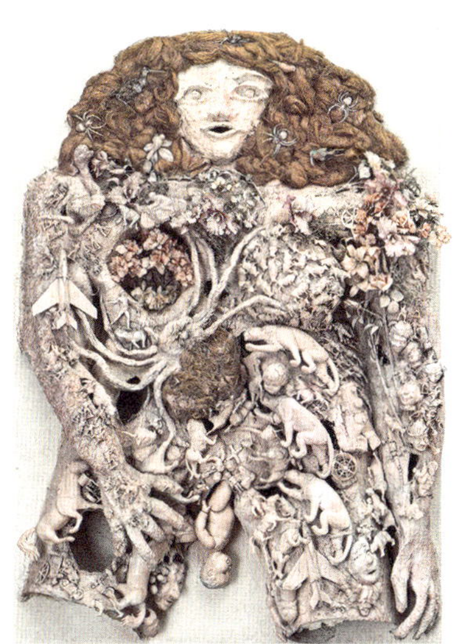

Niki de Saint Phalle: *L'accouchement rose* (The Pink Delivery), 1964. Mixed media, relief, 219 x 152 x 40 cm. Moderna Museet

show at Green Gallery. Kusama recalled that Patty Mucha, Oldenburg's wife and an artist in her own right, led her to his *Soft Calendar for the Month of August* (1962) and "said to the effect, 'Yayoi, I am sorry we took your idea.' I was surprised to see the work almost identical to my sculpture."[20] Lippard later wrote that Kusama's bristling soft sculptures "constituted some of the most memorable art shown in New York in the early 1960's."[21] Yet Oldenburg's oversize soft hamburgers and cakes brought him instant fame and have become international symbols for the Pop era.

The American artist Jann Haworth also made soft sculptures before Oldenburg, but in his 1990 survey of Pop, Marco Livingstone argued that her "choice of subject matter and especially her use of procedures associated with 'women's work'", including its "handcrafted, sometimes folksy look", relegated her art to Pop's periphery.[22] Haworth began studying at the Slade School of Fine Art in London in 1961 and made her first soft sculptures there, a move she has called an act of rebellion partly in response to the department's "male-dominated zone".[23] She used cloth, latex, and sequins, she said, because "it was a female language to which the male students didn't have access".[24] *Donuts, Coffee Cups and Comic* (1962) includes a table setting made entirely from textiles: a stitched *Sunday News* showing a *Dick Tracy* comic alongside "chinoiserie" fabric tea cups and saucers and a variety plate of doughnuts. That same year she made *Old Lady*, a full-scale soft sculpture of a woman sitting in a chair. The figure's white hair is a confection of hand-sewn lace, and the wrinkles in her face and neck are quilted from variously coloured fabrics – methods, for Haworth, of beautifying female old age.[25] The woman's body, however, is an illusion: her legs form the chair's front legs, and her torso comprises the seat and back. Haworth recognised that older women were often ignored in life and underrepresented in art. In other words, she said, "They were furniture."[26]

At the same time, Saint Phalle moved from making her *Tirs*, or shooting paintings,[27] to three-dimensional depictions of brides, witches, and mothers – beautiful, monstrous figures studded with small dime-store objects such as guns, insects, dinosaurs, warplanes and heads. These sculptures and reliefs reflected women's vulnerability and ambiguous power and led to the creation of her *Nanas* in the mid-1960s: brightly coloured, buoyant celebrations of womanhood. In Saint Phalle's drawings and sculptures, the *Nanas* are temples and goddesses, structures to be climbed on and entered, women in love, at play, and in romantic entanglements. The erotic exuberance of Saint Phalle's work finds a complement in Dorothy Iannone's radically liberated art. In 1968, Iannone made the artist's book *Lists (IV)*, a joyous record of her lovers that includes explicit drawings of each sexual encounter. Kusama's experience ran counter to Saint Phalle's and Iannone's. *Accumulation No. 1* (1962) is an armchair thickly barnacled with hand-sewn phalluses. The work, and the series of *Accumulations* that succeeded it, addressed Kusama's sexual anxieties. In affixing phalluses onto furniture and dresses, she literally superimposes the male gender atop traditionally female-gendered domestic objects in a stifling display of dominance and threat.

Dorothy Iannone: *I Was Thinking Of You III*, 1975/2006. Acrylic on wood, feathers and black and white video with audio, 190 × 100 × 37 cm Louisiana Museum of Modern Art

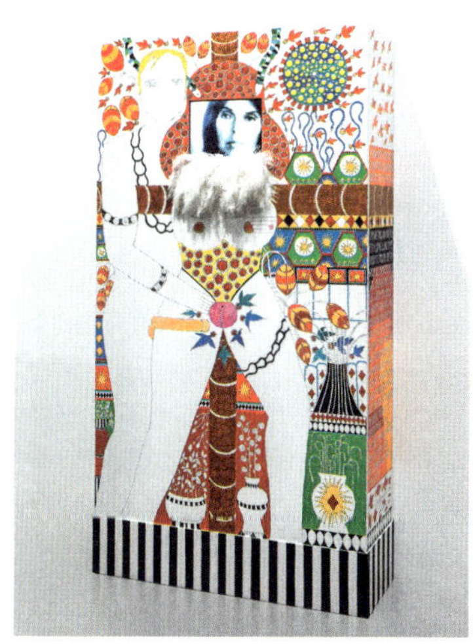

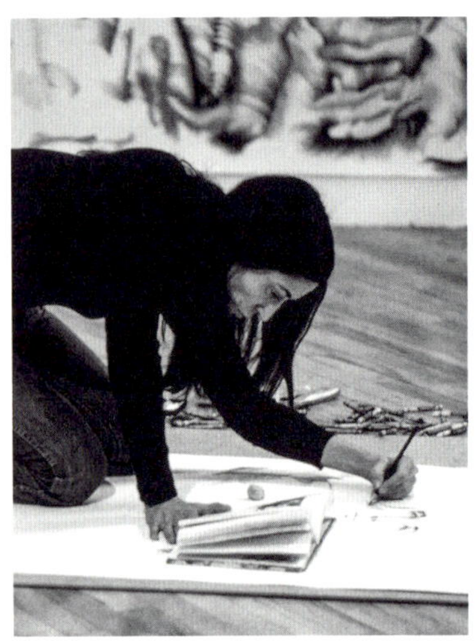

Marisol preparing works for *New Drawings and Wall Sculpture by Marisol*, Sidney Janis Gallery, New York, 1975. Marisol Papers, Buffalo AKG Art Museum

If the elements of Pop were a lingua franca, what that language signified was not the same for all who spoke it. When Brian O'Doherty, in 1967, attempts to get Marisol to "contemplate her own mystery", she responds, "Why is my own face one of my preoccupations? Because I can't find out what I look like."[28] For women, a response to the imagery of modern society might be openly adversarial or defensive.[29] Beginning in 1960, Marisol's drawings included outlines of her hands and face, and casts of her body parts appeared on her sculptural works. "The tracing of myself began in Paris in a hotel room", she later wrote. "Out of fear of losing my body and my mind I placed a sheet of paper on the floor and traced myself."[30] Even if the image is a familiar one, it may be unrecognizable. Perhaps that's why Kiki Kogelnik began disassembling the body in her paintings of the 1960s and augmenting them with cyborg parts. In works such as *Female Robot* and *Self Portrait* (both 1964), female bodies are dismembered or torn asunder. These future-forward, occasionally harrowing representations reimagine the corporeal form and offer escape from the reality not just of the kitchen but of Earth altogether. The "colourful indifferent universe", as Ashbery put it, may have seemed less hospitable than the planet on which women then (as now) fought for fundamental civil rights.

Pop clichés

Decades later, women were still being written out of Pop art history. In 2000, David McCarthy offered a blanket rationale for omitting women: "If, as is now commonly argued, modernism was largely an enterprise with men describing the world from their point of view, we should expect no less of Pop. A survey of Pop artists on both side of the Atlantic will turn up no major women within the movement [...] One way of explaining the gender bias in Pop is to focus on the age and interests of its practitioners. The concerns of the members – technology, science fiction, automobiles, advertising, pin-ups – were gender-specific in the post-war years. In an interview from 1982 [the British artist] Peter Phillips claimed that Pop was a movement initiated by young men who celebrated their most immediate interests, including pictures of women."[31]

The overwhelming evidence to the contrary makes this claim untenable; Pop's practitioners and their concerns were manifold. Lippard argued that Marisol's work wasn't tough enough to be considered Pop, but she also approvingly quoted the critic G.R. Swenson who, in defense of Warhol's technological "de-personalization", wrote that "it is the most common clichés, the most common stock responses which we must deal with first if we are to come to some understanding of the new possibilities available to us in this brave and not altogether hopeless new world".[32] Marisol and other women of the period created art that conveyed urgent, contemporary expressions of commonly held feelings as significant as any of those deemed universal by dint of their not engaging with gendered social issues. Women's concerns are universal, grounded in everyday experience. Symbols of innumerable social, political and cultural values, woman have been objects throughout the history of art. What better cliché to take aim at as we make our way into the bold future.

Kiki Kogelnik: *Liquid Injection Thrust*, 1965
Oil and acrylic on canvas, 139 × 93.4 cm
Louisiana Museum of Modern Art

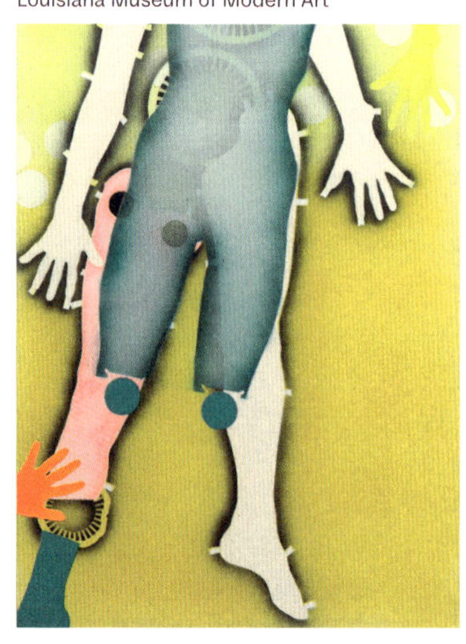

NICOLE RUDICK is an independent writer and editor. *What Is Now Known Was Once Only Imagined*, her book on the artist Niki de Saint Phalle, was published in 2022 by Siglio Press. Rudick's criticism has appeared most recently in *The New York Review of Books, Apollo, The New York Times* and *The New Yorker*, and her essays on art have been published in catalogues from the New Museum, the Drawing Center and Museum of Art, Rhode Island School of Design.

1. Lucy R. Lippard, "Household Images in Art", *Ms.* 1, no. 9 (March 1973). Reprinted in *From the Center: Feminist Essays on Women's Art* (Dutton, 1976), p. 56.
2. Peter Selz, Henry Geldzahler, Hilton Kramer, Dore Ashton, Leo Steinberg, Stanley Kunitz, "A Symposium on Pop Art", *Arts* (April 1963), pp. 35-45. Reprinted in *Pop Art: A Critical History*, ed. Steven Henry Madoff (University of California Press, 1997) pp. 65-81.
3. Lawrence Alloway, *Six Painters and the Object* (Simon R. Guggenheim Foundation, 1963), p. 3.
4. John Ashbery, preface, in *International Exhibition of the New Realists* (Sidney Janis Gallery, 1962), p. 2.
5. Ibid.
6. Jasper Johns, interview with G.R. Swenson, "'What Is Pop Art?' Answers from 8 Painters", Part II, *Art News* (February 1964). Excerpted in *American Artists on Art from 1940 to 1980*, ed. Ellen H. Johnson (Harper & Row, 1982), p. 89.
7. Carl I. Belz, "Pop Art and the American Experience", *Chicago Review*, vol. 17, no. 1 (1964), p. 109.
8. Irving Sandler, "In the Art Galleries", *New York Post* (20 May 1962), p. 10.
9. https://www.npr.org/transcripts/161162113
10. Lucy R. Lippard, *Pop Art* (Frederick A. Praeger, Inc., 1966), p. 101.
11. Ibid.
12. The art historian Barbara Rose, for instance, argued that "both post-painterly abstraction and pop art reacted against Abstract Expressionism in favor of a more impersonal, detached, and clearly articulated art." Barbara Rose, *American Art Since 1900: A Critical History* (Frederick A. Praeger, 1967), p. 213. Responding to Warhol's self-described "machine-like" approach to artmaking, Irving Sandler writes, "The upshot of this approach has been an art so dead-pan, so devoid of signs of emotion, that I have called it cool-art." Irving Sandler, "The New Cool-Art", *Art in America* (January-February 1965). In a panel conversation for a pair of Pop-themed exhibitions at the Guggenheim Museum in 1988 (all the panelists were men), George Segal complained, "Between Kaprow and Claes and myself, we're part of a minority group of passionate expressionist pop artists, and mostly, the critics have been celebrating pop art as this kind of cool, ironic, detached commentary on things ... I think what hasn't happened is some notation of the breadths of ambition in this group: what they wanted to tackle." From "Early Sixties: The Surge of American Pop", recorded on 15 November 1988, transcript, https://www.guggenheim.org/wp-content/uploads/2018/08/9009304_01_9009305_01_9009306_01-The-Surge-of-American-Pop.pdf). Pop's reproduction of mass-produced objects and imagery and contemporaneous technological advances may have had an outsized effect on the attitude some critics brought to bear on the work, inspired by certain artists' embrace of the wonders of automatization. In an interview from the mid-1960s, Warhol commented on his studio environment: "Factory is as good a name as any. A factory is where you build things. This where I make or *build* my work ... Mechanical means are *today*, and using them I can get more art to more people." Quoted in Benjamin H.D. Buchloh, "Andy Warhol's One-Dimensional Art: 1956–1966", *October Files*, ed. Annette Michelson (MIT Press, 2002), p. 5. Roy Lichtenstein balked at the Americanization of Pop, arguing instead that Pop is "actually industrial painting. America was hit by industrialism and capitalism harder and sooner ... I think the meaning of my work is that it's industrial, it's what all the world will soon become." Roy Lichtenstein, interview with G.R. Swenson, "'What Is Pop Art?' Answers from 8 Painters", Part II, *Art News* (February 1964). Excerpted in *American Artists on Art from 1940 to 1980*, ed. Ellen H. Johnson (Harper & Row, 1982), p. 86. Warhol's rumination on a painting machine could easily be used as ad copy for a washing machine: "I really think you could have a machine that paints all day long for you and do it really well, and you could do something else instead, and you could turn out really wonderful canvases." Buchloh, "An Interview with Andy Warhol", *October Files*, p. 127.
13. Quoted in Ali Smith, "Ali Smith on the prime of pop artist Pauline Boty", *The Guardian* (22 October 2016).
14. Translation by Jill Carrick in "Phallic Victories? Niki de Saint Phalle's *Tirs*", *Art History* (November 2003), p. 716.
15. John Canady, "Art: Constructions on the 'Tensegrity' Principle", *New York Times* (16 April 1966), p. 16.
16. Grace Glueck, *New York Times*, "It's Not Pop, It's Not Op – It's Marisol", *New York Times* (7 March 1965), p. 34.
17. "Art: Marisol", *Time* (7 June 1963), p. 76.
18. "Wood Carvers' Comeback: Young US Sculptors Revive Neglected Art", *Life* (14 July 1958), p. 59.
19. "One the Scene: Marisol: Artful Assembler", *Playboy* 15 (September 1968), p. 176.
20. Interview with Grady T. Turner, *Bomb* (Winter 1999), https://bombmagazine.org/articles/1999/01/01/yayoi-kusama/.
21. Lucy Lippard, *Eva Hesse* (New York University Press, 1976), p. 217, note 41.
22. Marco Livingstone, *Pop: A Continuing History* (Abrams, 1990), p. 168.
23. Bob Chaundy, host, *Considering Art*, podcast (8 February 2021), https://consideringart.com/2021/02/08/considering-art-podcast-jann-haworth-pop-artist/.
24. *Seductive Subversion: Women Pop Artists, 1958-1968*, eds. Sid Sachs and Kalliopi Minioudaki (University of the Arts, Philadelphia and Abbeville Press Publishers, 2010), p. 22.
25. Chaundy, *Considering Art*.
26. Jann Haworth, "Mistakes, Omissions, and Iconoclasts: From Sgt Pepper to Work in Progress", TEDx Talk, Provo, UT (March 2017), 14 min., 7 sec., https://youtu.be/Mm5kNNxbnZ4?si=JoYaMuVP8LZJK8I.
27. Saint Phalle began making her *Tirs* in 1961. These were performances in which she used a gun to explode bags of pigment and other substances embedded in canvases. "I was shooting at MYSELF, society with its INJUSTICES", she wrote in an epistolary artwork from 1992. "I was shooting at my own violence and the VIOLENCE of the times." From Saint Phalle's "Letter to Pontus", produced for the catalogue *Niki de Saint Phalle* (Verlag Gerd Hatje, 1992). Reproduced in Nicole Rudick, *What Is Now Known Was Once Only Imagined: An (Auto)biography of Niki de Saint Phalle* (Siglio, 2022), p. 80.
28. Brian O'Doherty, "Marisol: The Enigma of the Self-Image", *New York Times* (1 March 1964).
29. John Berger's well-known line applies here: "Men look at women. Women watch themselves being looked at." Berger, *Ways of Seeing* (Penguin, 1977), p. 47.
30. Quoted in Cathleen Chaffee, "Hereafter, Marisol" in *Marisol: A Retrospective,* ed. Cathleen Chaffee (Buffalo AKG Art Museum and Delmonico Books, 2023), p. 39.
31. David McCarthy, *Pop Art* (Tate Publishing, 2000), p. 25. I'm grateful to Sue Tate's "A Transgression Too Far: Women Artists and the British Pop Art Movement", for alerting me to McCarthy's discussion of gender bias. Tate's excellent essay appears in *Seductive Subversion: Women Pop Artists 1958-1968*, eds. Sid Sachs and Kalliopi Minioudaki (Abbeville Press, 2010).
32. Lippard, *Pop Art*, p. 10.

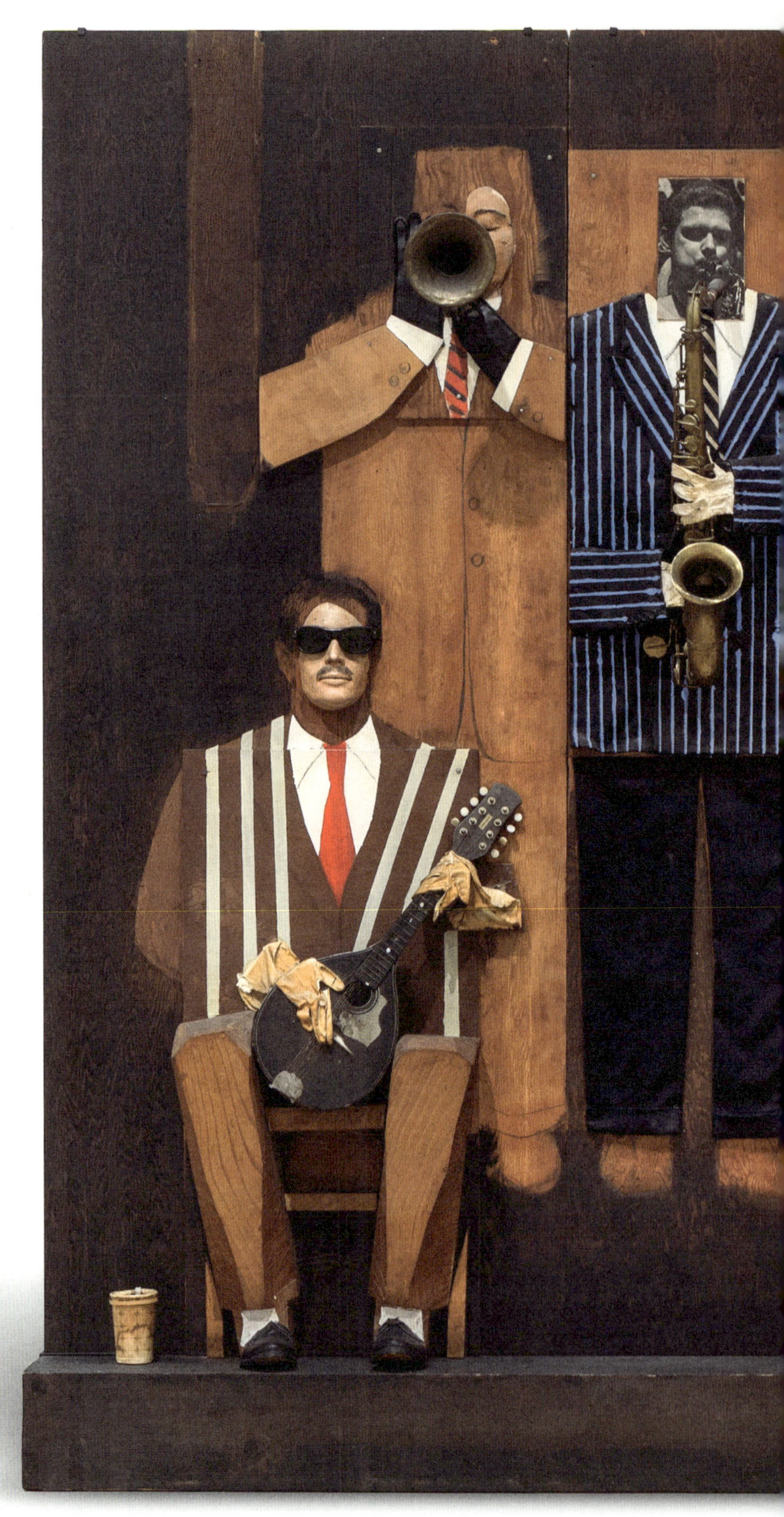

 20. *The Jazz Wall*, 1963

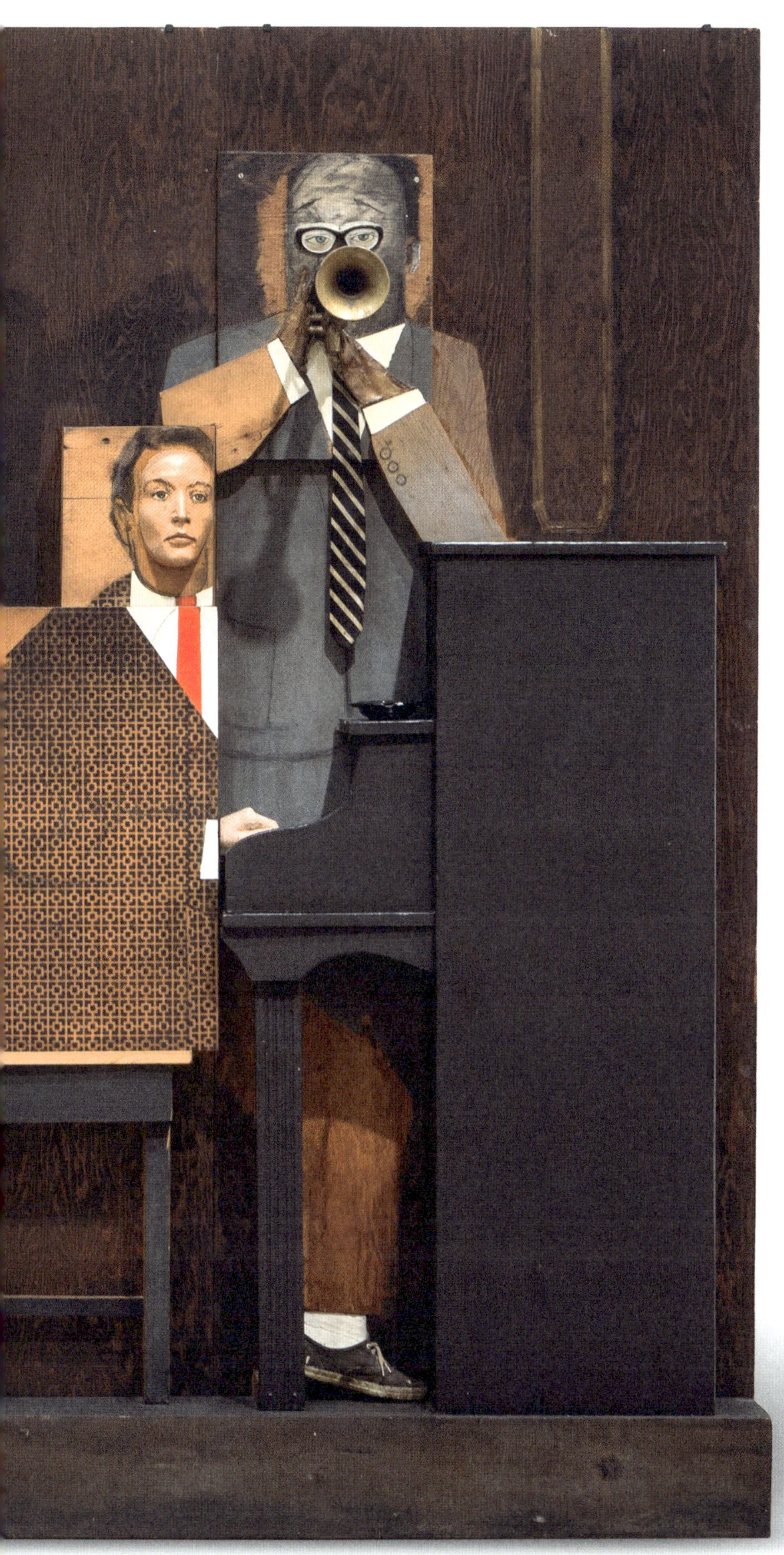

29. *LBJ*, 1967

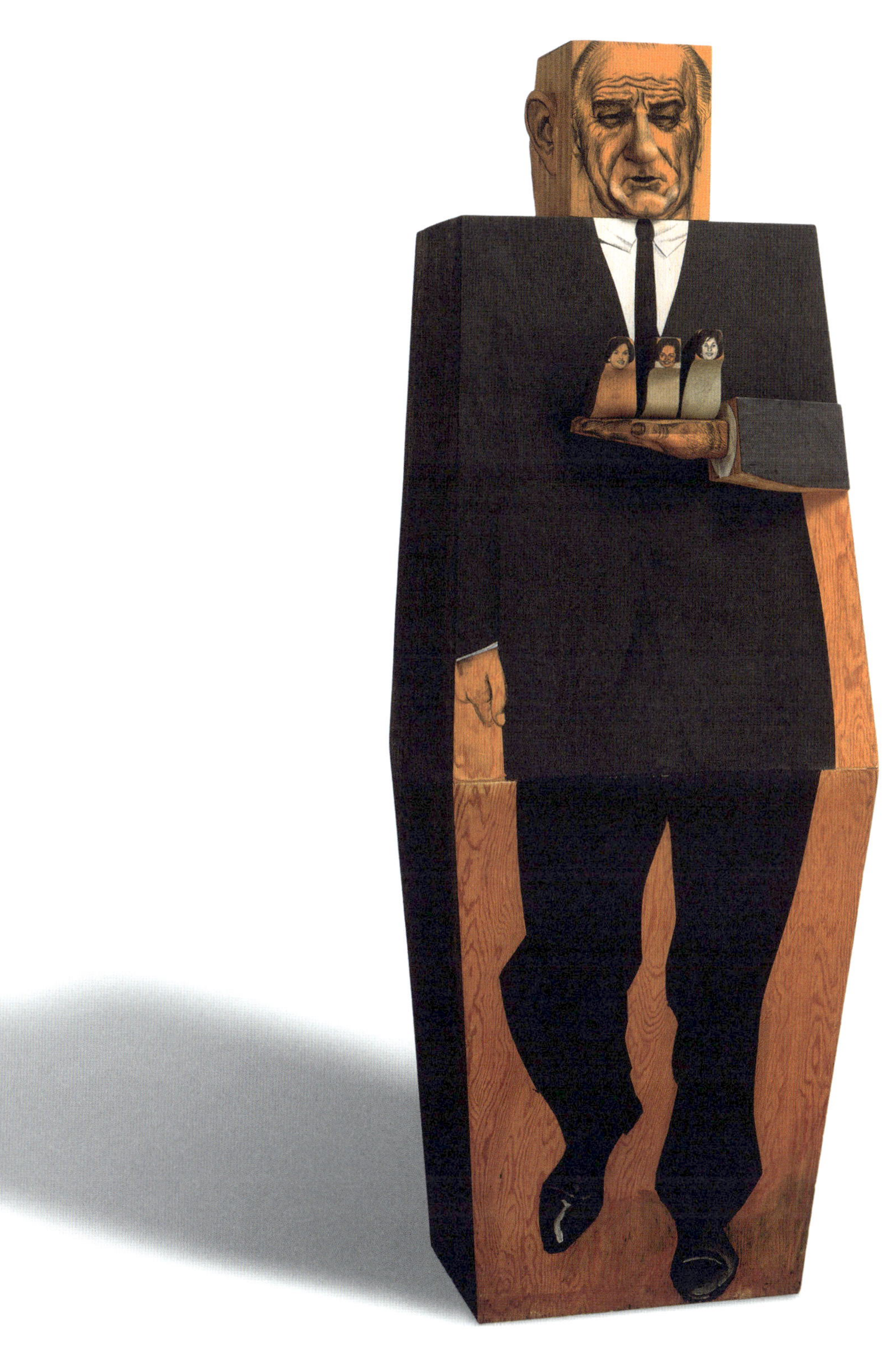

31. *The Royal Family*, 1967

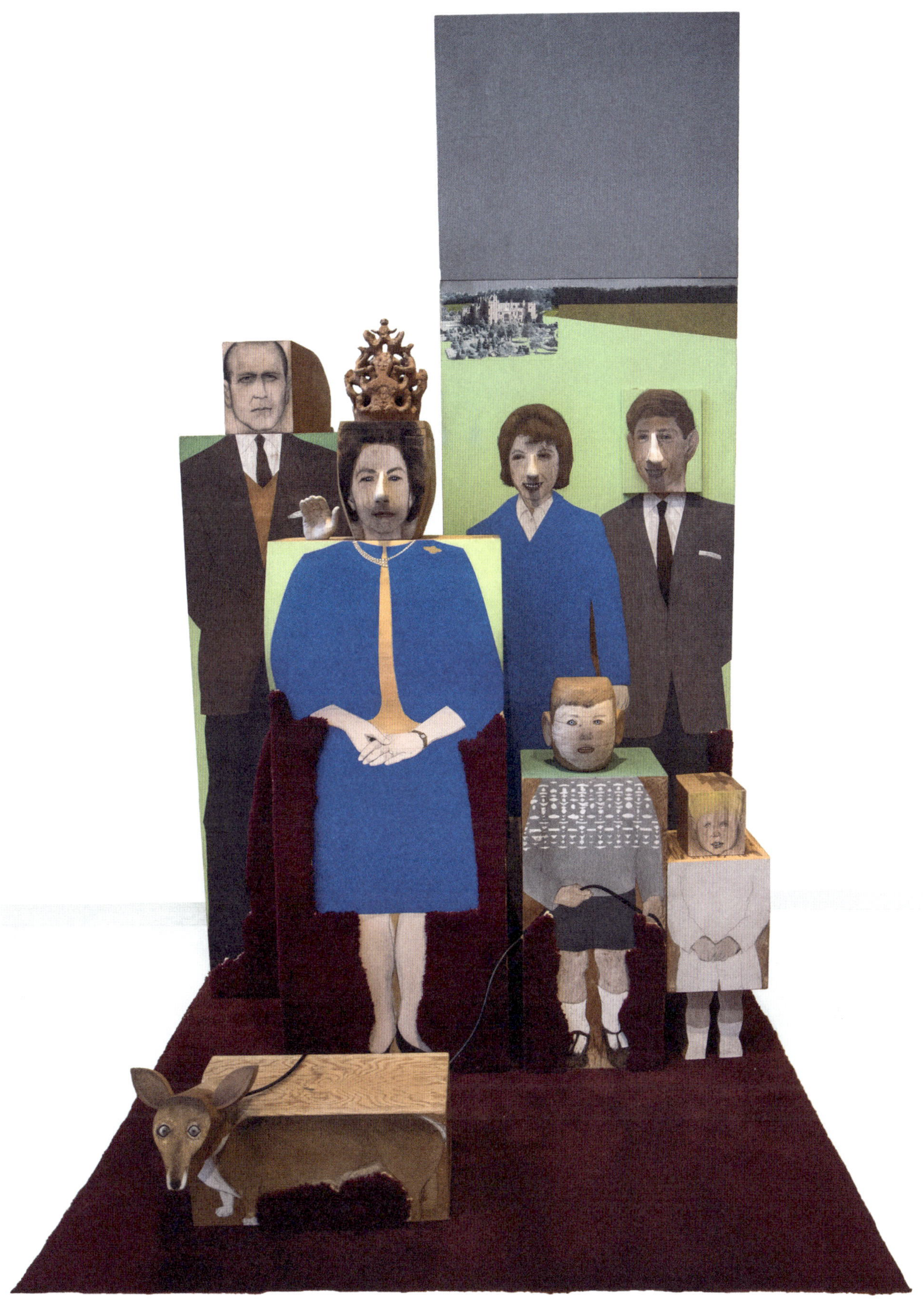

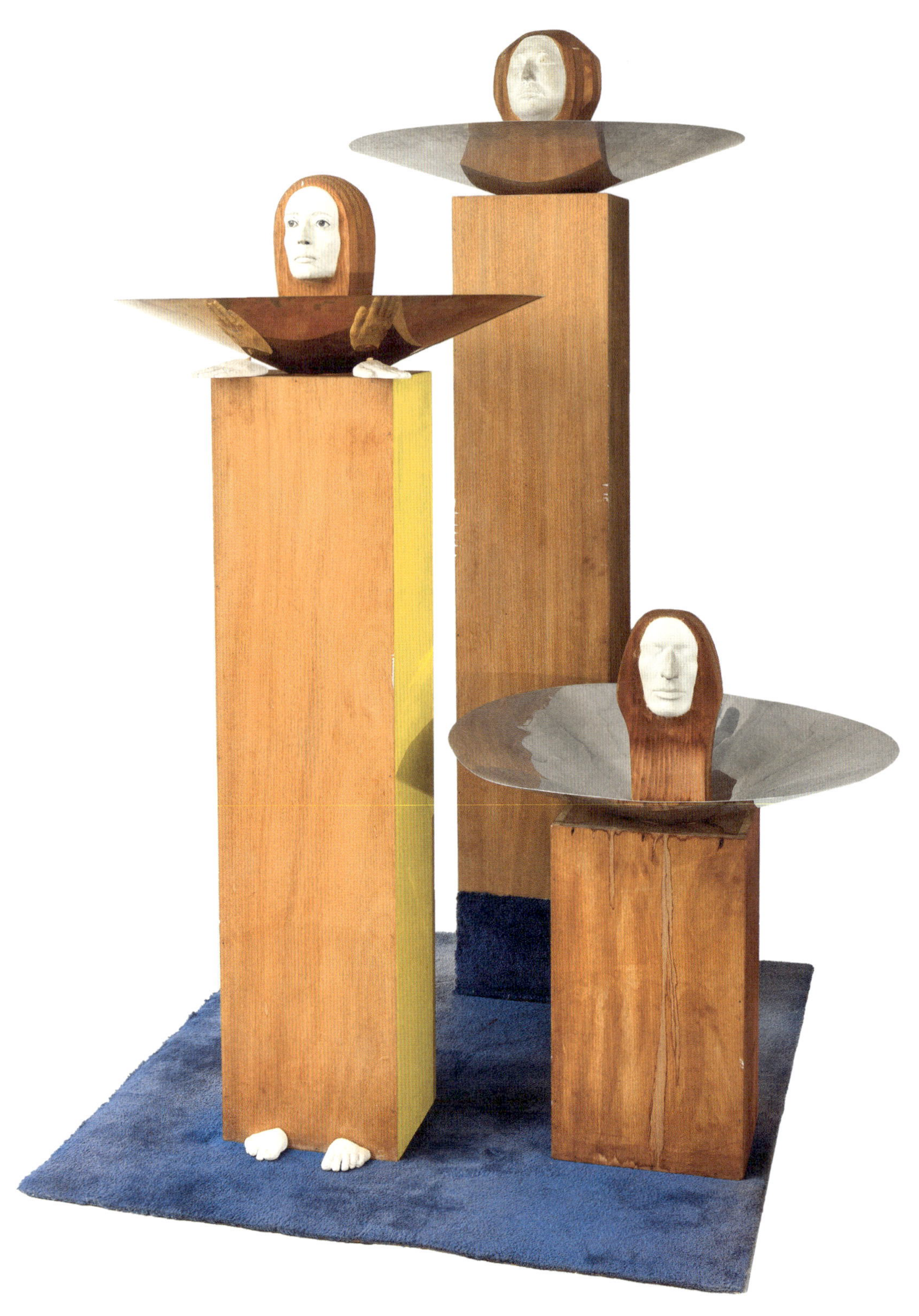

33. *The Sun Bathers*, 1967

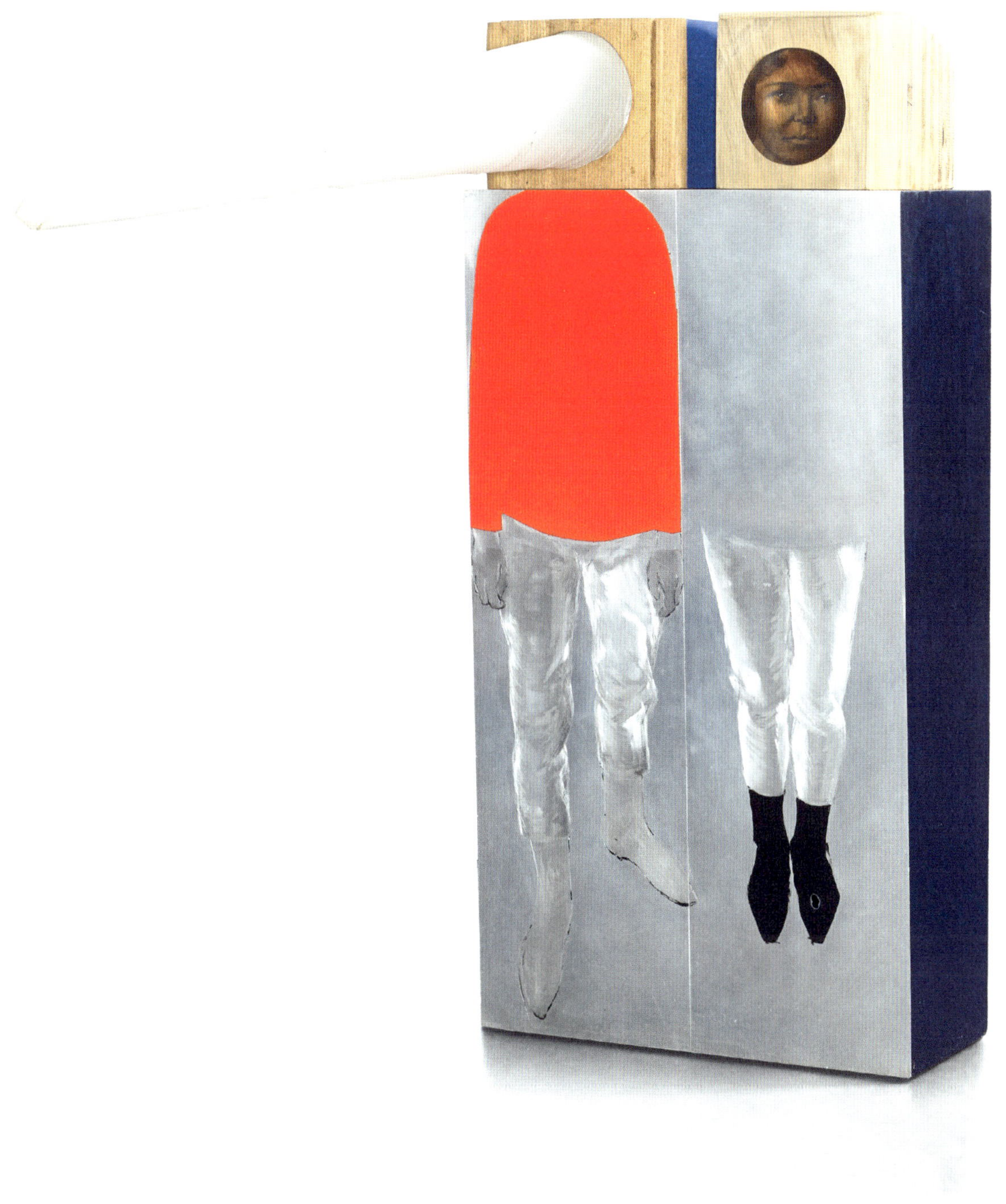

25. *Couple No. 1*, 1965–66

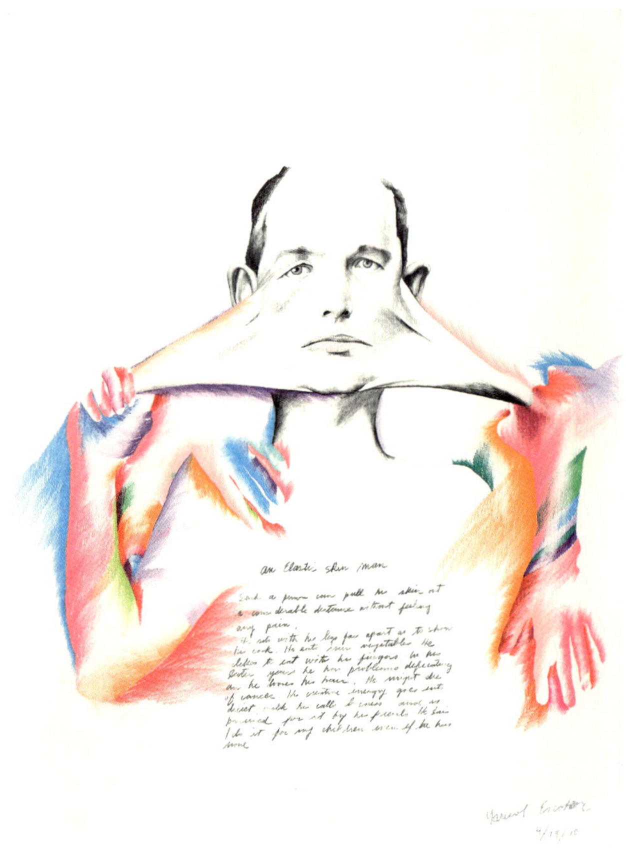

72. *An Elastic Skin Man*, 1975

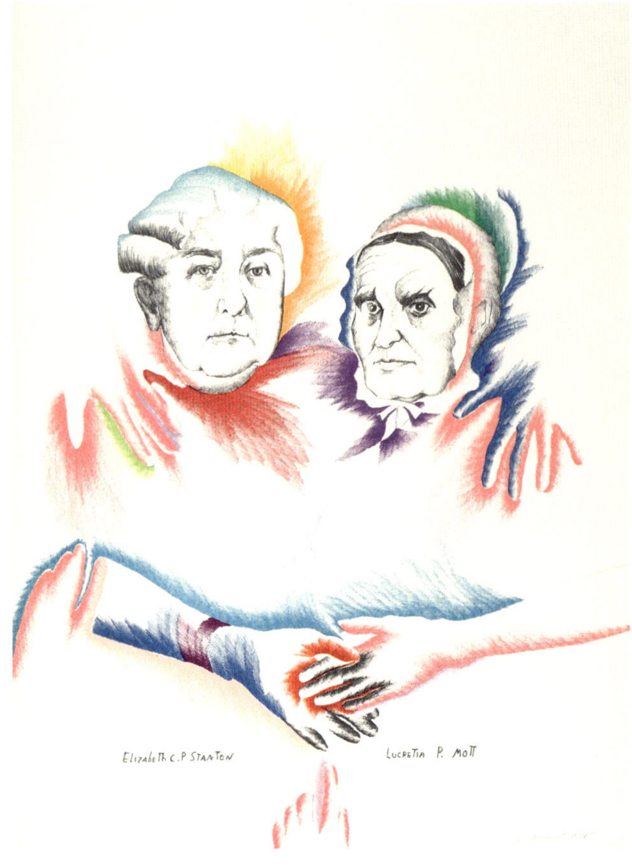

77. *Women's Equality* from the *Kent Bicentennial Portfolio: Spirit of Independence*, 1975

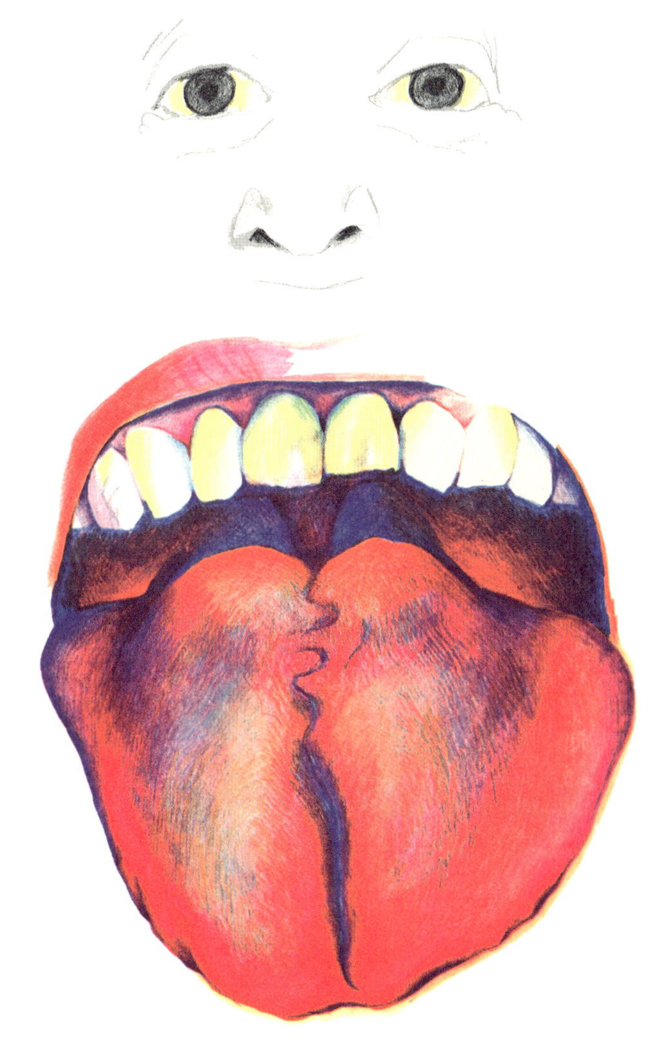

52. *Saca la Lengua*, 1972

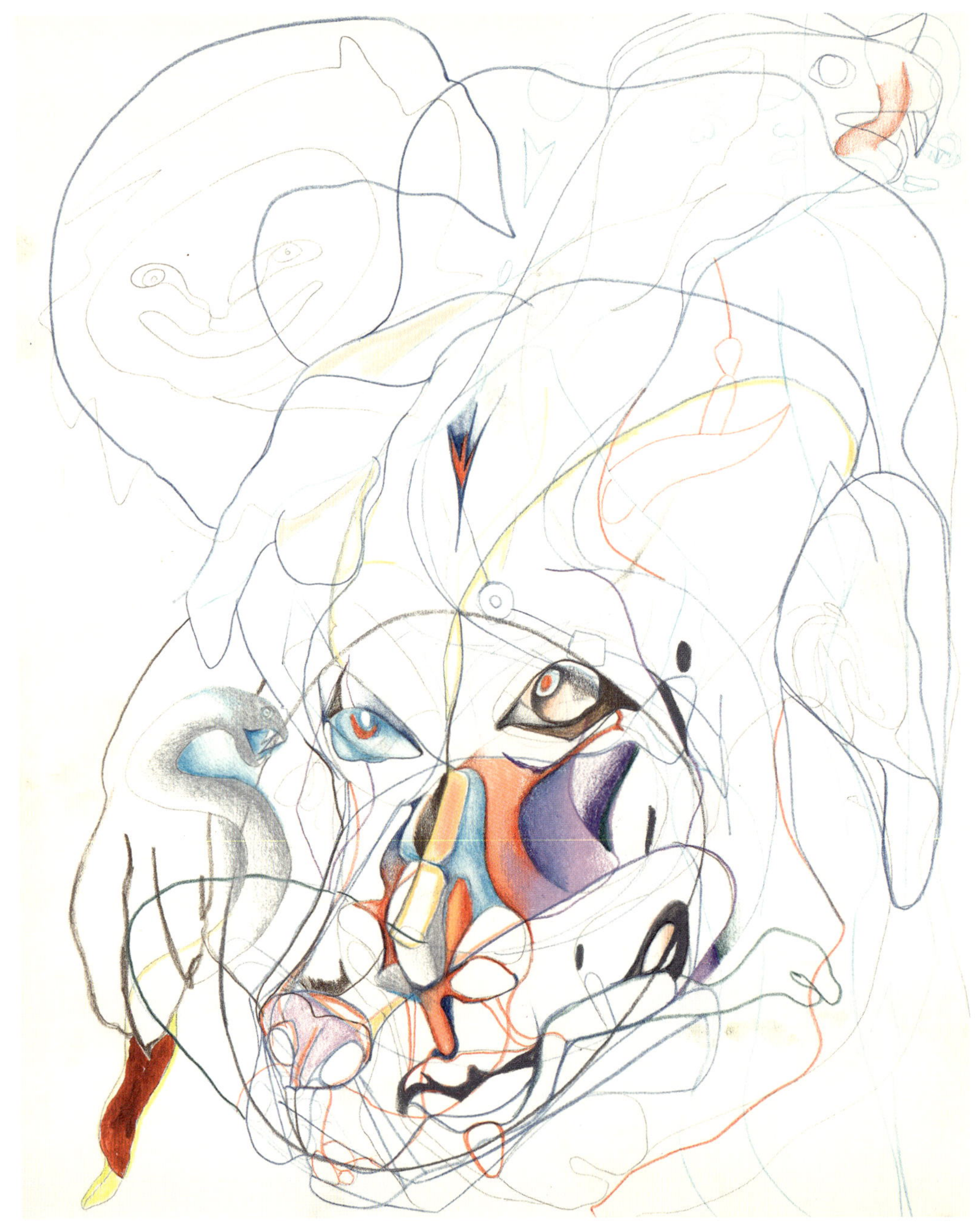

50. Untitled, c. 1972

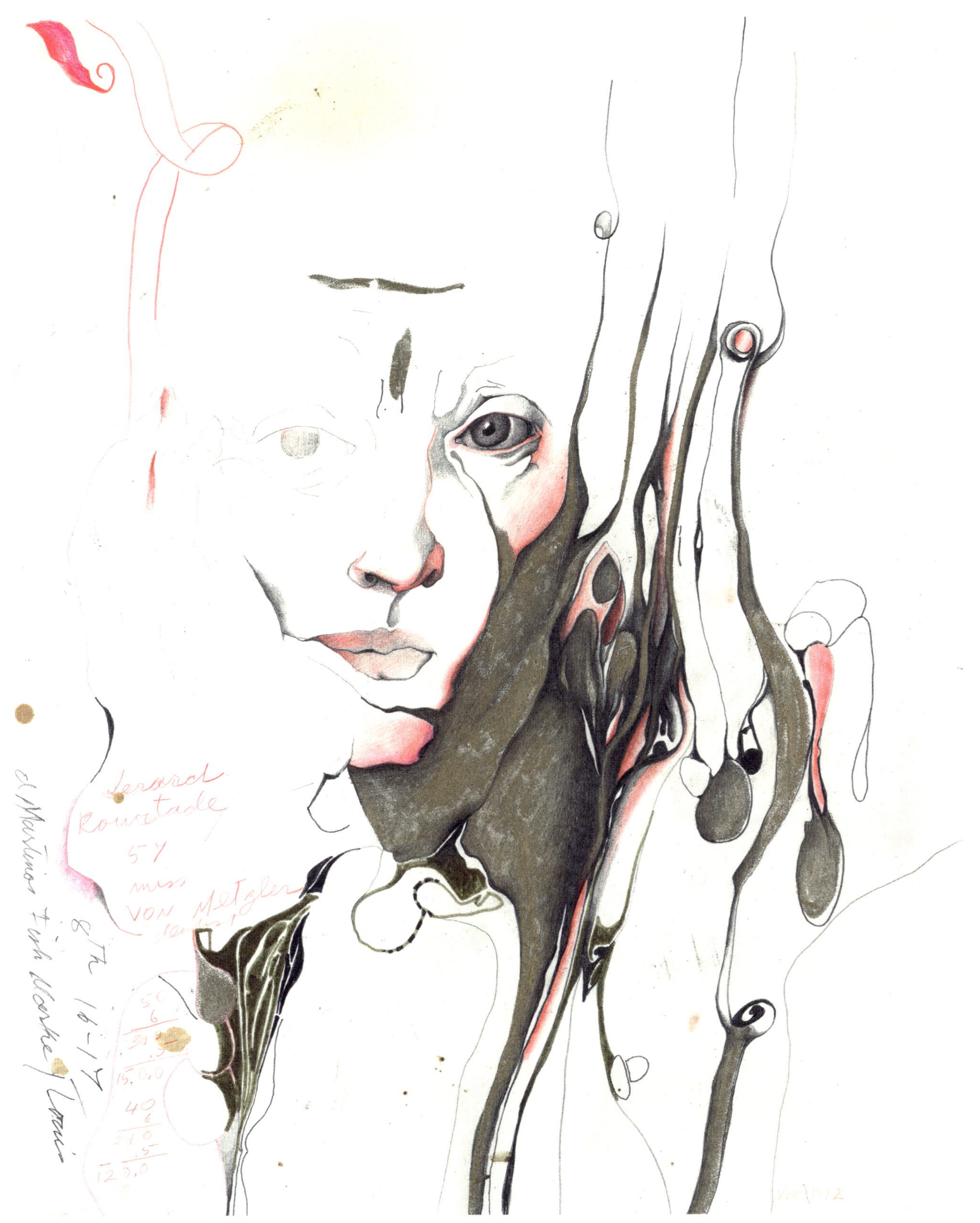

55. Untitled, 1972

Marisol's Accessories and Sculpture's Genders in the 1960s

David J. Getsy

In the 1960s, Marisol occupied a unique and highly visible position as one of the most prominent *figurative* sculptors in American art. Such a role is notable because, in the 1960s, American sculpture had a problem with the human form. Many sculptors spurned it, seeing it as tied too strongly to the traditions of the statue and the monument. Marisol, by contrast, made caricatures of the statue and the figure with her blocky sculptures onto which figurative elements were drawn or attached. She developed a new kind of statue – one that spoke to and anticipated developments in such movements as Minimalism and Pop. More importantly, her sculptures posed questions about the minimum number of traits we need to see the human figure, to assign its gender, or to map desire onto it. With her playful and often irreverent exaggerations and repetitions of gendered signs, Marisol's works open up a conversation about how mobile and contingent assignments of gender and sexuality can be.

While not the only sculptor who retained the human form in this decade of repression and return, Marisol was certainly the most prominent. Others, such as George Segal, Ed Kienholz, Bruce Conner and Paul Thek also created figurative sculptures, but Marisol captured the American popular imagination. Early on, she developed her signature style for the 1960s: life-size or oversize geometric blocks of wood onto which were added drawings and life-casts of the body's parts. She made statues that played with the mass cultural image, like Pop, and that occupied space, like Minimalism, with her faceted monolithic statues. Anticipating the sculptural questions that would shape 1960s sculpture, Marisol unabashedly created wildly popular sculptures of

25. *Couple No. 1,* 1965–66

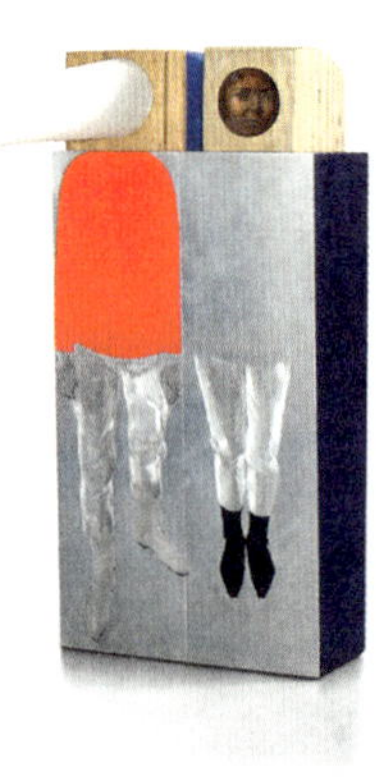

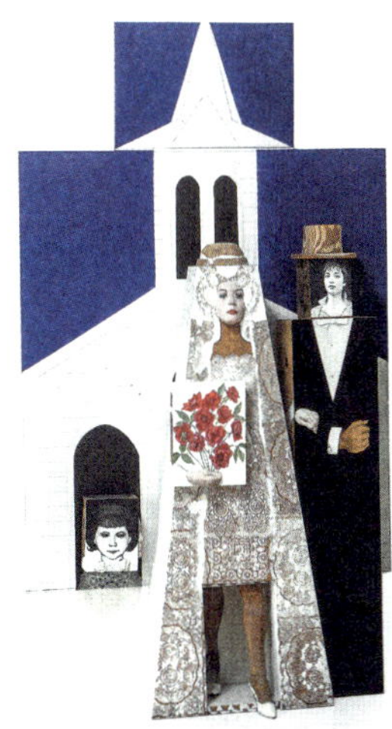

The Wedding, 1962-63. Oil and pencil on wood with fabric and collage, 279.4 × 161.3 × 101.6 cm. Private collection

people. Despite their approachability and generous irony, her sculptures nevertheless did something new with the tradition of the statue. She did not give us images of the body or the face that were singular – sometimes even in a solitary statue. Multiplying facets and faces, Marisol fractured the wholeness of the body, asking us to see it always as more than what we might at first think we recognise.

Generic forms

Central in debates about American sculpture in the 1960s was the role of the human body – either as depicted image or implied analogy. In particular, questions about the assignments of gender or desirability to the human form escalated as sculptors pursued alternatives to the statue. Increasing degrees of abstraction and non-figuration in sculpture rejected the *image* of the human form but nevertheless clung to the idea of the body as sculpture's frame of reference. Even a 1.8 metre steel cube conveyed "a kind of latent or hidden naturalism, indeed anthropomorphism", as the American art critic Michael Fried famously wrote in 1967 about Tony Smith's Minimalist sculpture *Die* (1962).[1] When bodies were evoked but not imaged, viewers (and its makers) ask *just what kind of body* was being analogised. Thus, the assignment of gender became a central and contentious issue. In conversations or writings about such sculptures, competing views of the body's sex or gender could be proposed. Inadvertently, abstract sculpture prompted questions of gender's multiplicity and mutability.[2] As well, the different ways that viewers or artists might desire those bodies became debated as non-normative sexualities became increasingly visible (and monitored) throughout the decade. Art criticism of the decade was riddled with the implications of gender and sex, and writers such as Fried, Lucy Lippard and Gregory Battcock evaluated contemporary sculpture in such terms.[3] Because sculpture (even an abstract sculpture) evoked the body, the assignment of gender to that body became a slippery and persistent question for those seeking to make sense of three-dimensional art.

Marisol's statues engaged with these questions through the partial abstraction of the human form, reducing markers of identification to a sometimes-humorous minimum. She often confronted her viewers with stereotypes and exaggerations of gender even as she insisted on a generic (indeed, interchangeable) form for the bodies of her statues. Her big, blocky sculptures become the screens onto which individual markers of gender are projected in the form of drawings, plaster casts, or commodity objects such as shoes, garments, and other accessories. She demonstrated an arbitrariness to how we might read these figures by attaching gendered objects (like purses or hats) and body parts (like breasts or buttocks). Our recognition of the human body in Marisol's work is often the result of just a few of these elements attached to an otherwise indiscriminate wooden block.

Such an attention to the ways that gender could be ludicrous or restrictive was to some degree Marisol's response to how, as an artist, she was seen in gendered terms. Her critics and peers looked for traits of femininity in her work (as they did with all women artists) and obsessed about how it was that a woman could be making sculpture. This context

Tony Smith: *Die*, 1962. Steel, 183.8 × 183.8 × 183.8 cm. Whitney Museum of American Art

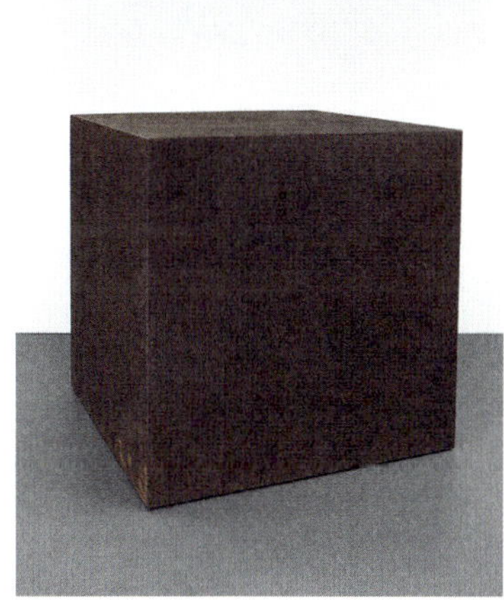

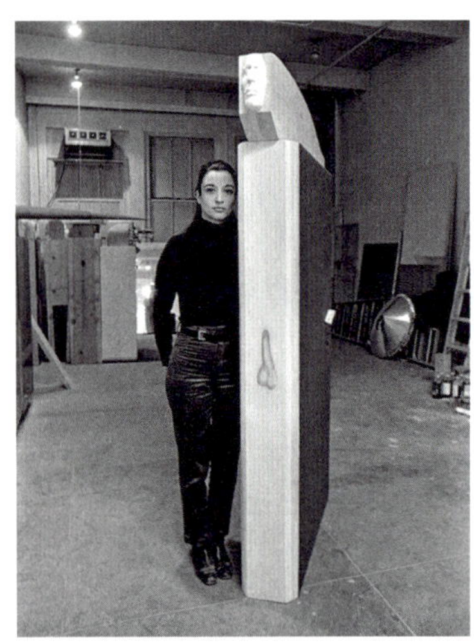

Marisol in her studio with the sculpture *Guy*, 1983. Photo: Jack Mitchell/Getty Images

is essential to understanding the unique role of Marisol in these debates. In defence, she developed a mercurial and enigmatic public persona which, like her faceted sculptures, could not be apprehended at a glance.[4] She made increasingly bold and large-scale figurative sculptures, and her interventions into this supposedly masculine medium were often noted in the press. Perhaps also in response to others' focus on her gender, Marisol's sculpture of the 1960s came to question and to exaggerate the signs and symbols that we customarily read as feminine, masculine or personal.[5]

Noting these exaggerations and caricatures, much of the writing about Marisol highlights the ways that she parodied or engaged with the trappings, excesses and limitations of femininity and its stereotypes.[6] She tackled clichés head on, often lovingly lampooning not just feminine ideals but also masculine pomposities, as well as the complexities of familial relations.[7] But I want to go further to ask how Marisol also questioned how we look for and assign all genders – and how her works offer an account of gender as mutable and contingent. As Cathleen Chaffee has discussed about the artist's long-standing interest in doubling and playful coding of gender across media, Marisol "mocks the inherent meaningfulness of sexual difference, often playfully undermining the default premising of sexual difference on the familiar gender binary".[8] Building on Chaffee's astute account of Marisol's artistic strategies, I will discuss how this general tactic of parodying or multiplying gender markers yields distinct readings in two very different sculptures in this exhibition from the 1960s: *The Sun Bathers* (1967, cat. 33, p. 60 and this spread) and *Portrait of Betty* (1961, cat. 14, p. 21 and following spread).

Building blocks

Whether blocky or curvaceous, Marisol's sculptures of bodies are characterised by their accessories – drawn faces or limbs, added objects being held or worn, and casts of body parts and her own face. These accessories are clearly added to the sculptures but never fully integrated in the material itself. One could imagine the drawn or sculpted parts could be replaced or moved to another sculpture; there is an arbitrariness in these bodily fragments.

This interchangeability is particularly clear in a work like *The Sun Bathers*, with its three figures of different heights. On a blue carpet, three cuboid columns are topped with a sculpture of a head, surrounded by a reflective disc reminiscent of the sun-reflecting face tanners that were in vogue in the 1960s. The heads are based on casts – including one of Marisol's own face. There are speculations as to the identifications of the other faces, and the shortest of the three is believed to be based on a boyfriend of Marisol's named Guy – who is also featured in another similarly featureless statue, *Guy* (1967-68, this spread). But the identification of the faces matters little. All are treated similarly and anonymously with each embedded in a carved wood cowl-like form. We might take the surrounding wood to signify long hair – a gendered marker in the 1960s – but that identification then complicates how we read the features of the tallest and the shortest statues. Indeed, there is no hint of what kind of body (or what gender) these three statues might be. The only other body parts indicated are the hands and feet on the

33. *The Sun Bathers*, 1967 (detail)

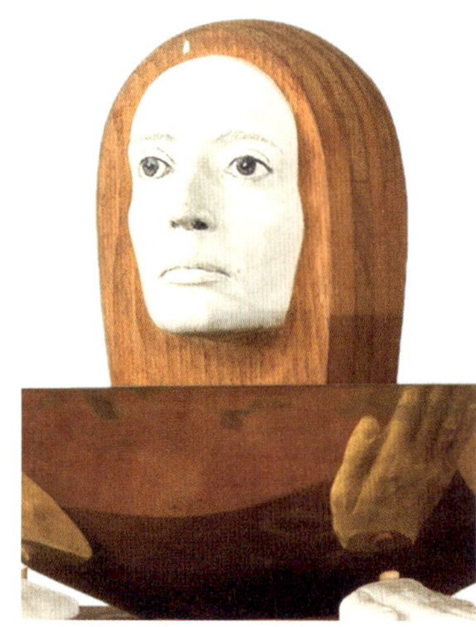

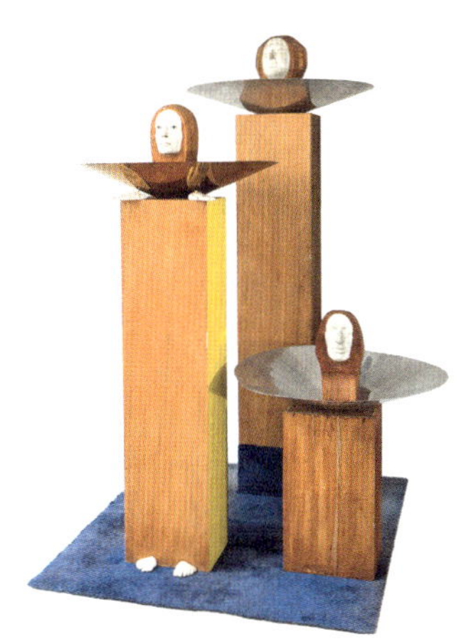

33. *The Sun Bathers*, 1967

one statue, but these too give little anchoring of sex or gender. (Indeed, in earlier photographs of this sculpture the cast feet were placed at a short distance from the shortest of the three figures.) As well, the height or proportions tell us little, and any attempt to see these statues as gendered must try to discern it in the faces (with their nearly matching hair) alone. Rather than individuality, it is interchangeability that Marisol emphasises in this trio of statues.

Marisol's visual language often leaves gender only tenuously suggested (or not at all). In other works, Marisol might add accessories to her statues, but they are minimal and seem superfluous to the sculptural body itself. More fundamental is the underlying presence of the blocky forms themselves, which defy – or rather, seem to precede – those additions. In some works (such as *La visita*, 1964, cat. 24, pp. 40-41 or *The Bathers*, 1961-62, cat. 16, p. 45), she has gone so far as to make secondary sex characteristics (like breasts or buttocks) look as if they are seemingly detachable additions to her blocks, indicating how *superfluous* these signs are. Like the feet in *Sun Bathers*, they could be moved to new generic blocks to dress them up in different ways. In other works, there are barely any indicators of gender assignment or of being a statue other than the titles, as with *Six Women* (1965) or *Three Figures* (1967). These statues are, at their core, ungendered blocks that are then decorated with a small number of almost cartoonish traits or accessories that appear as if they could be taken on or off for show – like the exaggerations of drag.

Marisol further demonstrated this strategy of arbitrariness with her own face, which she frequently used in her sculptures and assemblages. Whether as a plaster cast or a photograph, it gets repeated and altered across her sculptures and collages. While some of these works play with self-portraiture, she also used her own face to see how it could mutate and suggest new possibilities in different assemblages and combinations. In her works, the repeated face does not guarantee a gendered reading, and Marisol's practice of replicating her own face was a means to turn it into an object that could suggest multiple identifications.[9] She sometimes used it in sculptures that imply masculinity – such as at the centre of *The Jazz Wall* (1963, cat. 20, pp. 54-55 and this spread). In a work from around the same time, *The Wedding* (1962-63, p. 67), she presents both bride and groom with images of her own face. Marisol's multiplications of her own image not only shift personalities in each sculpture, they also serve as reminders that we can never really know a person (or their gender) solely on the basis of their facial features or bodily characteristics. We might assume there are masculine or feminine traits to faces, but those same features can be easily altered or exaggerated to suggest a different gender, a different personality, or a different category – again, like drag. Or, as with *The Sun Bathers*, such readings are reliant on a coordination of other supposed signs of gender like the implication of long hair that all three faces of the sculpture share. It is not that gender is always ambiguous in Marisol's sculptures, but rather that any security of an assignment of gender is called into question by the arbitrariness and contingency of these accessories to the otherwise abstracted or nondescript sculptural bodies. Indeed, asking just what kind of person (or people) a Marisol

20. *The Jazz Wall*, 1963 (detail)

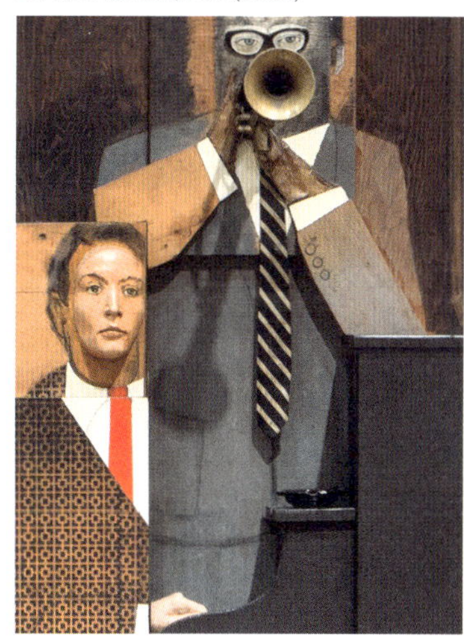

sculpture might be implying through its minimal signs is part of many viewers' fascination with these doll-like statues and their seemingly interchangeable parts.[10]

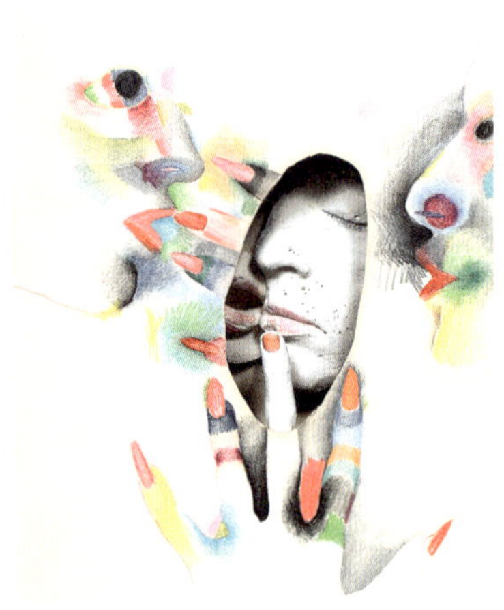

14. *Portrait of Betty*, 1961

Erotic doubles

To return to Marisol's use of her own face as multiple and mutable, the 1961 work *Portrait of Betty* contains two such casts, pressed adjacent at the lips. As well, a cast of Marisol's finger touches the closed lips of the face in profile, with the other mouth open as if to speak or take the finger into its mouth. These casts can be seen through a hole carved out of a box structure with a drawn surface depicting two faces (with many fingers) speaking from either side of the cut-out oval. This work relates to a series of such shadow-box reliefs Marisol was making in these years. It also connects to her long-running drawing practice in which faces and fingers in bright colours were used to multiply and transform images of bodies and their connections. The finger, in Marisol's drawings, sometimes stands in for other bodily parts (such as genitals of many kinds) as well as indicating hands and touching.[11] Indeed, there is a sensuality that is implied by the parted and closed lips in proximity to that sculptural finger and the drawn hands.

But this work is distinct from the other shadow-box sculptures or drawings because of its title, which tells us this work is a *portrait*. Marisol made many portraits throughout her career, but most of these still convey something about the likeness of the person, as with her 1960s portraits of artists, curators and collectors, including Andy Warhol, Sidney Janis, Henry Geldzahler and Ruth Kligman – each with their own sartorial and sardonic traits that give a sense of the individual she is monumentalising. *Portrait of Betty*, however, is rare for Marisol in that it did not recreate the visage or appearance of her sitter; rather, it substituted two casts of Marisol's own face. We should consider *Portrait of Betty* as a conceptual portrait, and with it Marisol engaged in American Modernism's long tradition of portraits that did not directly represent the sitter.[12]

Even with the generic faces and hands, however, *Portrait of Betty* does allude to a personal theme. The "Betty" of this work has been presumed to be Betty Parsons, the influential art dealer. Even though Marisol was not represented by Parsons's gallery, the two were friends for decades.[13] She was a regular visitor to the gallery and, on occasion, Marisol showed there. For instance, in 1963 Marisol contributed a work to an exhibition of Christmas toys organised by Parsons (and including Marisol's friend and collaborator Andy Warhol).[14] Parsons was a unique and influential figure in the New York art world of the 1950s. While her gallery helped to introduce American Abstract Expressionism, she was open in her advocacy for different types of artists and artworks. In addition to showing key figures in American Art (such as Barnett Newman) she made space for women artists and, notably, for artists working from nonnormative genders and sexualities (such as Forrest Bess, Sonja Sekula, and Robert Rauschenberg, just to name a few). An artist herself, Parsons was a lesbian who navigated the sexism and homophobia of the 1950s to establish a wide conversation in her gallery about what art could be – and who could make it.[15] Seeing *Portrait of*

14. *Portrait of Betty*, 1961 (detail)

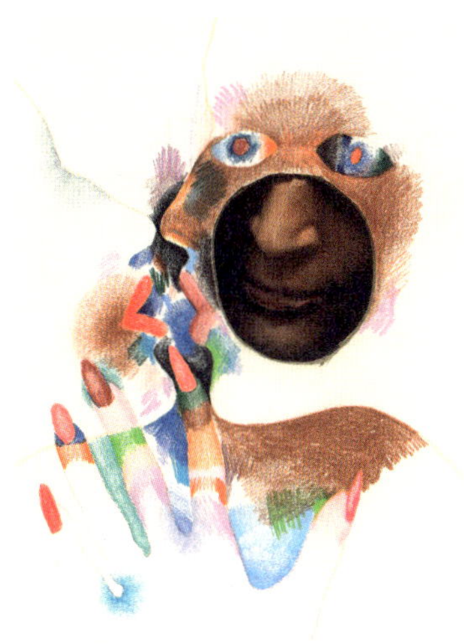

12. *Face Behind a Mask*, 1961

Betty as a conceptual portrait of Parsons helps to clarify the ways this relief sculpture mobilises gender and sexuality. The doubled faces and their painted lips imply kissing, with the finger reinforcing the sensuality of this cheek-to-cheek embrace. The intimate doubling of the faces, hands, lips, and fingers combine to convey sensual and erotic potential among their repetitions.[16] In these years, Marisol made other drawings and sculptures of the same face kissing itself, as with the related work *Untitled* (1960) or *Kiss* (1966, cat. 8, p. 28 and this spread). Indeed, in a related and probably earlier work, *Face Behind a Mask* (1961, cat. 12, p. 20 and this spread), Marisol combines a cast of her own face behind two faces whose painted lips seem to approach for a kiss. In such works, there may be assumed to be an implication of homoerotic or same-gender desire, but that is not the only option. Rather, it is an erotics generated by the shared traits of the two faces pressed lip-to-lip. It is only through the mere accessories (nails, lipstick) that we can propose femininity to these partial faces. As with *Sun Bathers,* these are tenuous signs. Marisol's duplications and shifting uses of the face speak to this capacity of multiple genders and combinations. The sexuality of her images of kissing and touching are, for this reason, properly understood as polymorphous and open-ended.

Nevertheless, seeing this depiction as a "portrait" compels us to think about this work in relation to an individual and their life. Regardless of how we might think about the possibilities of gender in this work, it unabashedly presents an erotic and sensual moment of intimacy between two doubles. That is, the sameness of the pressing faces proposes a homoeroticism.[17] The work cannot be reduced to a simple reading of that potential, but it nevertheless questions a normative account of desire or love as being defined as a relation of two halves of a gender binary. This context of nonnormative desire is reinforced when we remember that it is more than the kiss that is contained in *Portrait of Betty*. The drawings that surround the pair seem to speak at the couple within the box as well as to each other. The finger touching the closed lips also resembles a gesture of silence – of telling one not to speak. We might ask if the drawn figures seem to whisper about this embrace. The homoeroticism of *Portrait of Betty* is coupled with these talking figures hounding the moment of intimacy within the shadow box. In these years, any nonnormative sexuality or gender was a topic of scandal, conversation, and gossip. Marisol puts this intimate embrace in such a social context through the speaking figures that surround it.[18] The presentation of homoeroticism in this work is counterposed with the actively speaking faces. This combination can be understood in relation to the gossip and homophobia that were rife in the New York art world of the 1960s – the social world in which women such as Parsons had to navigate.[19] Even if the referent of this work was not Parsons (or even if there were no actual Betty), this work's intimate combinations of doubles allegorises the experience of scrutiny of outlaw desire. The addition of the word "portrait" compels us to look at this four-faced work as representing an individual. That individual, however, is given no singular likeness and is instead reduced to an image of outlaw desire as a topic of others' talk.

8. *Kiss*, 1966

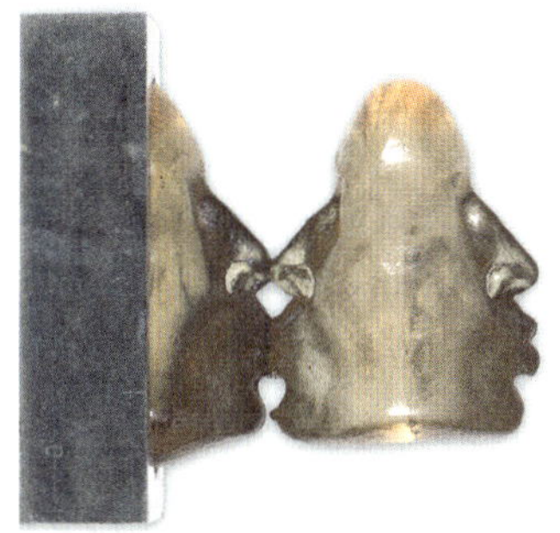

Multifaceted

In each of the many works that repeated it, Marisol made much of her own face. She evacuated it as a unique image of a self (herself), and instead used it to imply other people, other experiences, and other possibilities. It is a different face when it appears in *Sun Bathers* than in *Portrait of Betty* (or *Jazz Wall*, for that matter). It gained its specificity through the company it kept in each new sculpture. That face shifted ages, genders, identities and meanings in relation to what it was surrounded by and put into dialogue with. With both her own face and with the other accessories added to her statues, Marisol posed questions about just what we think we know when we see a person's exterior, bodily traits or clothing. In her work, any of those supposedly meaningful components could be superfluous, caricatural, interchangeable, and unnecessary. She exemplified this through her use of her face – alone or multiplied – showing how it produced new possibilities in different contexts and combinations. This might be understood as Marisol's account of personhood and gender in which one can never be reduced to the image others see. Her famously enigmatic persona and sardonic artworks were built around this very idea: that we are all more than we appear.

DAVID J. GETSY writes about modern and contemporary art and performance from the 19th century to the present. He has published eight books, including *Queer Behavior: Scott Burton and Performance Art* (Chicago 2022), *Abstract Bodies: Sixties Sculpture in the Expanded Field of Gender* (Yale 2015) and the widely-read anthology of artists' writings *Queer* (MIT 2016). He is the inaugural Eleanor Shea Professor of Art History at the University of Virginia and a 2025 Guggenheim Fellow.

1. Michael Fried, "Art and Objecthood", *Artforum* 5, no. 10 (June 1967), p. 19.
2. The capacity of abstract sculpture to speak to questions of gender's multiplicity and mutability is discussed at length in David J. Getsy, *Abstract Bodies: Sixties Sculpture in the Expanded Field of Gender* (Yale University Press, 2015).
3. Gender and sexuality were central to Lucy Lippard's most important writings on abstract sculpture in the 1960s, including "Eccentric Abstraction", *Art International* 10, no. 9 (20 November 1966), pp. 28, 34-40; and "Eros Presumptive", *The Hudson Review* 20, no. 1 (Spring 1967), pp. 91-99. For a reading of Fried's "Art and Objecthood" in relation to homosexuality, see Christa Noel Robbins, "The Sensibility of Michael Fried", *Criticism* 60, no. 4 (Fall 2018), pp. 429-454. On Gregory Battcock's art criticism, see Jennifer Sichel, "Gregory Battcock's 'Quiticism' and the Queer Underground Press", *Selva: A Journal of the History of Art* 6 (Spring 2025). For more on the importance of gender and sexuality in sixties sculpture, see Jo Applin, *Eccentric Objects: Rethinking Sculpture in 1960s America* (Yale University Press, 2012).
4. For a lucid account of Marisol's own elusiveness and multiplicity, see Alex Da Corte, "You Will Not Catch Me Alive" in *Marisol: A Retrospective,* ed. Cathleen Chaffee (Buffalo AKG Art Museum and DelMonico Books, 2023), pp. 179-193.
5. Marisol has also toyed with these themes in other works, including with the caricatures of masculinity. See, for instance, Della Solomons, "Marisol's Antimonument: Masculinity, Pan-Americanism, and Other Imaginaries", *The Art Bulletin* 102, no. 3 (2020), pp. 104-129.
6. See the important discussion in Cécile Whiting, "Figuring Marisol's Femininities", *A Taste for Pop: Pop Art, Gender, and Consumer Culture* (Yale University Press, 1997), pp. 187-230. For a discussion of the importance of caricature and gender for Marisol, see Albert Boime, "The Postwar Redefinition of Self: Marisol's Yearbook Illustrations for the Class of '49", *American Art* 7, no. 2 (Spring 1993), pp. 6-21.
7. On the important theme of the family – and Marisol's sometimes critical relationship to it – see Marina Pacini, "Marisol's Families" in Marina Pacini, ed., *Marisol: Sculptures and Works on Paper* (Memphis Brooks Art Museum, 2014), pp. 73-98.
8. Cathleen Chaffee, "Hereafter, Marisol" in *Marisol: A Retrospective,* ed. Cathleen Chaffee (Buffalo AKG Art Museum and DelMonico Books, 2023), p. 43.
9. Here, I find a useful counterpoint in the sculpture of Nancy Grossman from the late 1960s in which she sculpted (and subsequently covered) faces in ways that similarly complicated the assignments of gender to those facial characteristics. Unlike Marisol, Grossman considered those faces (which did not resemble her) to be self-portraits. See Getsy, *Abstract Bodies*, pp. 147-207.
10. See discussion in Delia Solomons, "Babies, Nuclear Giants, and Other Monsters", in *Marisol: A Retrospective,* ed. Cathleen Chaffee (Buffalo AKG Art Museum and DelMonico Books, 2023), pp. 67-85.
11. See Anna Katherine Brodbeck, "Sexually Frustrated: The Radical Potential of Eroticism, Violence, and Hybridity in Marisol's Drawings" in *Marisol: A Retrospective,* ed. Cathleen Chaffee (Buffalo AKG Art Museum and DelMonico Books, 2023), pp. 123-138.
12. For a broad history of this practice, see Anne Collins Goodyear, Jonathan Frederick Walz and Kathleen Campagnolo, eds., *This Is a Portrait If I Say So: Identity in American Art, 1912 to Today* (Bowdoin College Museum of Art and Yale University Press, 2016).
13. For instance, in the Betty Parsons Papers, Archives of American Art, Smithsonian Institution, there is a copy of a menu for the restaurant Chanterelle, for which Marisol provided a cover drawing. On this item, Marisol hand-copied the courses on the interior and wrote on the cover "for Betty with Love, Marisol. May 22 1980."
14. See Jessica Beck, "Marisol and Warhol: An Influential Friendship" in *Marisol and Warhol Take New York,* ed. Jessica Beck (Andy Warhol Museum, 2021), pp. 14-23.
15. See Ann Gibson, "Lesbian Identity and the Politics of Representation in Betty Parsons Gallery" in Whitney Davis, *Gay and Lesbian Studies in Art History* (Hayworth Press, 1994), pp. 245-270.
16. As the important painter and chronicler of lesbian art Harmony Hammond wrote of Marisol's many drawings of hands and faces, "In Marisol's drawings and lithographs, hands or fingers carry pocketbooks, form suggestive shapes, or just float in from the edges of the paper. The hands both refer to another part of the body and remain hands, the touching organ. The gesture is not completed but implies a sexuality of touching, allowing us to feel out or complete our own fantasies." Harmony Hammond, "A Sense of Touch" [1981] in *Wrappings: Essays on Feminism, Art, and the Martial Arts* (TSL Press, 1984), pp. 81-82.
17. Marisol also hinted at homoerotic potential in other works. For instance, see the discussions in Solomons, "Marisol's Antimonument" and Chaffee "Hereafter Marisol".
18. The social and interpersonal contexts for Marisol's artistic choices are explored in Jessica S. Hong, "Marisol's Social Networks" in *Marisol: A Retrospective,* ed. Cathleen Chaffee (Buffalo AKG Art Museum and DelMonico Books, 2023), pp. 89-120.
19. On gossip and homophobia in the New York art world, see Gavin Butt, *Between You and Me: Queer Disclosures in the New York Art World, 1948-1963* (Duke University Press, 2005).

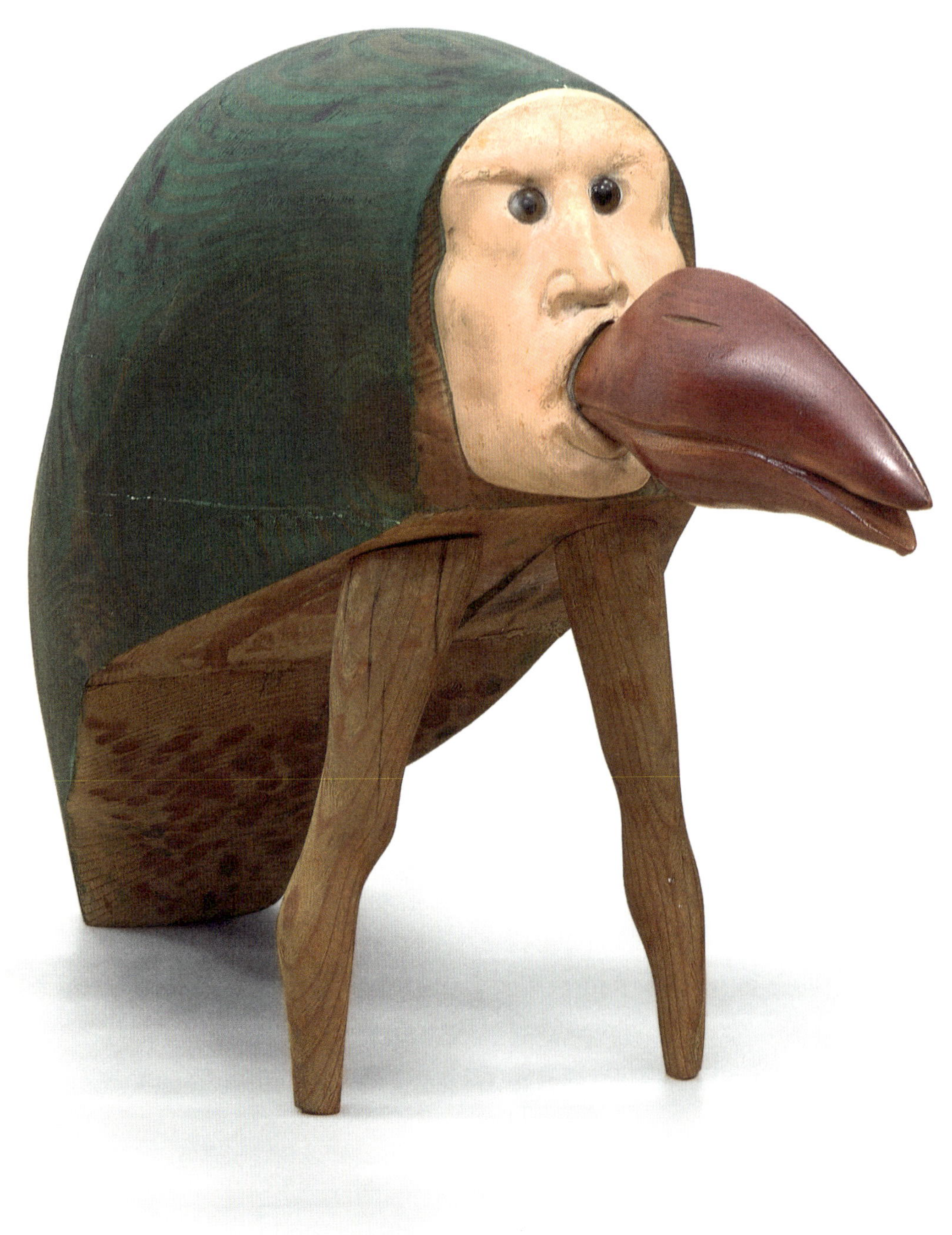

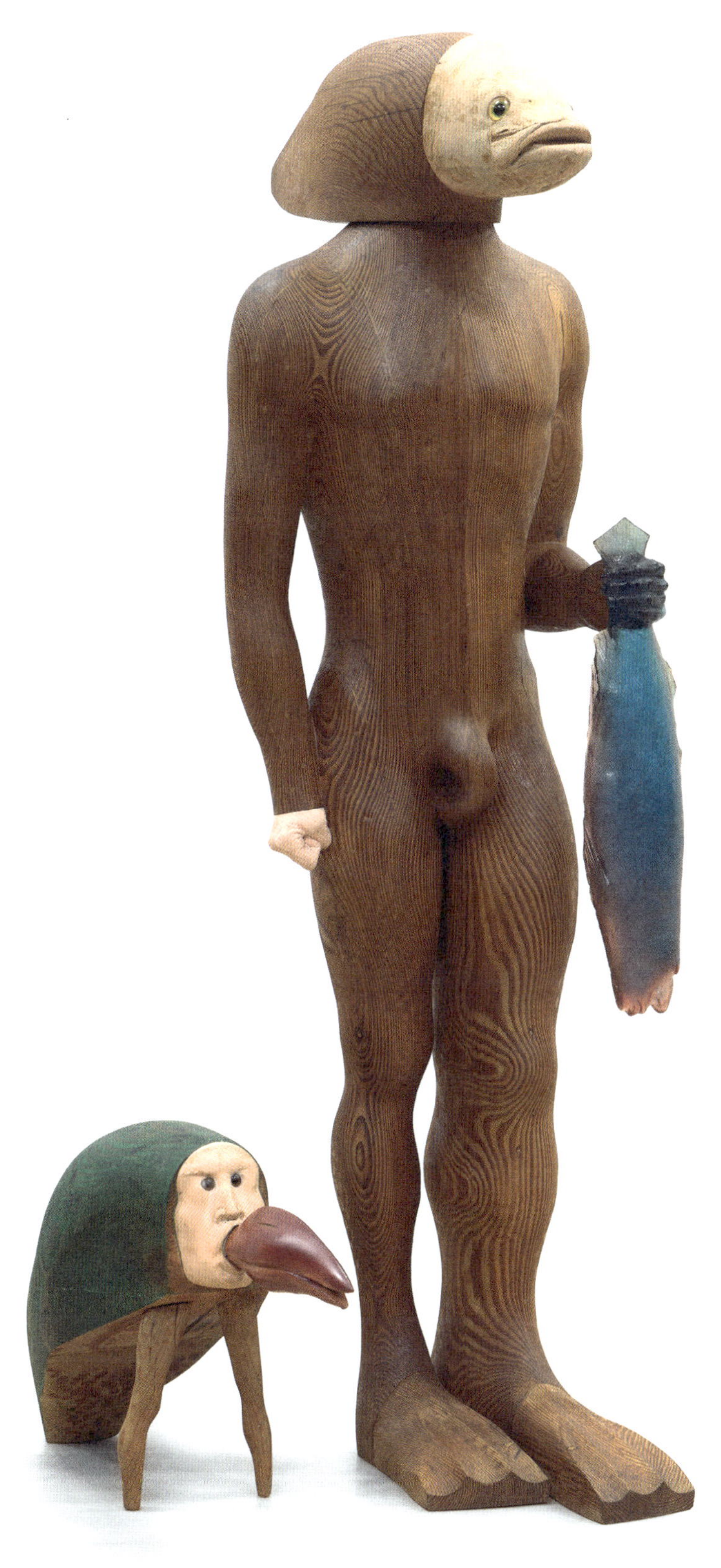

58. *The Fishman*, 1973 (detail opposite)

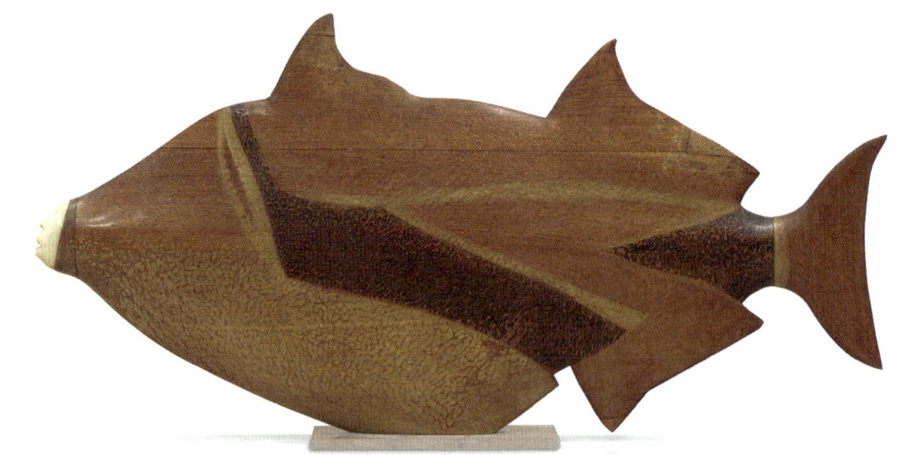

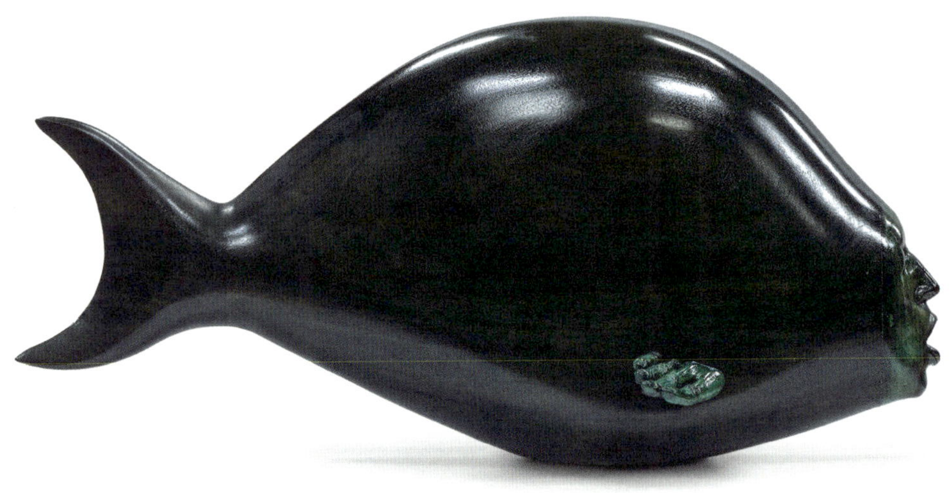

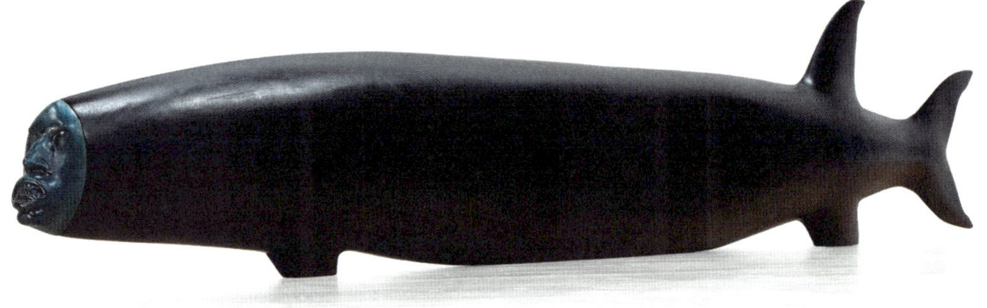

53. *Triggerfish II*, 1972

43. *Greenfish*, 1970

46. *Barracuda*, 1971

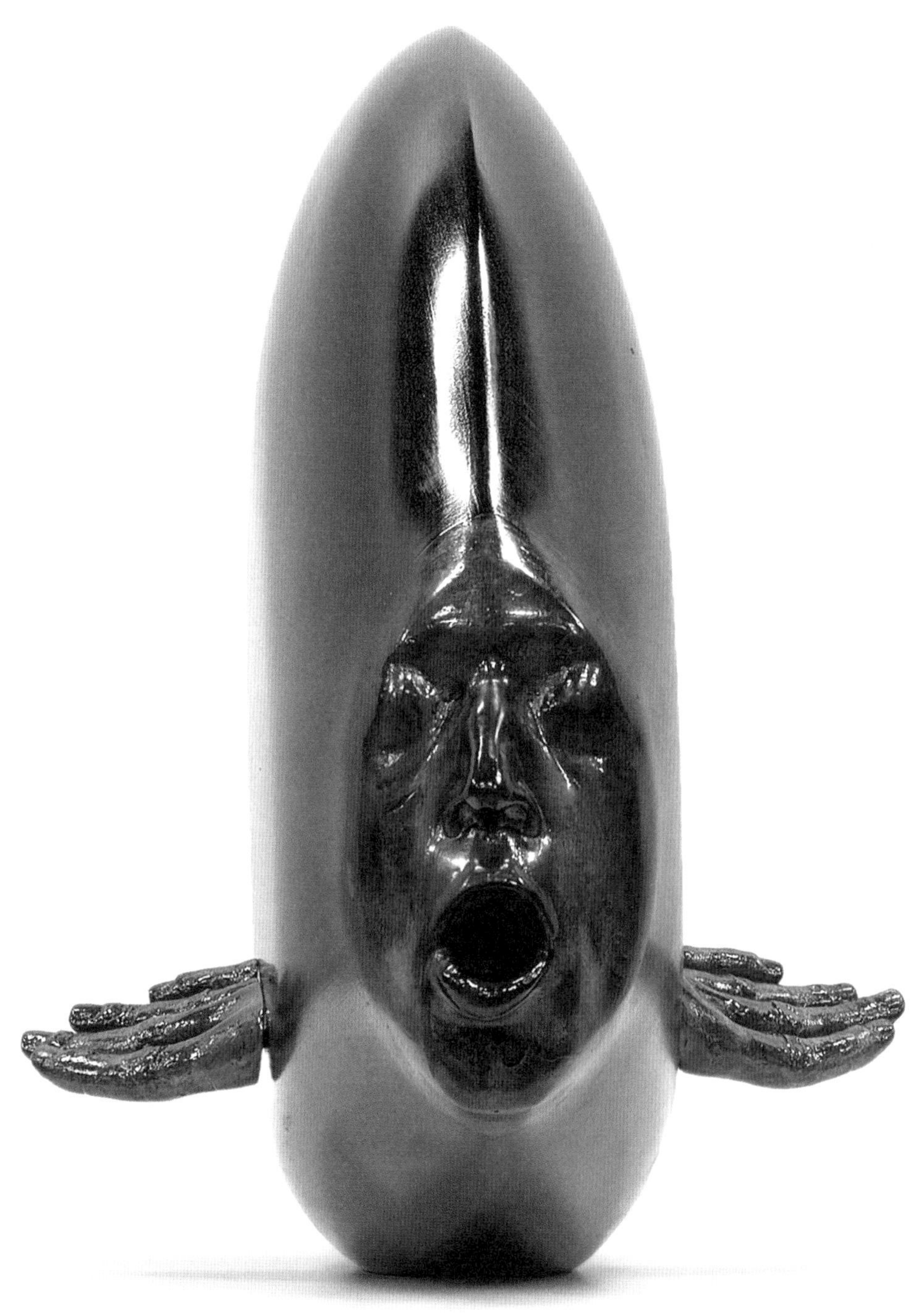

43. *Greenfish*, 1970

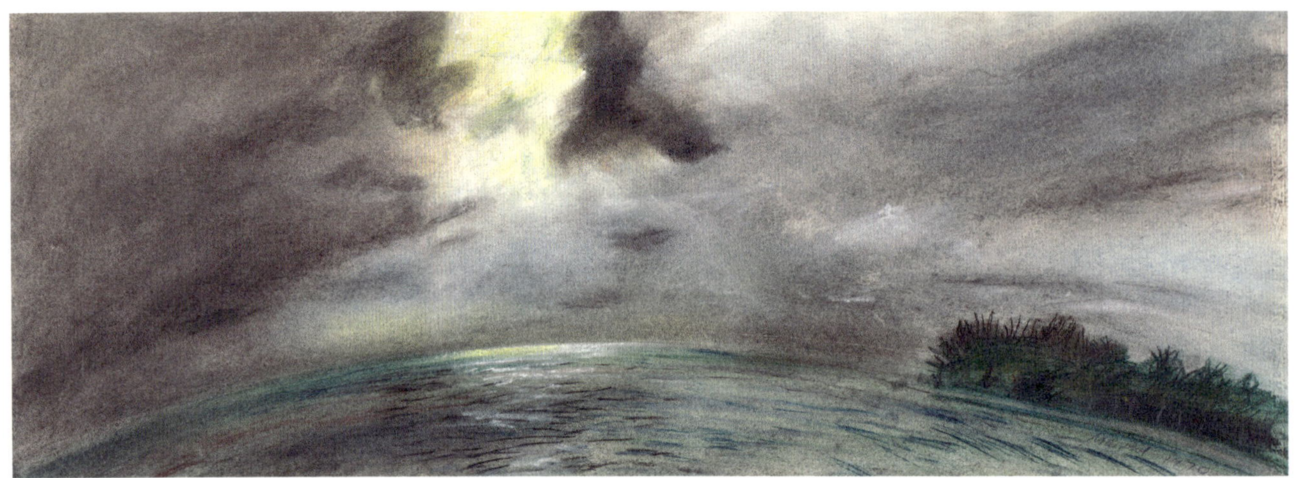

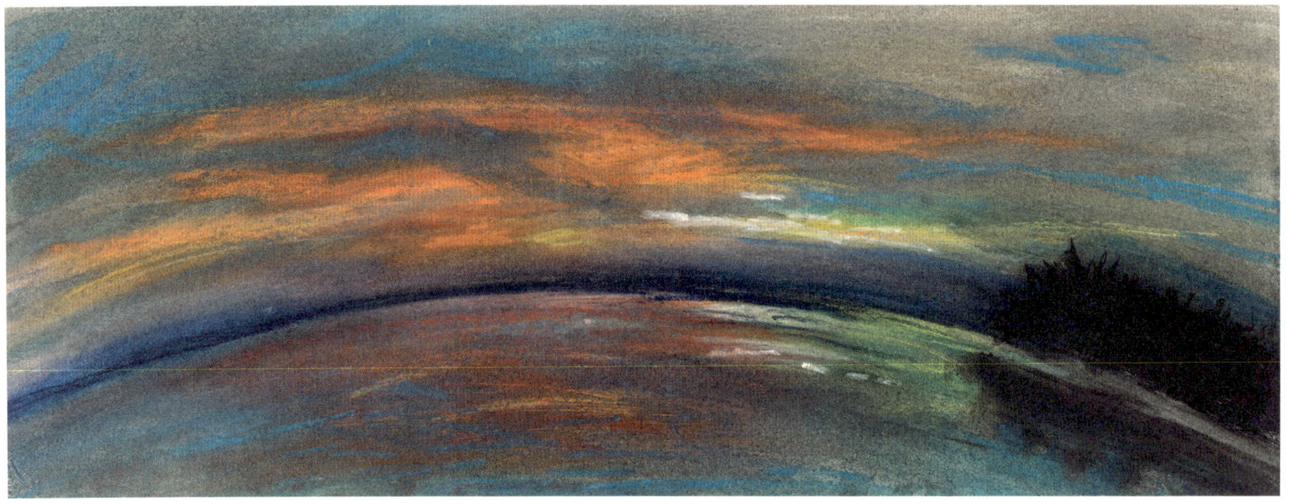

45. *Untitled Landscape*, 1970

44. *Untitled Landscape*, 1970

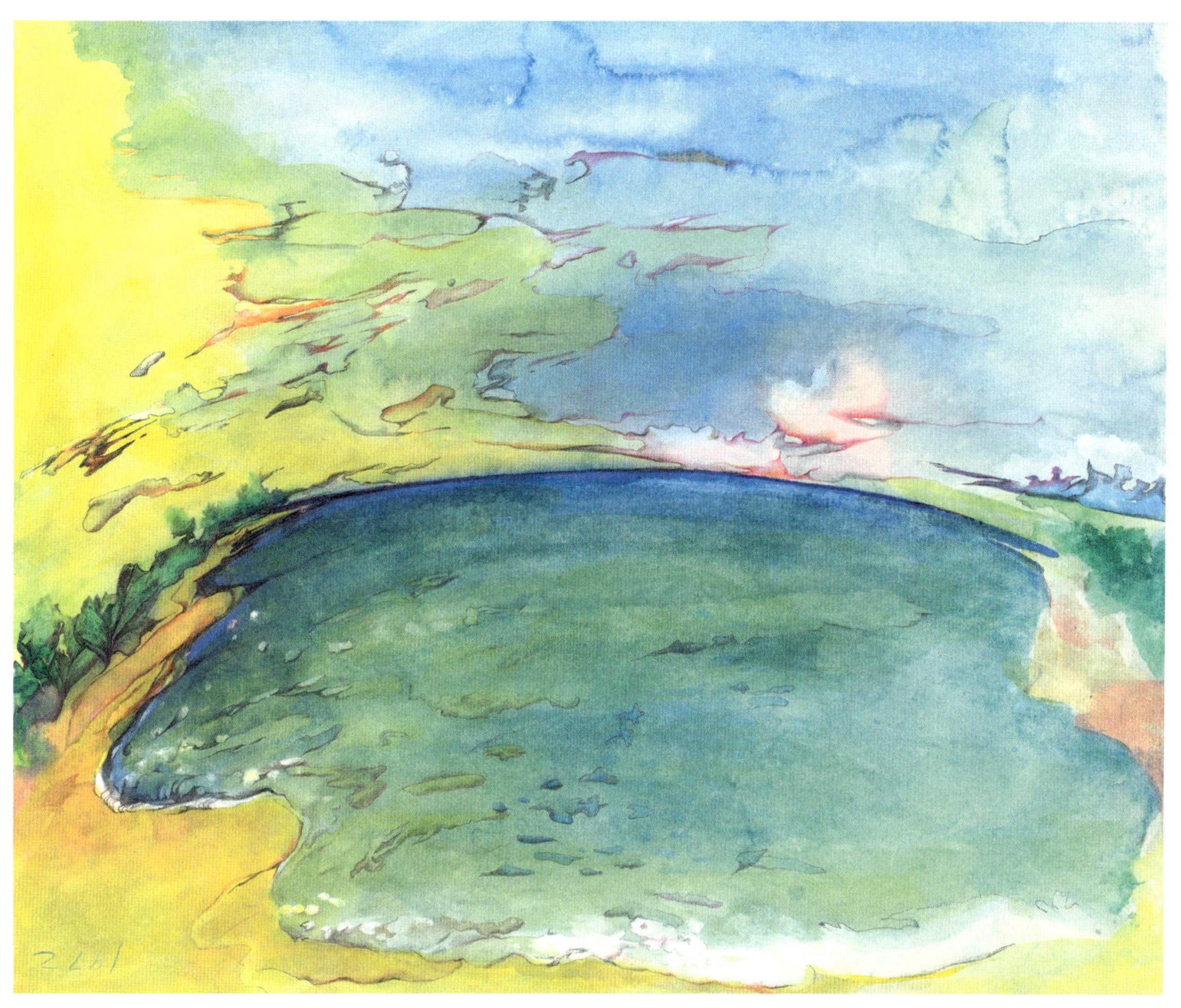

54. Untitled, 1972

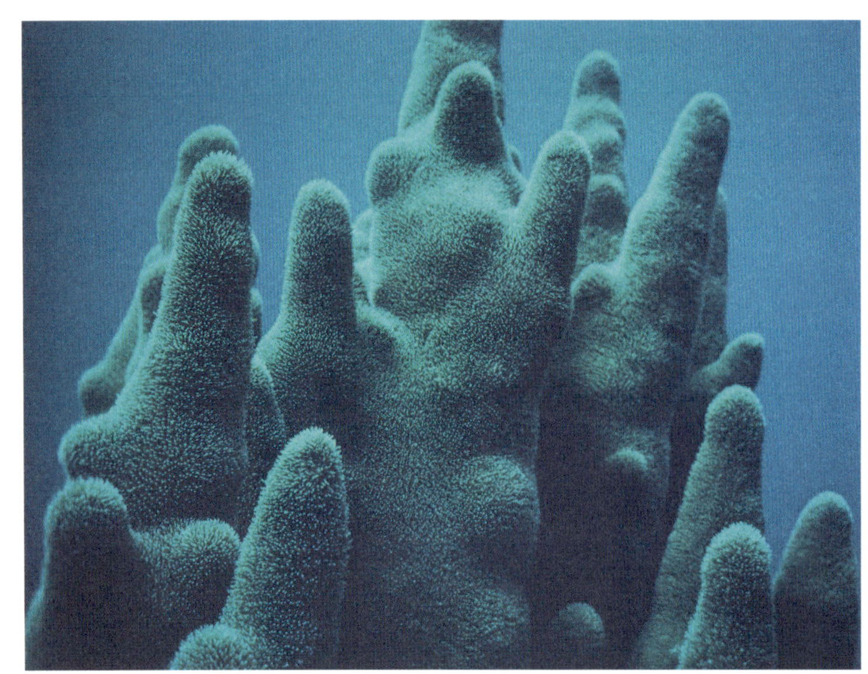

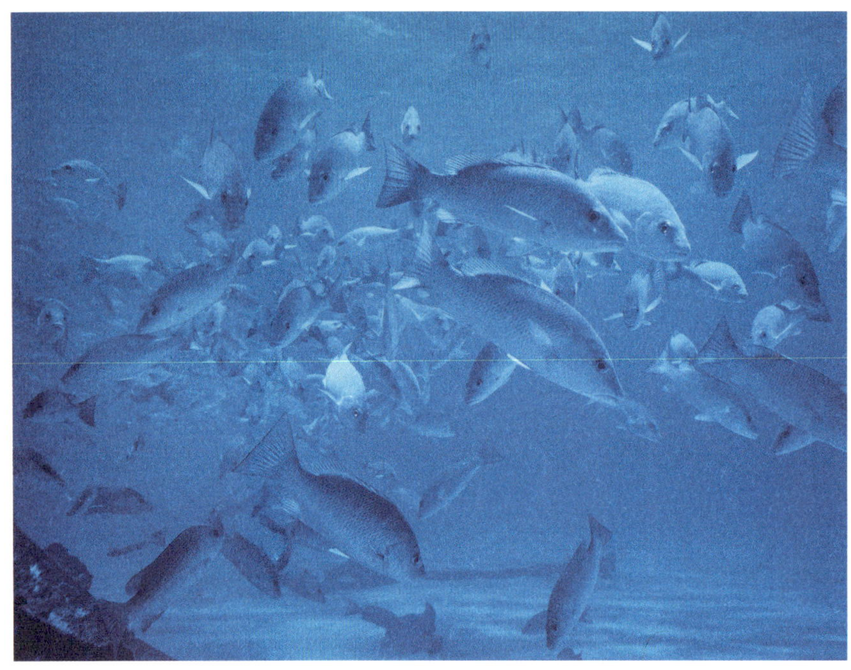

93. Underwater photograph taken in Bonaire, 1979–80
Collection Buffalo AKG Art Museum. Bequest of Marisol, 2016
82. Untitled, c. 1976

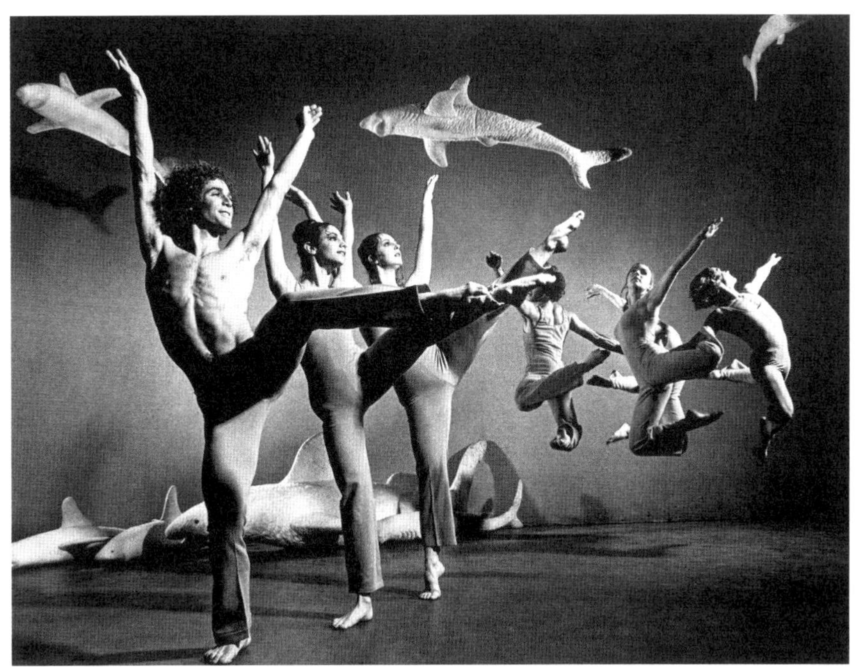

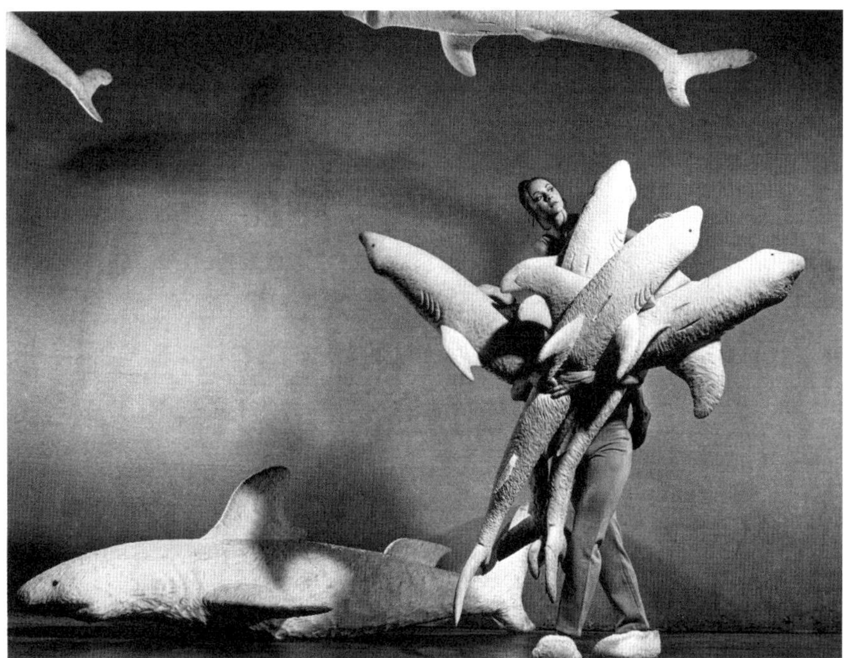

The Louis Falco Dance Company's performance of *Caviar*, 1970
Marisol's décor and costumes for The Louis Falco Dance Company's performance of *Caviar*, 1970
Décor and costumes by Marisol. Marisol Papers, Buffalo AKG Art Museum

Breath Work

Delia Solomons

During Marisol's brief stint in therapy in the 1950s, her psychoanalyst encouraged her to practice a version of what is now called "breathwork", in which a person devotes attention to their own breathing as a means to foster deeper embodiment, grounding and calm. However, in an interview (in her only known comment about therapy), Marisol recounted that for her this approach was destabilising on an existential level: "[The therapist] really screwed me up [...]. He was talking about your insides and how your heart beats and how you breathe [...]. So then I started feeling that I wasn't breathing [...]. And then I had to be conscious about my breathing [...]. And I went through some horrible times where I could almost faint."[1]

For all the good mindfulness practices centering breath can bring, I also understand her response. It is dizzying to think of how our very survival utterly depends on this automatic operation of taking in air, and then releasing it, that we typically enact unconsciously. What's more, while attunement to our breathing provides remarkable psychological benefits, it can also activate traumatic memories held in the mind and body, as Marisol's experience perhaps conveys.[2] In this essay, I am not interested in psychoanalysing Marisol or pinpointing what traumas might have been activated, but rather in accessing her sensitivity to and deep exploration of breath in her artworks and writings, a subject that is absent from extant literature on the artist.

Marisol's distressed reaction to breathwork proves all the more arresting when we consider that over the next few decades two of her core artistic and personal pursuits involved intensive – indeed harrowing

85. Untitled, c. 1970-80

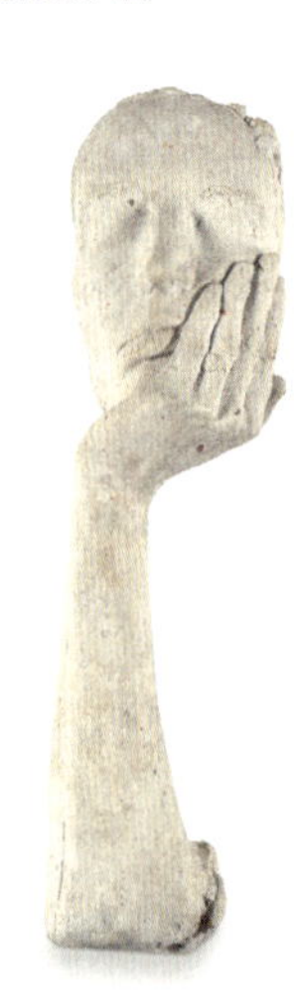

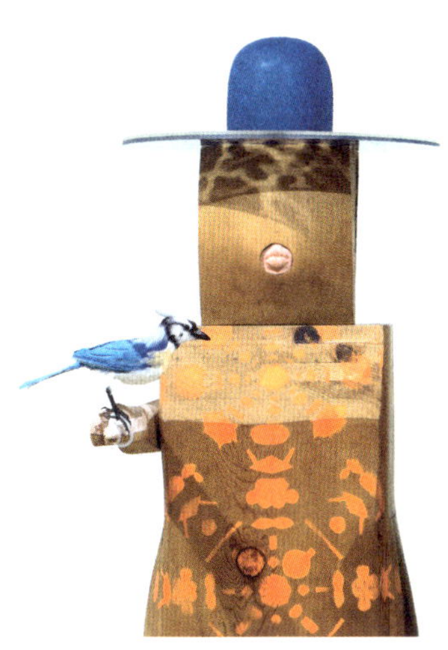

26. *Three Women with Umbrella*, 1965-66 (detail)

– breath constriction: facial casting and deep-sea scuba diving. Analysis of these practices and related unpublished archival interviews and writings reveals the striking role breath plays in Marisol's artistic process, imagery, training as a deep-sea diver and conceptual relationship to the world. This short essay unpacks her exploration of breath as a marker of survival versus death and an operation that blurs traditional boundaries between self and environment. These considerations, placed in dialogue with the emerging field of Breath Studies in the conclusion, open new existential, ecocritical, relational and embodied readings of Marisol's work.

Casting: when breath becomes air[3]

By the early 1960s, Marisol made casting her own face a key component of her sculptural practice. She engaged this smothering process over and over – temporarily covering her face in plaster and probably breathing through small tubes as the plaster contracts and hardens. In fact, most of her cast faces likely index unique casting sessions, as descriptions of her chosen materials and process indicate that she would rarely have produced multiples from a single mould.[4] Some viewers recognised that her methods involved a direct threat to her own respiration and asked her how she breathed when she made these works.[5]

Once completed, the finished objects themselves recall death-masks and life-masks, which record "the immobilised features of someone who is already dead or will die".[6] These casts conjure that terrifyingly thin line between life and death marked by the ability to breathe, of being and remaining properly oxygenated. As ossified body imprints, they invoke the moment we become as still as statues, the split second after our working lungs push our chest up and down one last time. Marisol's facial casts function as self-memorials, capturing a moment of breath restriction in an object that survives after the artist/model ceases to breathe.

Marisol's uncanny sculptures look like they might suddenly draw breath and, as noted by art critics since the 1960s, come alive.[7] The musicians in *The Jazz Wall* (cat. 20, pp. 54-55) appear on the verge of activation, like they could suddenly start pushing air into the saxophone and trumpets, strumming the guitar and tapping the piano keys; some party-goers joked the musicians could do just that when the sculpture was originally installed in the New York City nightclub L'Interdit. Several of Marisol's figures even appear to hold their breath with puffed out cheeks (for example, in *The Family* (1963) and *Three Women with Umbrella* (1965-66), cat. 26, p. 37 and this spread); perhaps once we turn our backs to the sculptures they can release a relieving exhale. In multiple sculptures, Marisol suggests such kinetic potential not only through eerily veristic body parts, but also through equipment designed for movement; the wheels in *The Car* (cat. 22, pp. 38-39) and *Mimi* (cat. 106, p. 112 and this spread), and the rockers in *Tea for Three* (cat. 10, p. 6) appear capable of setting her creaky wooden automatons into robotic motion.

106. *Mimi*, 1997

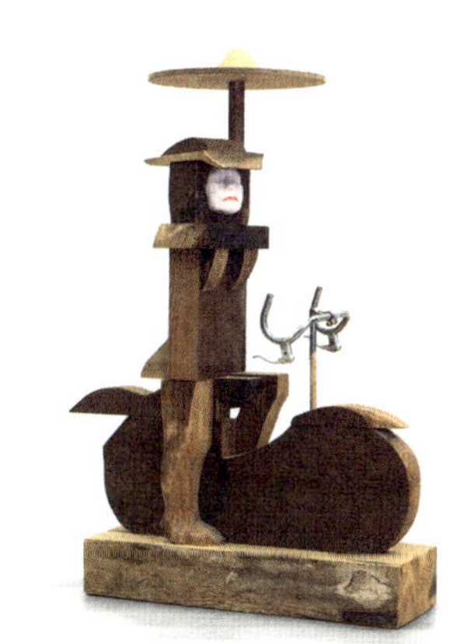

In the 1970s, Marisol made a devastating series of cast faces bearing the brutal imprints of attacks from beer cans and soda bottles (cats. 63-67, 70-76, pp. 90-91). The visages recall surviving or deceased victims of

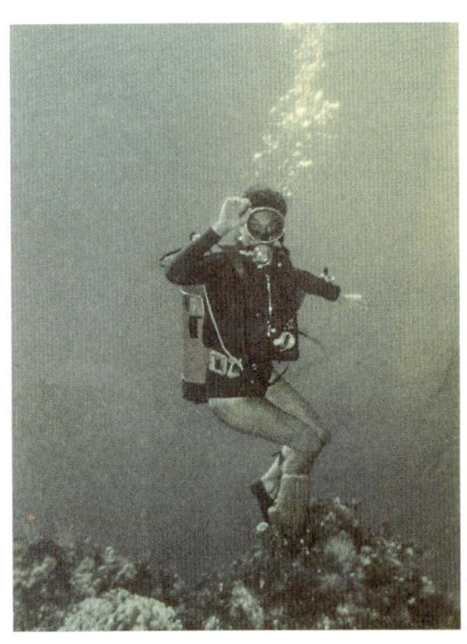

Marisol, underwater in Cozumel, 1974
Marisol Papers, Buffalo AKG Art Museum

domestic and/or sexual violence; some even carry the assault weapons as evidence dangling below. Breath, if possible, looks desperately pained. These figures have been deprived of the protective boxy body armour Marisol gave her 1960s sculptures, and are left profoundly vulnerable. They conjure not only Marisol's lived experience of violation but also feminist movements' intensifying outcry against sexual violence in the early to mid-1970s, as art historian and curator Anna Katherine Brodbeck has explained.[8] This excruciating series underscores the fact that Marisol's engagement with casts and breath is not just about clever animation (detailed above), but rather reflects survival and precarity in a dangerous world. She integrates these reminders of mortality in not only her most grim depictions but also as ominous undercurrents in her bright, Pop leisure subjects.

To breathe underwater

By the early 1970s, Marisol's attunement to breath and survival had been intensified by her experiences deep-sea scuba diving, as reflected in her journals and artworks inspired by her subaquatic immersion.

Marisol pursued death-defying diving adventures throughout the 1970s in at least nine different countries across the Pacific and Caribbean. She dove as deep as 235 feet below sea level.[9] For context, Jeppesen's *Sport Diver Manual* (1975) – the industry standard, which Marisol owned in her personal library – suggested a 100-foot limit and stated that most divers were satisfied at 30 feet.[10] In the Navy's chart of recommended time limits for specific depths (21 minutes at 100 feet, 5 minutes at 150 feet, etc.), 200 feet was literally off the chart because some divers experience nitrogen narcosis that renders them unable to "perform simple motor or mental tasks", leading to diving catastrophes and fatalities.[11]

A scuba diver's life depends upon measured, constant breathing. Even in an emergency, the most critical rule is to "never hold your breath under water while using scuba. Always keep breathing".[12] Breathing too little or too much is life threatening, yet holding breath is a natural response to the body submerged in water and our respiration automatically quickens when we face stresses. It is easy to panic – you lose all sense of direction and time in this immersive, highly stimulating aquatic world. Marisol captured the seemingly endless nature of the undersea environment in photographs and film (see cats. 82, 93, p. 80). In her drawing *Mexico* (1978), her silhouette wears scuba and snorkel gear set against a backdrop of blue aquatic submersion, while glowing translucent passages course around her articulating perhaps air-as-life-force or ocean currents brushing past.

In her journals, Marisol described the revitalising potential and the terror awaiting her underwater. Often she felt "reborn – cleansed and purified", submerged among the quiet, the coral and the incredible fish with whom she'd commune.[13] In her 1976 Cozumel journal she wrote, "All that matters is, if I can have a good dive to become healthy again, maby all will be fine again" [*sic*].[14] However, she also recounted perilous experiences: for example at 200 feet she panicked when she couldn't clear her ears after her pressure gauge had blown-up pre-dive; she wrote that her mind raced: "This is it. I'm going to die. I will never get out

Mexico, 1978. Coloured pencil on paper, 100.01 × 70.17 cm. Collection Buffalo AKG Art Museum. Bequest of Marisol, 2016 (2021:116)

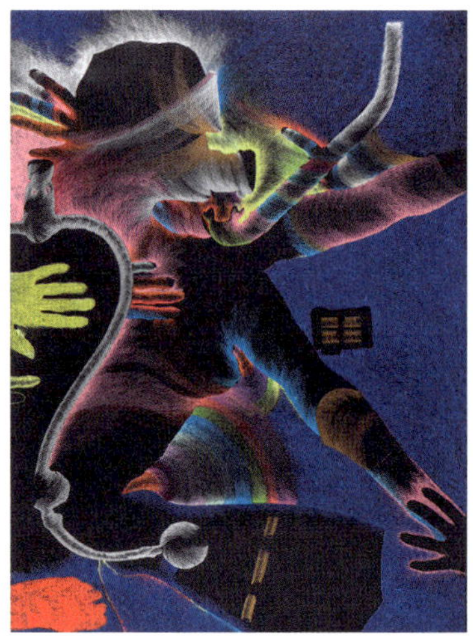

of this."[15] Elsewhere she described how frightened she became when her friend suffered a stroke while diving and how, in these early experimental days of scuba, she nearly gave up diving, as the development of new equipment and procedures led her to consider how little experts knew for certain about scuba safety.[16] At the same time, Marisol saw the magic of these inventions that made deep-sea exploration possible; she even designed an underwater dome habitat – *Aqua Bell* – which maintained air pressure and replenished oxygen for underwater spectators.[17]

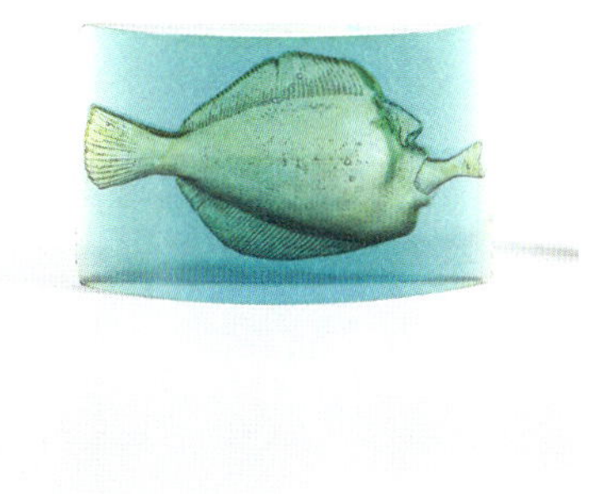

42. *Fished*, 1970

Shortly after she began diving, Marisol developed a new sculptural series: a hybrid aquatic bestiary suffused with questions about survival. Art historian and curator Julia Vázquez has insightfully related this series to the nuclear arms race, space exploration and the ecological movement.[18] Here, I seek to build upon her argument by emphasising breath's central role in articulating the survival imperative and by spotlighting additional unpublished quotes from the archives. In this sculptural series, multiple fish bear casts of the artist's face, thus pushing into new terrain her 1960s studio practice of suffocating casting to create breathless imprinted likenesses. *Greenfish* (cat. 43, pp. 76-77) and *Triggerfish I* appear to gasp for air; these facial expressions notably depart from the impassive, sedate ones Marisol typically utilised.[19] Perhaps these creatures aren't capable of breathing anywhere; undersea their human mouths would inhale water but when marooned on land they look desperate for watery submersion or like dead fossils in natural history museums. These sculptures – and counterparts like the missile-shaped *Barracuda* (cat. 46, p. 76) and ferocious *Triggerfish II* (cat. 53, p. 76) who bare their teeth to fend off predators or hunt prey – remind us that our world is indeed a dangerous place, so riddled with ecological, bellicose and colonial devastation that our survival often feels fragile.[20] If *Greenfish* and *Triggerfish I* open their mouths to scream (instead of gasp for air), this alternative offers little solace; human voices don't carry well underwater and above-ground pleas against wartime, interpersonal and environmental violence too often feel futile, as Marisol's silenced fish imply. The expressions on *Greenfish* and *Triggerfish I* also reflect, as Vázquez notes, Marisol imitating "the open-mouth yawn of a fish". As such, they invite us to consider potential inter-species empathy and the entanglement of our shared ecological fates.

In her diving journals, Marisol mourned humans' destruction of the underwater world. She wrote of Cozumel: "It's horrible they have killed the most beautiful coral in the world [...] Before this was like a paradise, which gave such energy [...]. Now it's grey and dead just like them [...]. I didn't think the destructive force of people was this powerful."[21] Here, Marisol grieves the death of the coral reefs through language that envisions an integrated human-animal-environmental total system of vibrant matter struggling between generative energy and destructive force – all at the outset of the contemporary environmental movement. Throughout the 1960s, attention rose regarding not only contaminated waters but also the choking pollution of the air. A 1965 *Life* editorial explained the vastness of the air pollution problem, particularly in Marisol's home of New York, and opened with lines from Tom Lehrer's song "Pollution" (1960): "Just go out for a breath of air / And you'll be ready for Medicare."[22]

Marisol with *Greenfish* (1970), Trisolini Gallery, Ohio University, Athens, 1974. Marisol Papers, Buffalo AKG Art Museum

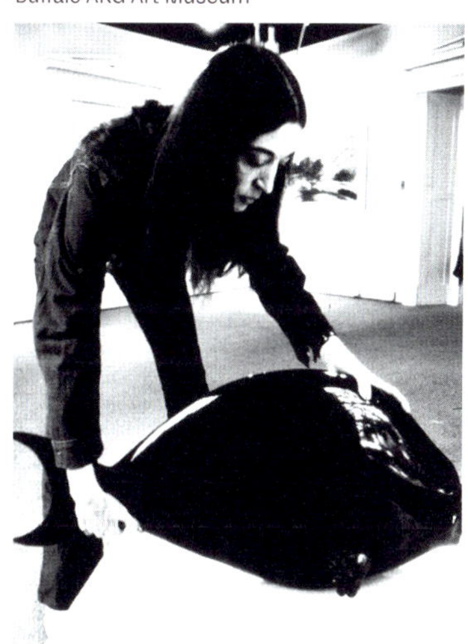

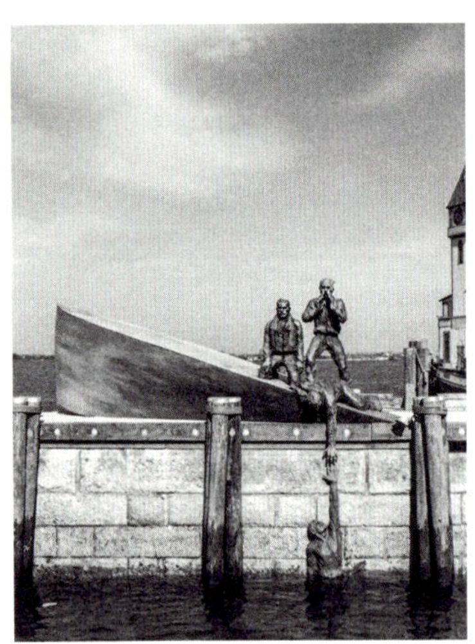
American Merchant Mariners' Memorial (1991), The Battery, Manhattan, New York. Marisol Papers, Buffalo AKG Art Museum

Marisol's attunement to breath may have been heightened by her eight-month study of Buddhist temples while travelling through India, Thailand, Cambodia and Sri Lanka in 1968-69, just months before she so intensively took to the water.[23] Her personal library held five books by Yogi Chien-min Chen published between 1968-72 and other texts exploring Buddhism. Given how central meditative breathing – particularly the anapanasati sutta – is to not only Buddhist practice but also the Western appropriations of Buddhism circulating in New York contingents close to Marisol, she likely had some familiarity with these practices.[24] Through her studies of not only Buddhism but also Catholicism (in which she engaged intensively in her youth), Marisol perhaps invested a spiritual dimension into her breath-related artworks, conjuring breath as a spirit and soul connected to a higher power, which proliferates across many religions in disparate nuanced incarnations.

Later in her career, Marisol again entangled breath, water and survival in her public monument *American Merchant Mariner's Memorial* (1991), which shows four sailors clinging to a sinking boat. She installed the sculpture in the Hudson River, collaborating with the choppy waters to image desperate struggles against drowning, with one sailor "half-submerged [...] [perpetually drowning] or surfacing with each tidal cycle".[25] This recurring drama stresses the precarity of human breath when facing ferocious open waters.

Ultimately, Marisol's breath-centered oceanic images and texts viscerally remind us that we are but brief contingent visitors – just one of many species-visitors – to this gorgeous, complex ecosystem. This brevity is magnified for humans underwater but is true on land as well, and we must work thoughtfully and communally to become a less devastating invasive species.

Relational and embodied readings of Marisol

At first glance, relating Marisol's work to breath may seem strange given the solid, obdurate nature of her sculptures. Indeed, her sculptures are a far cry from contemporaneous participatory breath-related art actions like Yoko Ono's event score "take the sound of the room breathing" (1963) and Lygia Clark's sensorial object *Respire comigo* (Breathe with Me) (1966), a found rubber diving tube the viewer handles to approximate our lungs' rhythmic breathing.[26] However, not only does breath play a core role in Marisol's imagery, process and inspiration (as described above), but also multiple interviews and journal entries reveal that Marisol established a dialectical relationship between her grounding, concrete sculpture and her own experiences of feeling like vapor. For example, she stated:"Sometimes I feel like I'm being blown away. People say they pinch themselves to see if they are awake. This restores them to reality. When I do a portrait, but really do myself in the portrait, or use my own hands or shoes, it brings me back to reality."[27] "My work brings me down to earth. I'm such an abstracted person that these figures somehow concretize me. Through them I feel I exist."[28]

Other evocative statements from the 1960s-70s include: "I feel like a shadow, like a black vapor with two holes through which I look."[29] "Be careful with that vacuum cleaner you are vacuuming my soul out of

24. *La visita*, 1964 (detail)

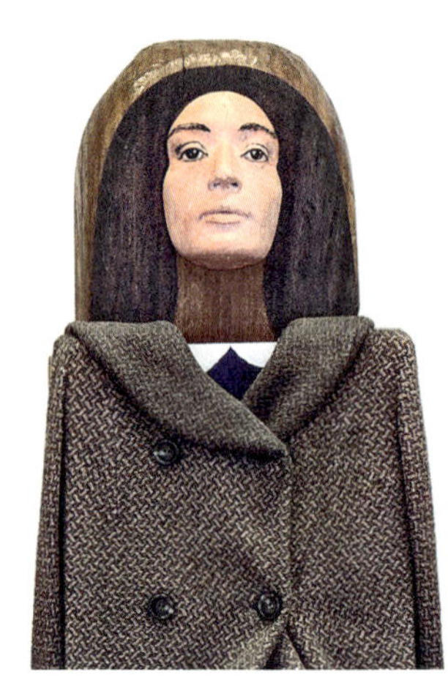

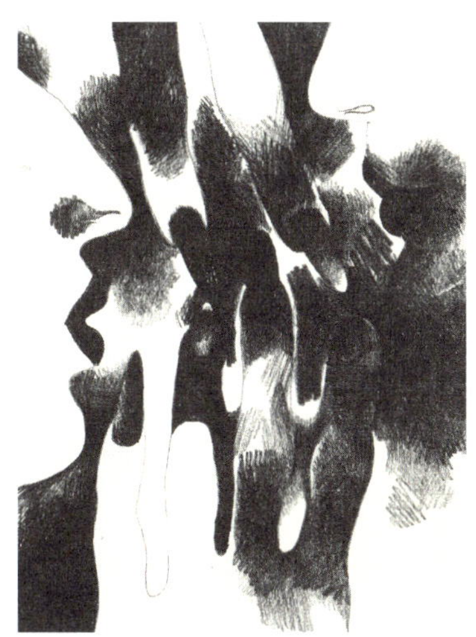

13. *Fingers and Faces*, 1961 (detail)

your room with it."[30] "I saw myself once, one evening when lying in bed, a shadow flying through the air, like a silhouette."[31]

Marisol's poetic invocations of feeling vaporous, shadowy and abstract establish an inverse dialectic with her solid sculptures but find compelling analogues in her prints' and drawings' many atmospheric passages. As a draughtswoman, she typically shaped forms by shading the diaphanous air around them, foregoing hard contours. For example, in *Fingers and Faces* (cat. 13, p. 29 and this spread), positive and negative space compete to emerge in a densely hatched atmosphere. In an untitled drawing (cat. 86, p. 103 and this spread), glowing rainbow translucent air currents cascade across body parts (arms, hands, profile, buttocks, spread legs) in a disorienting, enveloping account of sexual contact – ambiguously terrifying or ecstatic. Other works, like *All My Shoes for Ten Years* (cat. 62, pp. 98-99), reflect blatantly cruel forms of violent touch; fingers and even gunshots trespass upon the silhouettes, cutting into bodies with air-burst passages that convey the scalding pain of corporeal violation. While Marisol's airy works on paper and her obdurate sculptures are often treated separately, attunement to breath and air helps establish a connective thread.

Revisiting Marisol's works through the matrix and framework of breath redirects us to focus on the experiential side of the works' construction and meaning-making – the challenges to breath posed by her casting and scuba diving as well as the eerie breathing potential of her figures. We can even become more attuned to our own experiences of breath when looking at her work. Is our breathing calm, halted, shallow, deep, laboured or panicked as we view her works and consider her themes? Interestingly, several of Marisol's key interdisciplinary collaborators explored breath as a compositional and experiential principle. Dance choreographer Martha Graham – who invited Marisol to design sets or costumes for five different projects in the 1970s and 1980s – based her famed Graham technique on breathing's contraction and release.[32] Poet Robert Creeley, who collaborated with Marisol to publish the book *Presences* (1976), used unconventional syntax and stanza breaks to approximate distinct breathing rhythms.[33] Marisol, Graham and Creeley draw us as readers, dancers and viewers into distinctive forms of respiration, which lead to new experiences of embodiment.

At the same time, while studying breath encourages us to pay greater attention to our body's somatic experiences, it also troubles the assumption that the I/self/body is a viable independent unit of analysis.[34] With every breath, we inhale the environment around us (its nourishing and toxic components), circulate those within our bodies and exhale part of ourselves back into the world. Attention to breath implores us to study ourselves less as entities with strict interior-exterior boundaries and more as porous, interactional subjects subsisting on constant interchange with our milieus (i.e. every living and non-living entity around us). If Marisol's sculptural boxes image firmer interior/exterior division, their potential for breath and her diaphanous drawings pierce that very divide and suggest alternative relational models.

86. *Untitled*, 1976

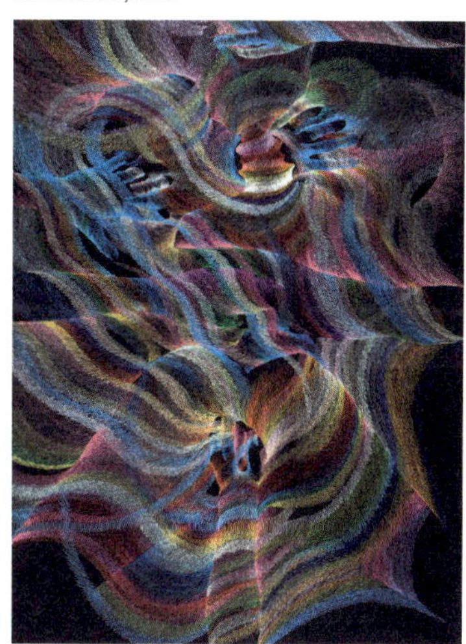

Our understanding of Marisol's work can be enriched by these modes of inquiry developed by scholars in the exciting, growing field of Breath Studies. While some writers like Jean-Christophe Bailey have pursued a universalising methodology grounded in the fundamental human experience of breathing, others have seen its potential for disruption of hegemonic discourse.[35] In the late 1990s Luce Irigaray declared that the late 20th century inaugurated the "Age of the Breath" in her critique of patriarchal assumptions underpinning Western philosophy.[36] Important recent publications by Ashon T. Crawley, Jean-Thomas Tremblay, Glenn Kaino, Mika Yoshitake, T.J. Demos and others working across Performance Studies, Environmental Humanities and Black Studies have interrogated the fact that many bodies cannot physically breathe or psychologically breathe easily in the white supremacist, heteropatriarchal, ableist, colonial present – perhaps most pointedly evidenced in Eric Garner's and George Floyd's shared last words "I can't breathe" and those words' afterlife in protests confronting the entangled histories of anti-Blackness, policing and state violence.[37] These scholars have also underscored how the politics of breathing have accrued intensified criticality today not only amid the Covid-19 epidemic (its respiratory impact and all it revealed about humanity's polarisation surrounding science and politics), but especially for environmental justice activists who warn us of our imminent breathlessness and draw attention to the economic and political elites' disproportionate harm to the climate by exporting their waste and polluting industries to disempowered regions. Marisol's engagement with breath intersects with several of these models; she explores our elemental human dependency on respiration, gendered vulnerability to corporeal and ideological violence in a patriarchal world, and environmental devastation's asymmetrically involved culprits and victims. I cannot, however, align Marisol's approach to race with the scholarship enlivening Breath Studies today. Her commentary about race is fraught – seemingly well-intentioned, informed by civil rights activism, and reflecting growing discourses about race as a social construct, yet also mired in racist allusions to blackface by covering her own cast face in black paint (see *The Car*). This subject requires much more than a single sentence and will be unpacked in my future book project.

As this essay has shown, breath crops up across Marisol's career, bringing together series traditionally separated – the 1960s "Pop" works, the fish series, her mid-1970s studies of sexual contact and violence and her later public monuments. Breath also connects her sculpture and works on paper in a compelling dialectic. This connective impact literalises an affective dimension of Breath Studies that multiple scholars have examined: how breath troubles tidy categorical separations – self/environment, human/non-human life, discrete disciplinary fields and more. Ultimately, attunement to Marisol's breath work, manifested across her art and archives, invites alternative relational and experiential readings of her work and underscores how much of her art reminds us of our absurd, terrifying contingency on these strange breathing machines we so briefly inhabit and their at once precarious and violent interplay with our environment.[38]

DELIA SOLOMONS is Associate Professor of Modern and Contemporary Art History at Drexel University. Her first book, *Cold War in the White Cube: U.S. Exhibitions of Latin American Art (1959-1968)*, examines a boom of exhibitions that framed Latin American art according to specific Cold War political and cultural ideologies for US audiences. Her current book project, *Marisol's Containment Culture,* explores Marisol's sculpture of the 1960s in relation to containment discourses proliferating in foreign policy, domestic agendas and psychological fields. Solomons' writing has also been published in *The Art Bulletin*; *Marisol: A Retrospective; Alex Da Corte: Mr. Remember; The Americas Revealed: Collecting Colonial and Modern Latin American Art in the United States; journal of visual culture;* MoMA's *post: notes on art in a global context* and *Journal of Curatorial Studies.*

1. "Marisol and John Jonas Gruen. Interview with Marisol", 3 June 1969, John Jonas Gruen and Jane Wilson papers, 1909-2016, Archives of American Art, Smithsonian Institution, Washington, D.C.
2. Bessel van der Kolk, *The Body Keeps the Score: Brain, Mind and Body in the Healing of Trauma* (Penguin Books, 2014).
3. This section's title nods to neurosurgeon Paul Kalanithi's heart-wrenching book about grappling with a fatal cancer diagnosis. *When Breath Becomes Air* (Random House, 2016).
4. Lawrence Campbell offers a detailed description of her working methods in "Marisol's Magic Mixtures", *Art News* 63 (March 1964), pp. 64-65. I'm grateful to sculptor Lewis Colburn for his insights into these materials and processes.
5. In response to this question, Marisol skirted the technical description and jokingly said "like this" before she enacted an exaggerated breath in and out, sparking laughter in the crowd. Recording of Q&A following Marisol's lecture at the Skowhegan School of Painting and Sculpture, 1965 (Series: Skowhegan School of Painting and Sculpture Lecture Archive, Folder: 118 Marisol. Museum of Modern Art Archives).
6. Marcia Pointon, "Casts, Imprints, and the Deathliness of Things: Artifacts on the Edge", *The Art Bulletin*, vol. 96, no. 2 (2014), p. 187.
7. See, for example, "Art: Sculpture – The Dollmaker", *Time* (28 May 1965), p. 80, and Daniel Chapman, "Marisol...A Brilliant Sculptress Shapes the Heads of State", *Look* (14 November 1967), p. 78.
8. Anna Katherine Brodbeck, "Sexually Frustrated: The Radical Potential of Eroticism, Violence, and Hybridity in Marisol's Drawings" in *Marisol: A Retrospective,* ed. Cathleen Chaffee (Buffalo AKG Art Museum and DelMonico Books, 2023), pp. 122-139. I am also indebted to the thoughtful connections Brodbeck and Chaffee develop between Marisol's drawings and sculpture in this book.
9. Julia Vázquez, "Marisol Underwater, 1970-1973" in ibid., pp. 104-121.
10. *Jeppesen's Sport Diver Manual* (Jeppesen Sanderson Inc., 1976), p. 2.41-42.
11. Ibid, p. 2.42, 2.46
12. Ibid, p. 1.64.
13. José L. Barrio-Garay, *Marisol* (Trisolini Gallery, Ohio University, 1974), np.
14. Journal entry "Esta vez todo esta cambiado...", dated 8 August 1976, in notebook labeled "Caraquiano en Agosto y Sep, 1976." Marisol Papers, Buffalo AKG Art Museum Archives.
15. Journal entry "Yesterday we decided to go on a deep dive...", approx. late September 1976. Marisol Papers, Buffalo AKG Art Museum Archives.
16. Transcript of an interview by Ana María Escallón, p. 6. Marisol Papers Buffalo AKG Art Museum. An edited version was published in Ana María Escallón, *Marisol* (Brenau University Galleries and Art Museum of the Americas, 1999). Journal entry "Maybe I will not dive again...", dated 10 September 1977, in black 1977 Journal. Marisol Papers, Buffalo AKG Art Museum Archives.
17. Three sketches of *Aqua Bell* appear in her archives, along with a description. Marisol Papers, Buffalo AKG Art Museum Archives.
18. See Vázquez, "Marisol Underwater".
19. These open mouths do, however, recall ones that appear in *Love* (1962) and *Self-Portrait* (1961-62).
20. See Vázquez, "Marisol Underwater".
21. "Es horrible han matado al coral más bello del mundo [...] Esto antes era como un paraíso, que daba tanta energía [...] Ahora está gris y muerto así como son ellos [...] No pensaba que la fuerza destructiva de la gente esa fuera tan poderosa." Journal entry "Querido Pajaro. Llegue a Cozumel...", in notebook labeled "Caraquiano en Agosto y Sep, 1976", Marisol Papers, Buffalo AKG Art Museum Archives. Translations mine unless otherwise noted.
22. "Editorial: The Big Sewer in the Sky", *Life* (13 August 1965), p. 4.
23. Draft of letter of complaint for *Smithsonian Magazine* (7 March 1984). Marisol Papers, Buffalo AKG Art Museum Archives.
24. Western interpretations of Buddhist practice almost certainly informed the psychoanalyst's descriptions of mindful breathing that so activated Marisol's anxiety in the 1950s.
25. Estrellita Brodsky, "Marisol's Irreverent Monuments" in *Marisol: A Retrospective,* ed. Cathleen Chaffee (Buffalo AKG Art Museum, 2023), p. 153.
26. While both Clark and Marisol source scuba iconography or materials, their works operate very differently. The parallels between Marisol and her Brazilian Neoconcretist contemporaries merit more consideration than I can explore in this short essay.
27. Lawrence Campbell, "The Creative Eye of the Artist Marisol", *Cosmopolitan* (June 1964), p. 68.
28. John Gruen, "Art: Marisol – Top to Bottom", *New York Herald Tribune* (8 March 1964).
29. "Me siento como una sombra, como un vapor negro con dos huecos por donde mireo." In "Ante de irme ...", dated August 3, 1978 in notebook with rainbow cover. Marisol Papers, Buffalo AKG Art Museum Archives.
30. "Querida pajaro, ahora me gusta..." in notebook labeled "Caraquiano en Agosto y Sep, 1976." Marisol Papers, Buffalo AKG Art Museum Archives.
31. Brian O'Doherty, "Marisol: The Enigma of the Self-Image", *New York Times* (1 March 1964), p. 23.
32. Johanna Heil, "Exercises in Discipline and Freedom?: The Graham Technique", *Dance Chronicle* vol. 39, no. 2 (Summer 2016), pp. 123-52.
33. Paul Diehl, "The Literal Activity of Robert Creeley", *boundary 2* , vol. 6/7, no. 3 (Spring-Autumn 1978), pp. 335-346.
34. See, for example, Jean-Thomas Tremblay, *Breathing Aesthetics* (Duke University Press, 2022).
35. Jean-Christophe Bailly, "The Slightest Breath (On Living)", *CR: The New Centennial Review* 10, no. 3 (Winter 2010), pp. 1-11, 269.
36. Luce Irigaray, "The Age of the Breath" in *Luce Irigaray: Key Writings: Part IV*, ed. Luce Irigaray (Continuum, 2004), pp. 165-170.
37. See for example Tremblay; Ashon T. Crawley, *Blackpentecostal Breath: The Aesthetics of Possibility* (Fordham University Press, 2016); and eds. Glenn Kaino and Mika Yoshitake, *Breath(e): Toward Climate and Social Justice* (Hammer Museum/DelMonico Books, 2024).
38. The ideas explored in this short essay will be expanded in my forthcoming book *Marisol's Containment Culture* (working title). I am deeply grateful that Cathleen Chaffee, Gabrielle Carlo, Julia Vázquez and many others at the Buffalo AKG Art Museum have so thoughtfully organised, cared for, represented and made available Marisol's Bequest and Archives. I also owe a hearty thank you to Faye Gleisser for her thoughtful feedback on this essay.

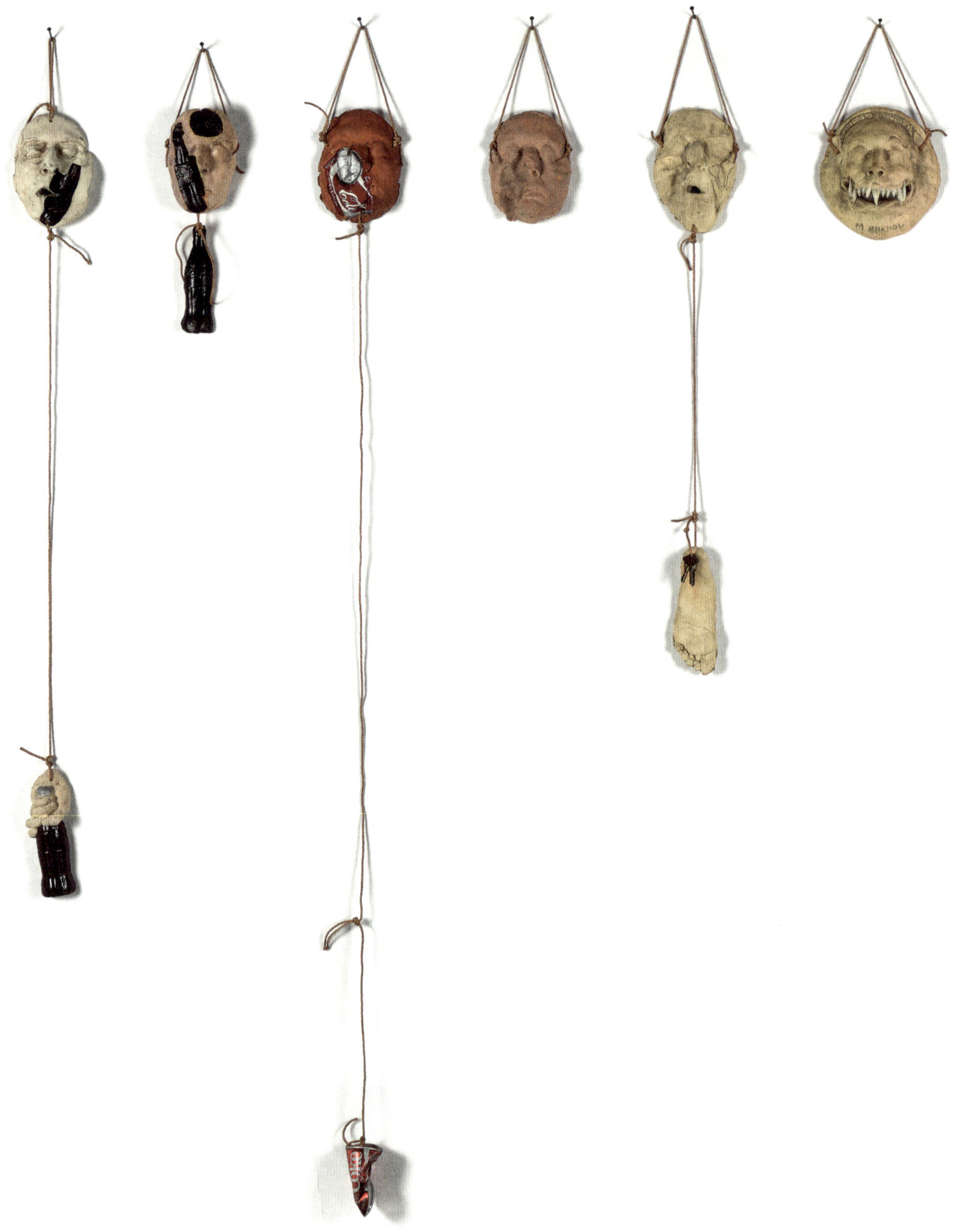

63. *Face and Hand with Coca-Cola Bottle*, 1974 67. Untitled, 1974 71. *Coke Can*, 1975 73. *Fido's Paw*, 1975
66. *Gus Key (also called Face, Foot and Keys)*, 1974 74. *M. Marisol*, 1975

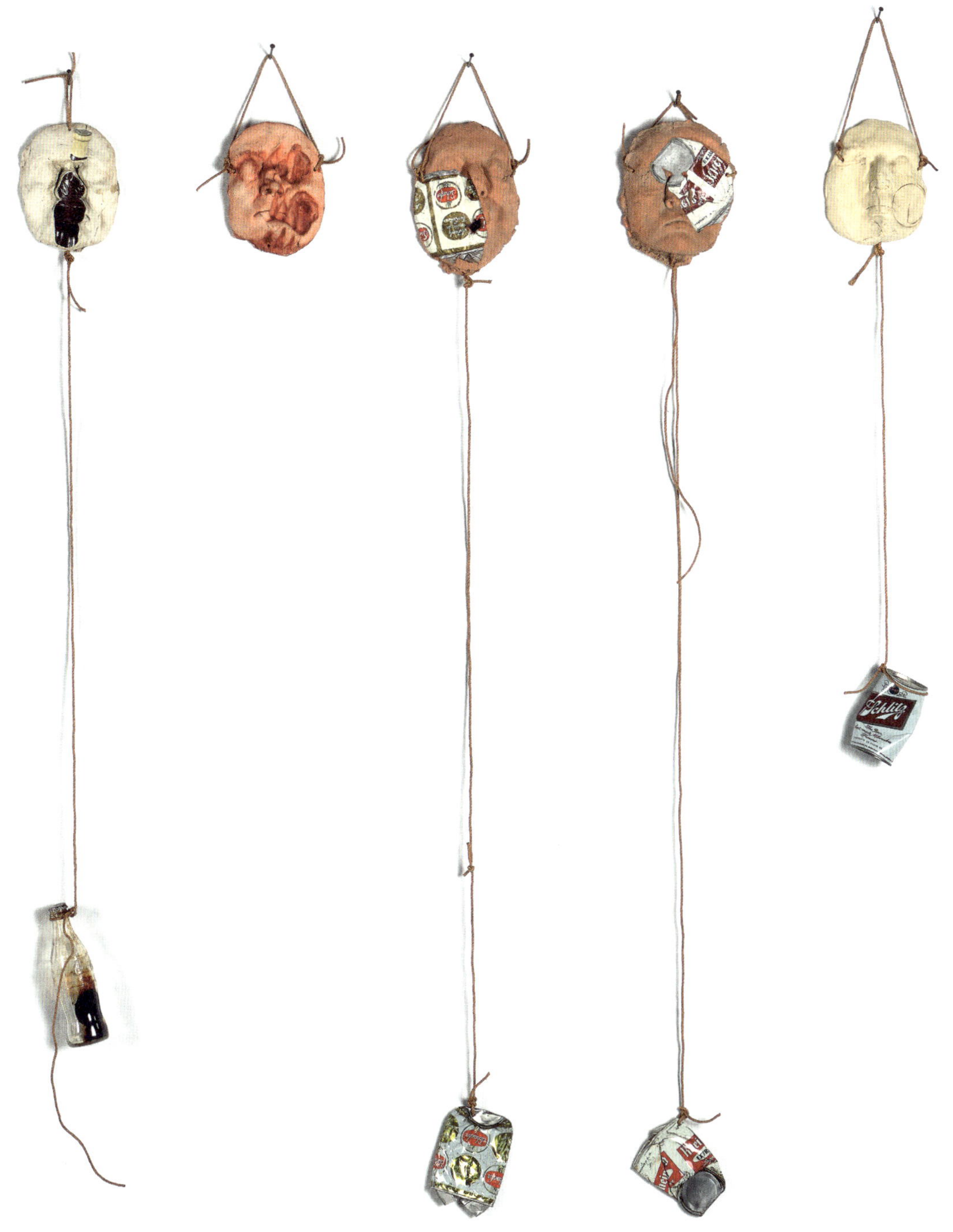

70. *Coke Bottle I*, 1975 75. *The Punch*, 1975 76. *Schaefer Can*, 1975 64. *Face with Rheingold Beer Can*, 1974 65. *Face with Schlitz Beer Can*, 1974

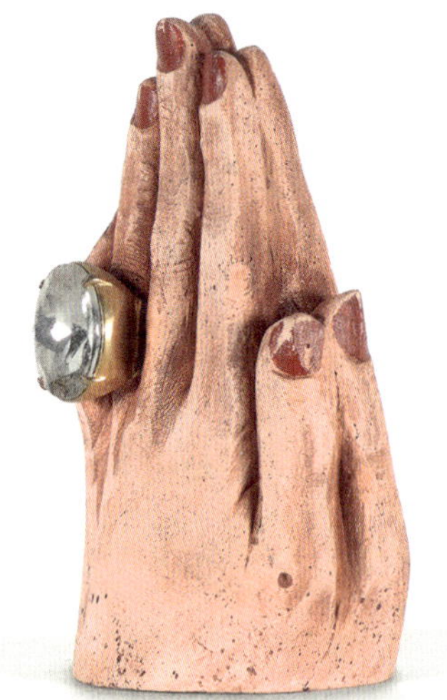
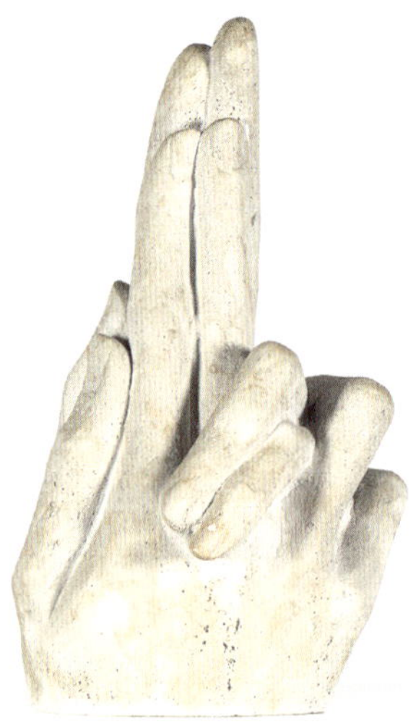
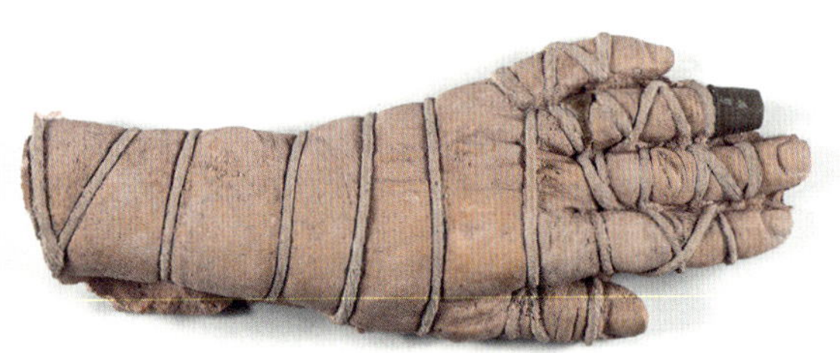
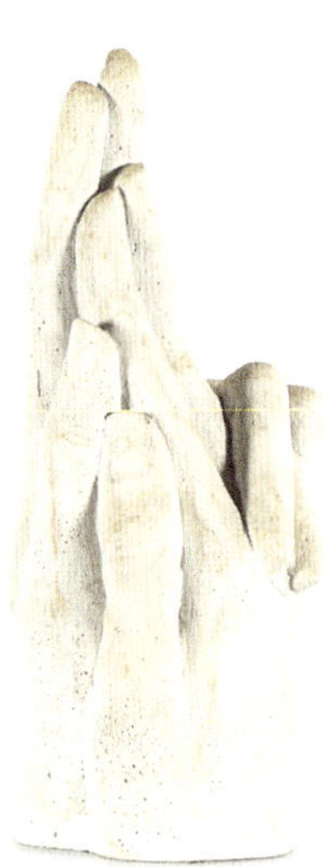
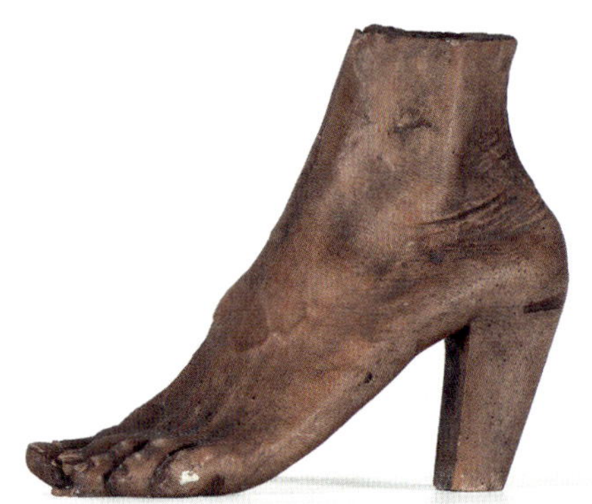

Top. 34. *Dominant Woman*, 1968 100. *Querube's hands*, 1987
Below: 90. *Thimble Thief*, 1977 101. Untitled, 1987 96. *Shoe*, c. 1982

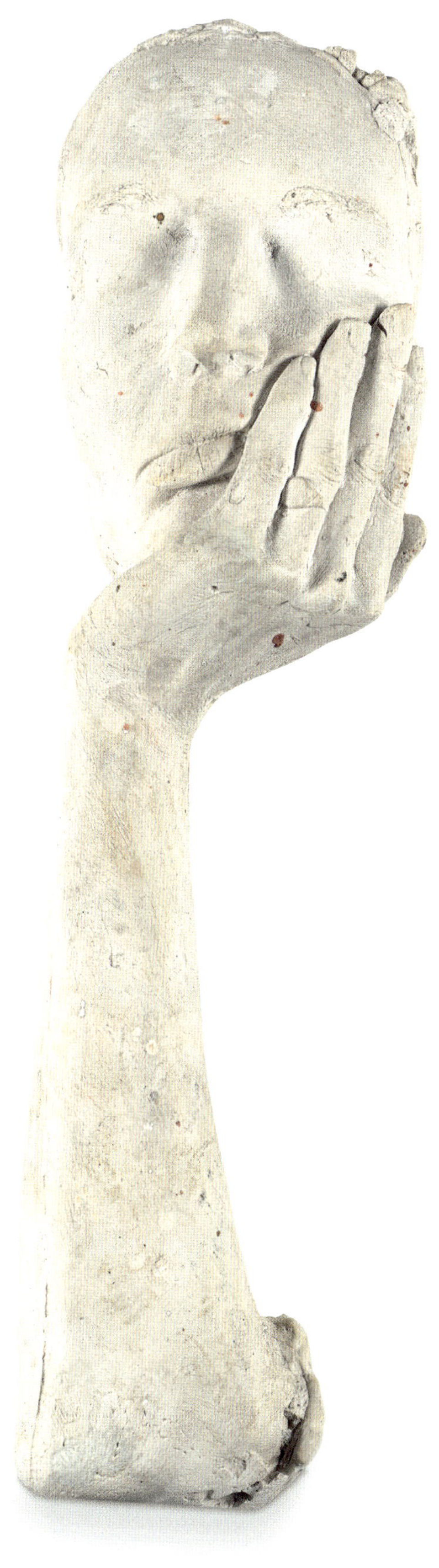

85. Untitled, c. 1970-80

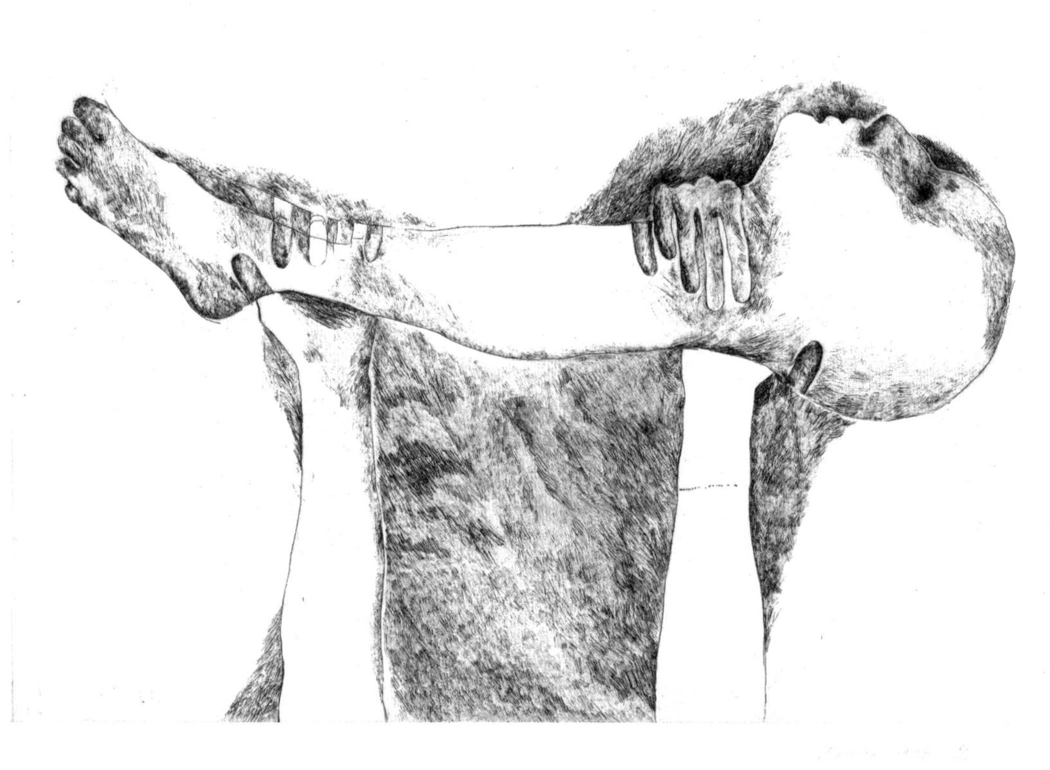

38. *The Death of Head and Leg*, 1969-73

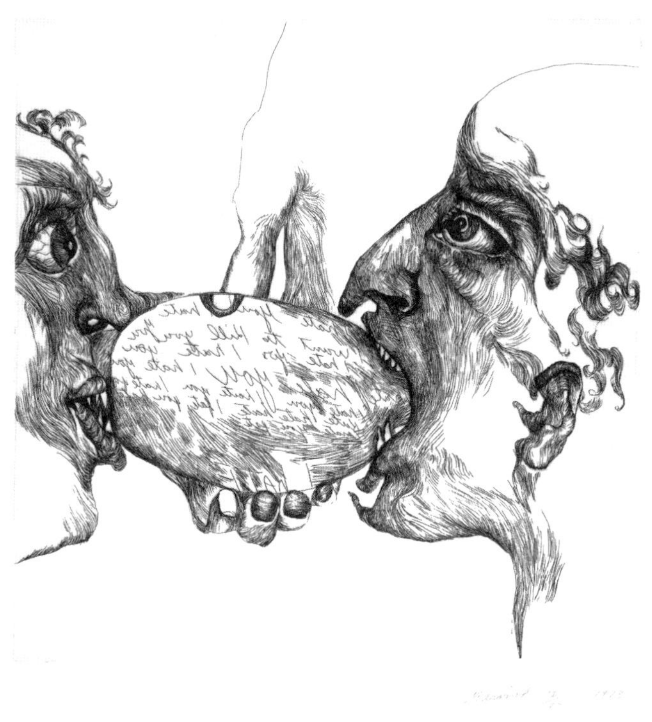

59. *I Hate You*, 1973

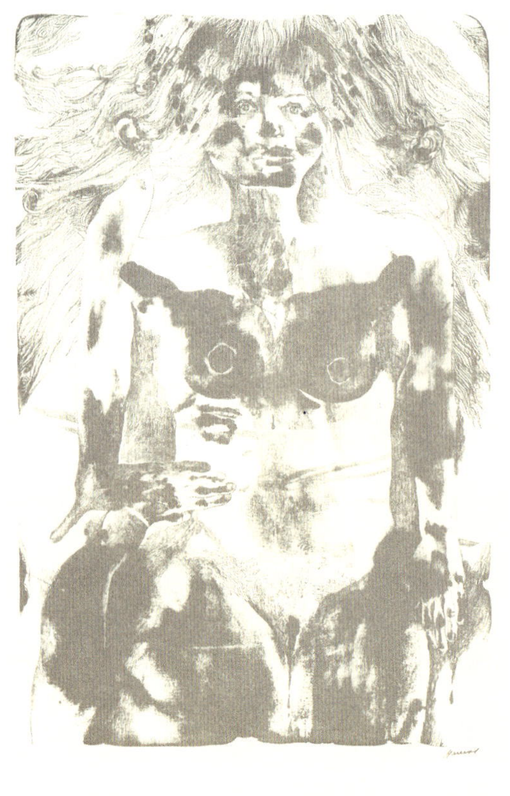

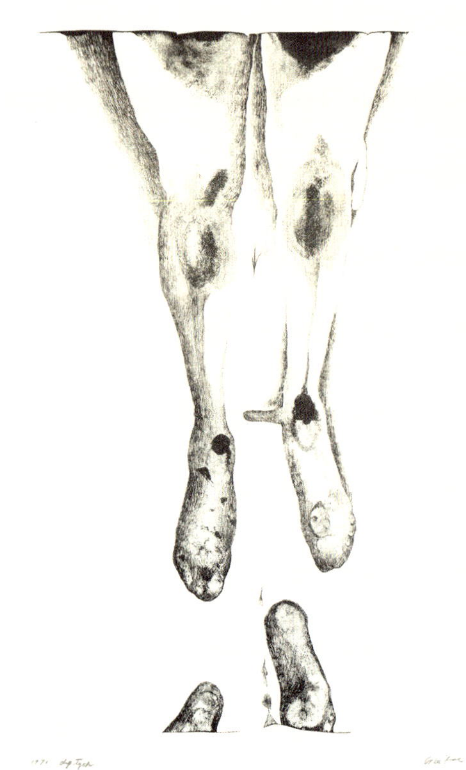

47. *Diptych*, 1971

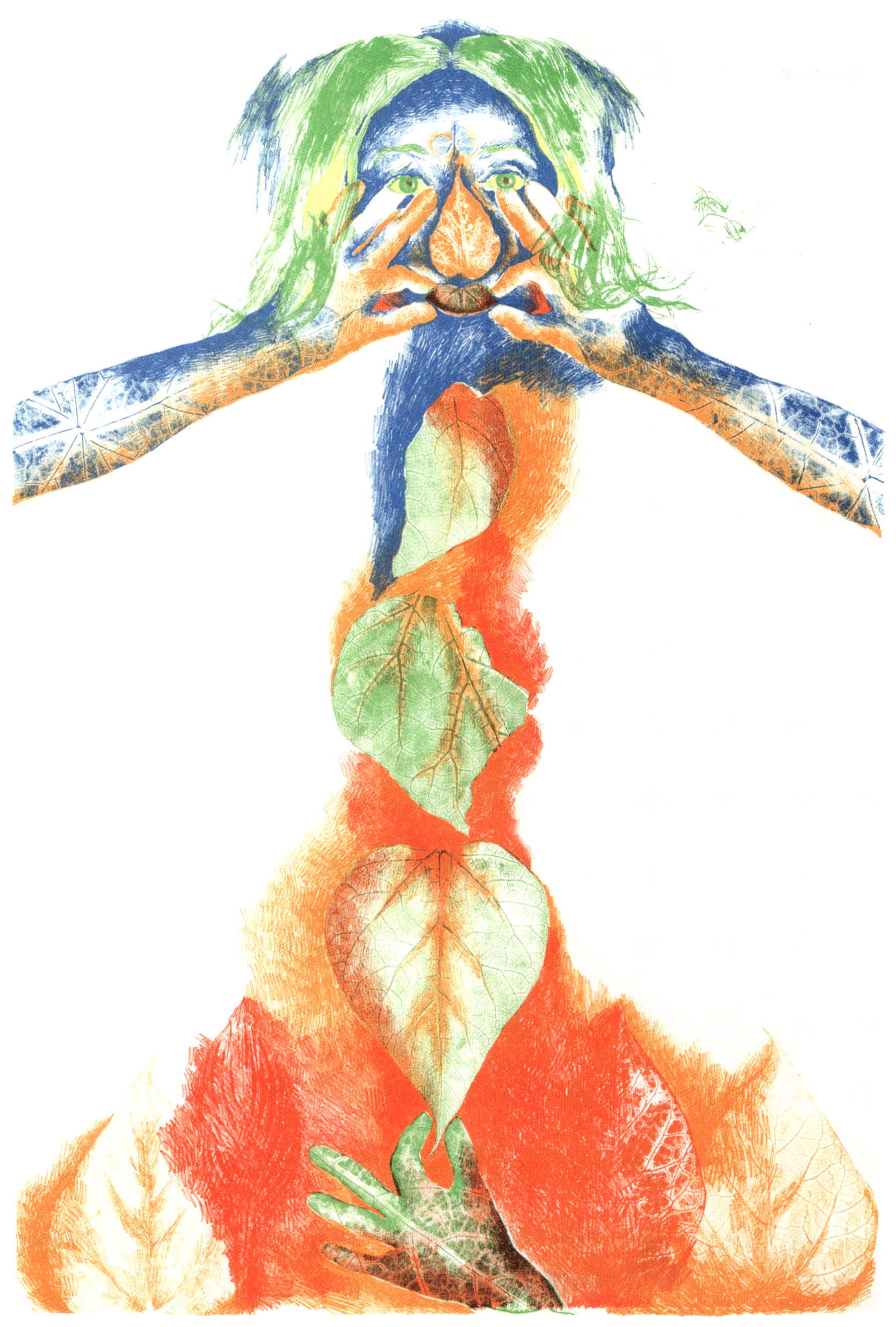

56. *Catalpa Maiden About to Touch Herself*, 1973

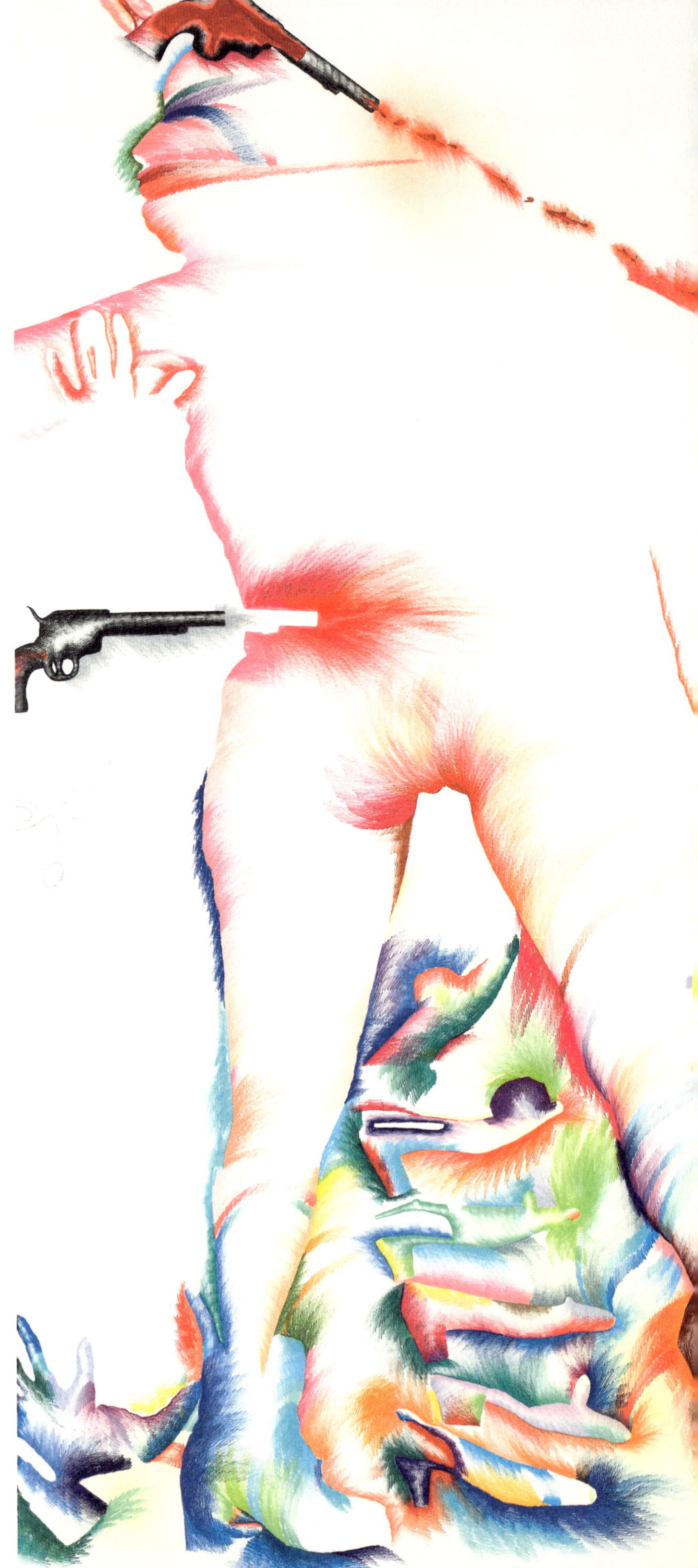

62. *All My Shoes for Ten Years*, 1974

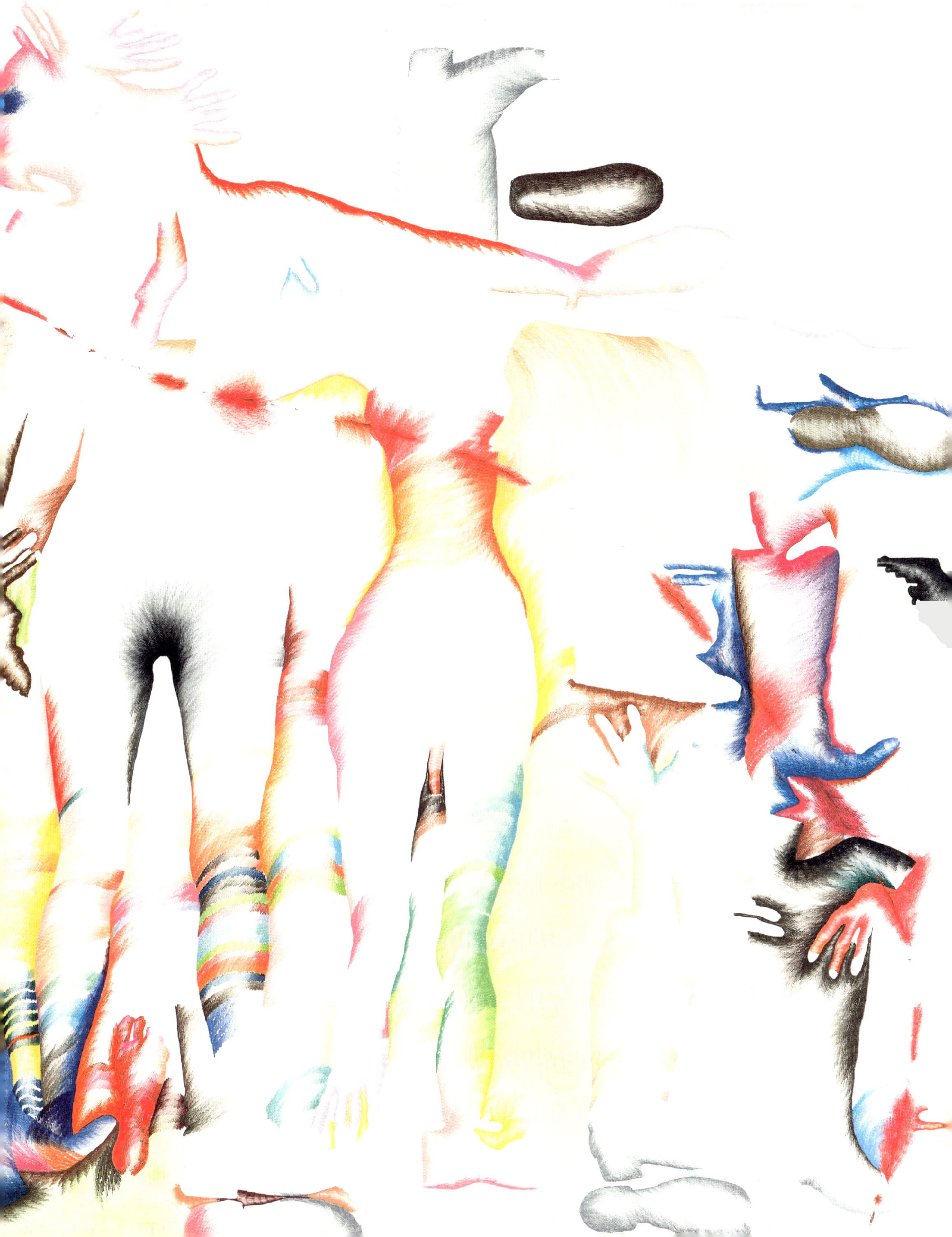

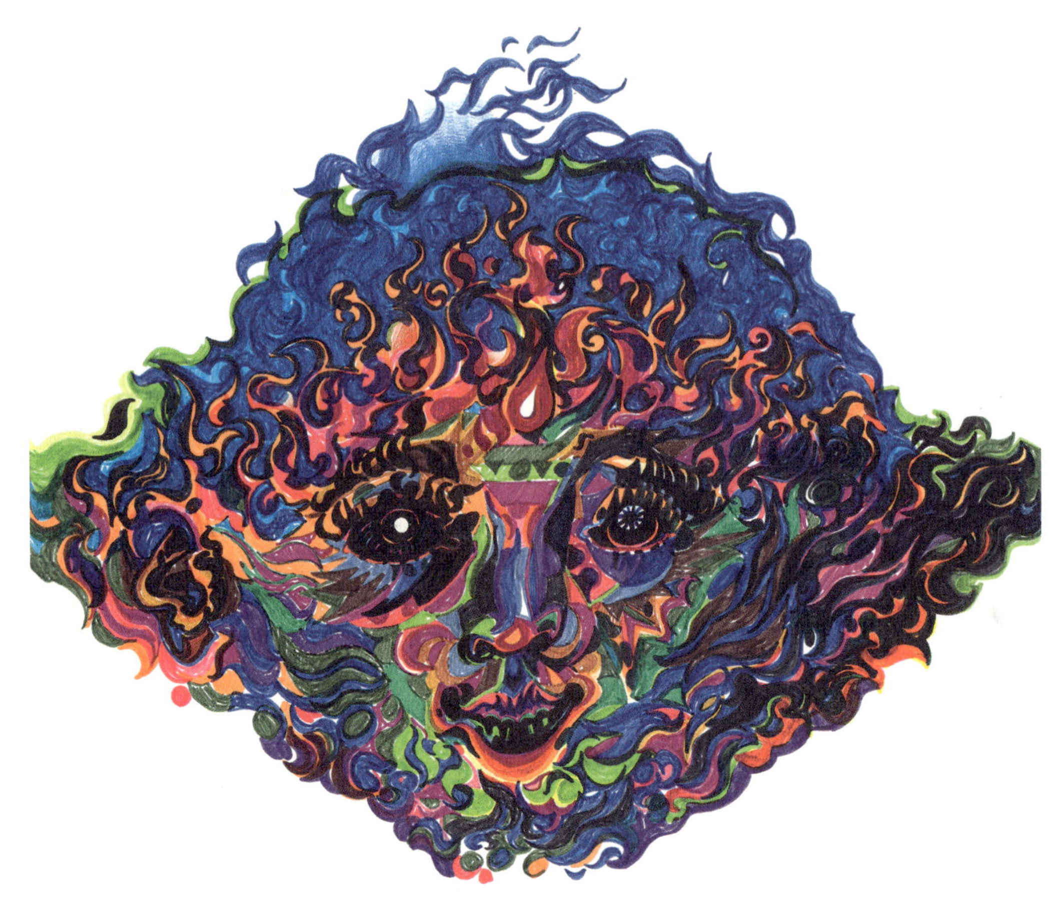

40. Untitled, c. 1970s

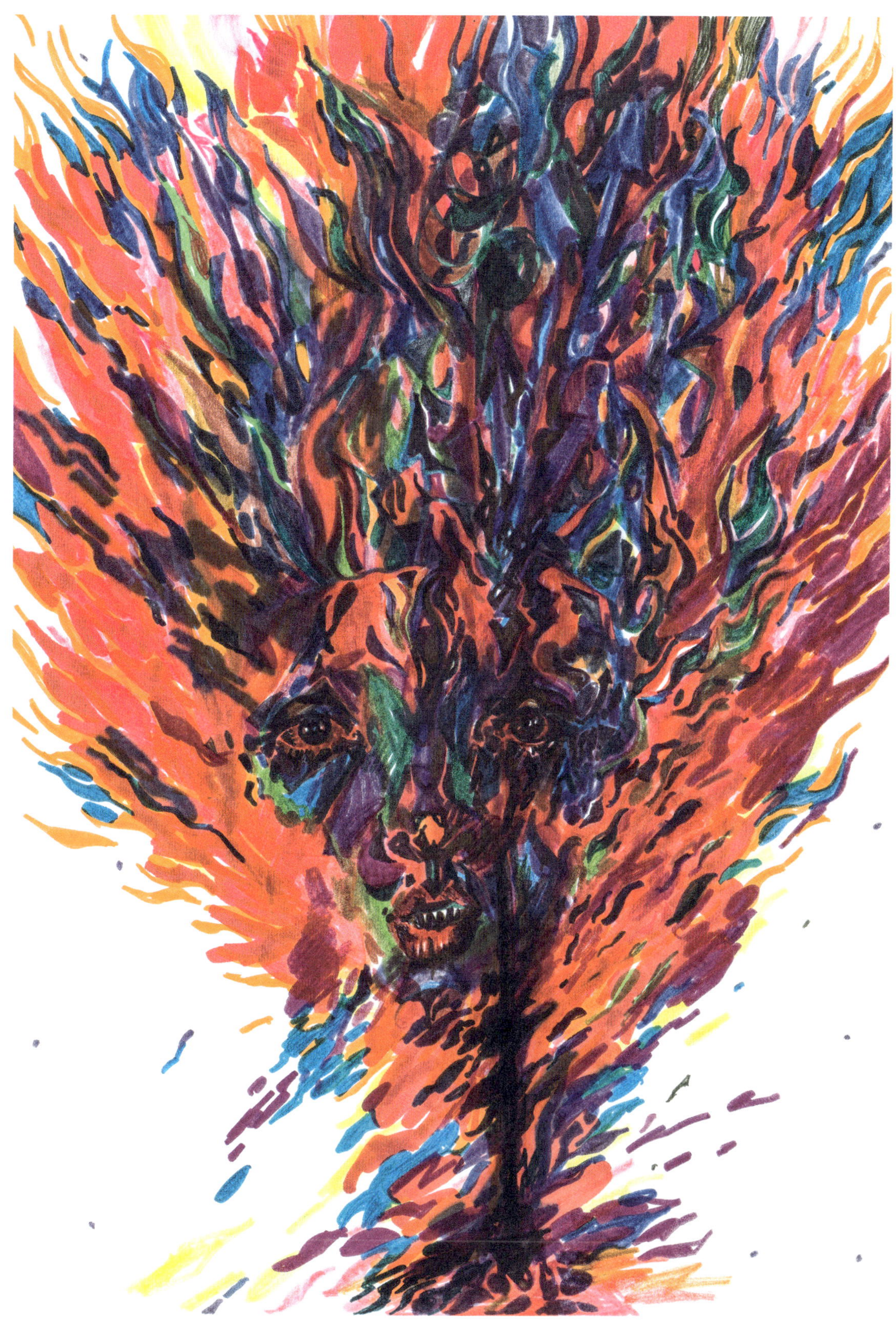

51. Untitled, c. 1972

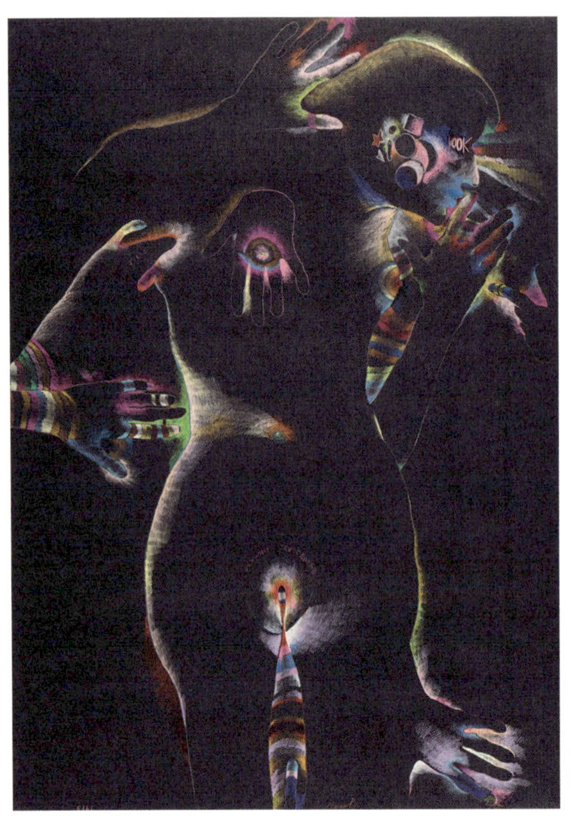

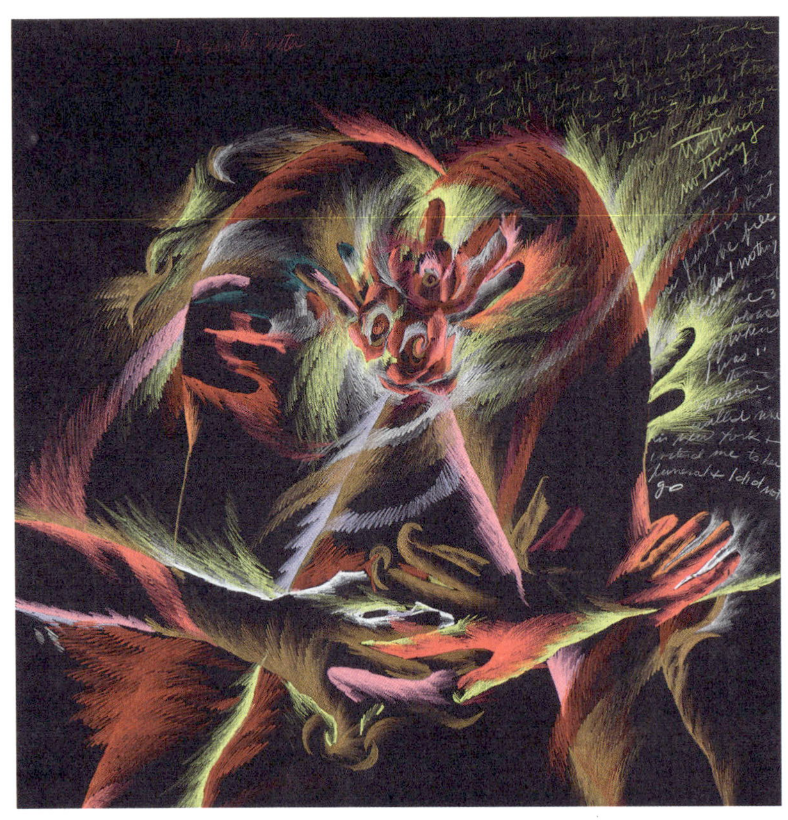

61. *Sexually Frustrated*, 1973

78. *The Scarlet Letter*, c. 1975–80

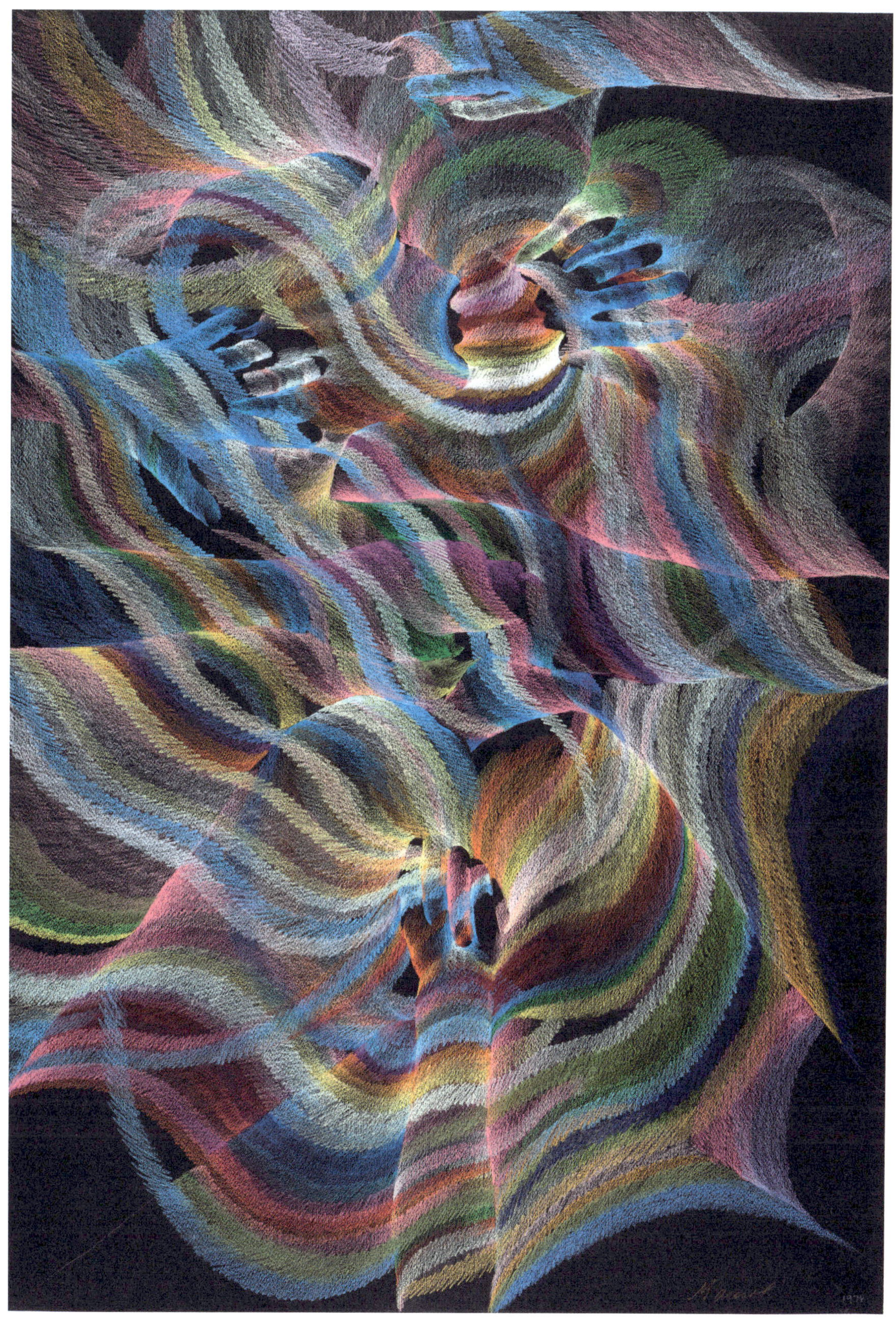

86. *Untitled*, 1976

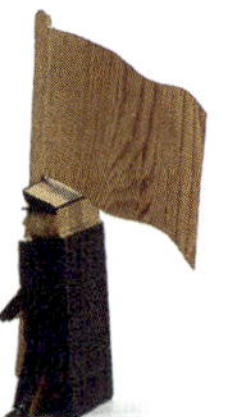
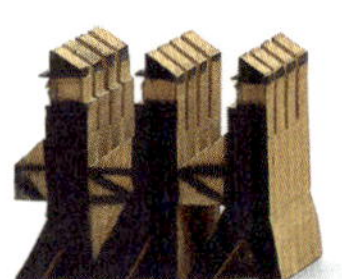
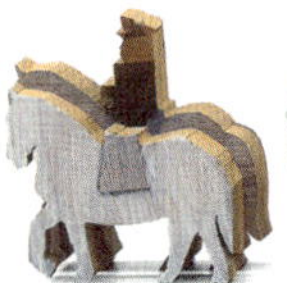
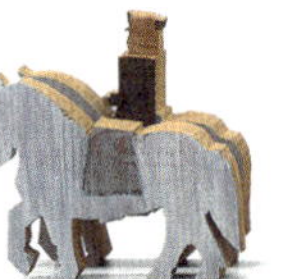

104. *The Funeral*, 1996

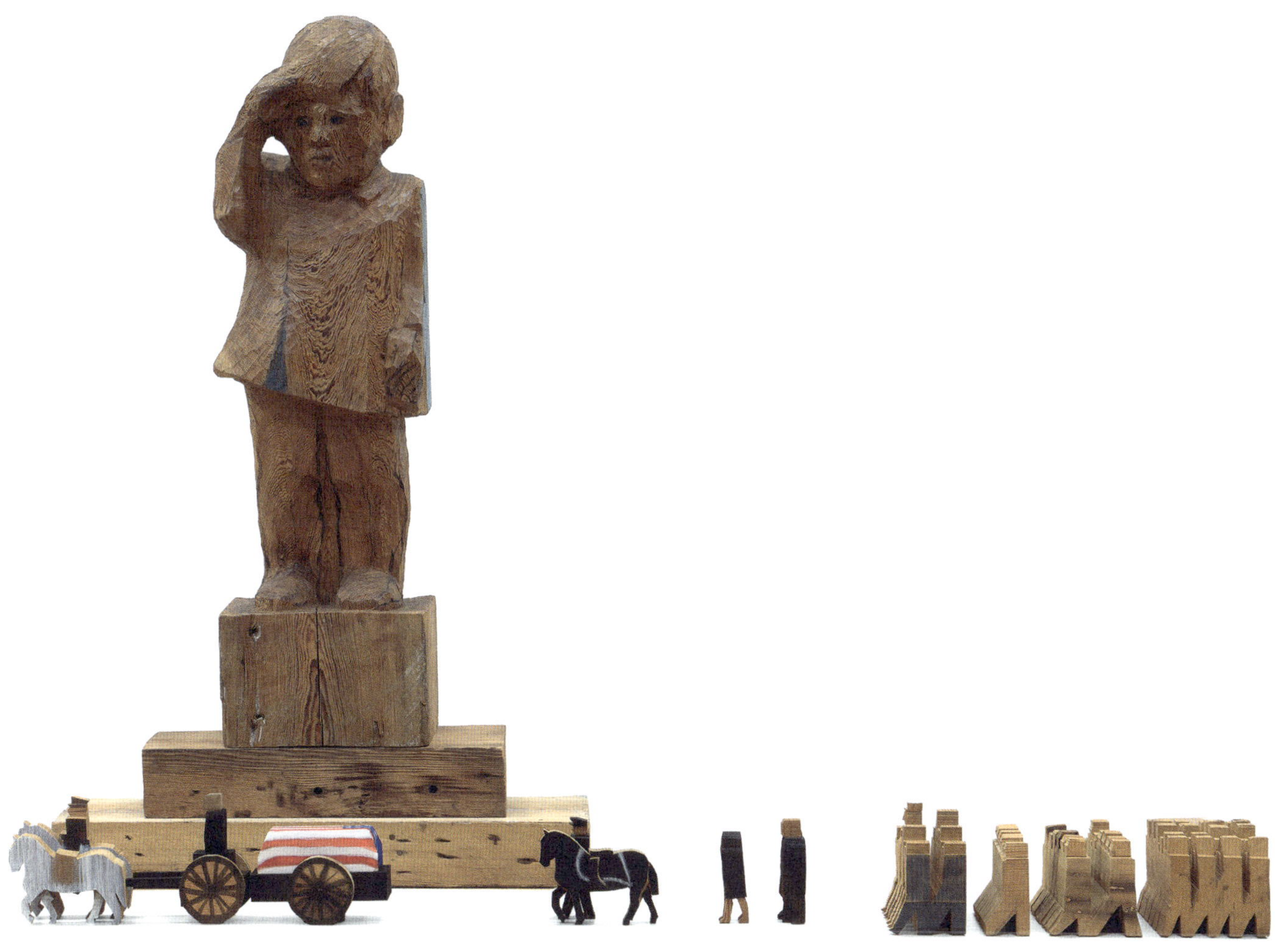

97. *Lincoln*, 1984

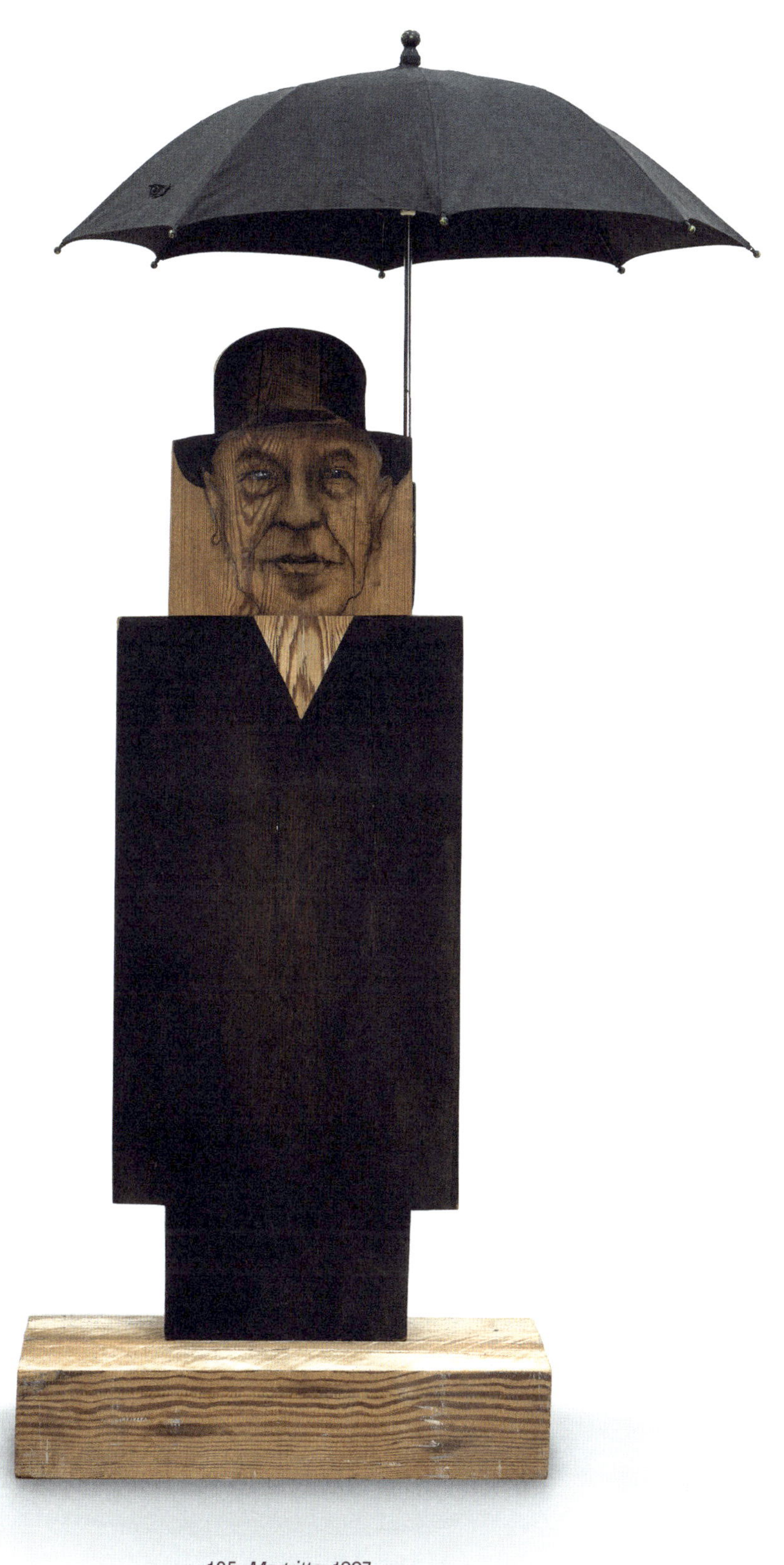

105. *Magritte*, 1997

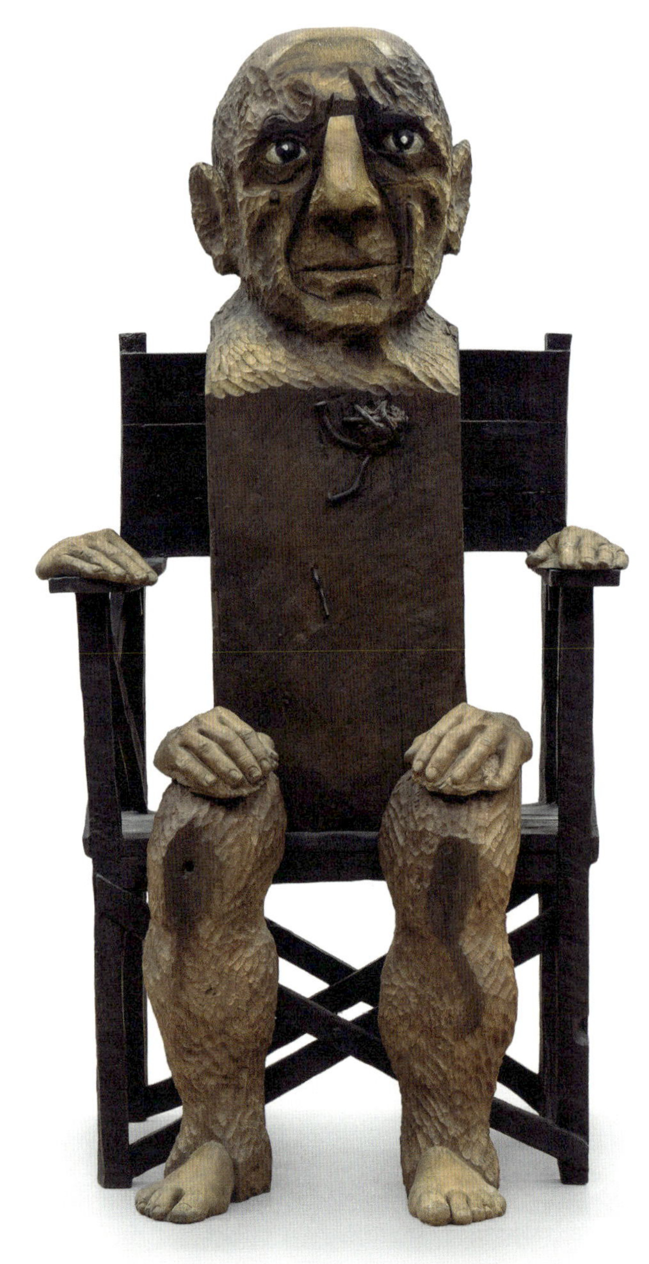

88. *Picasso*, 1977

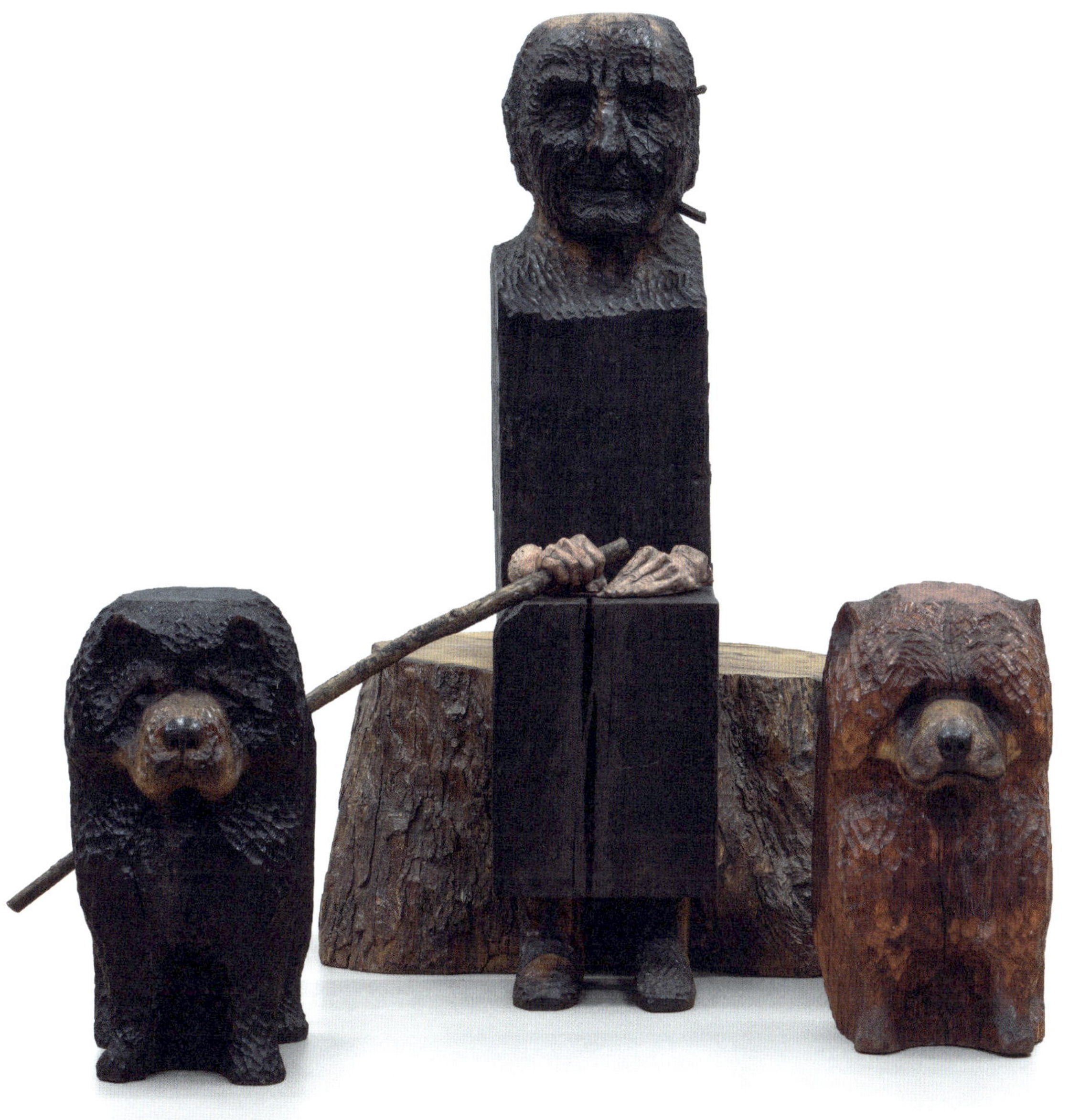

89. *Portrait of Georgia O'Keeffe with Dogs*, 1977

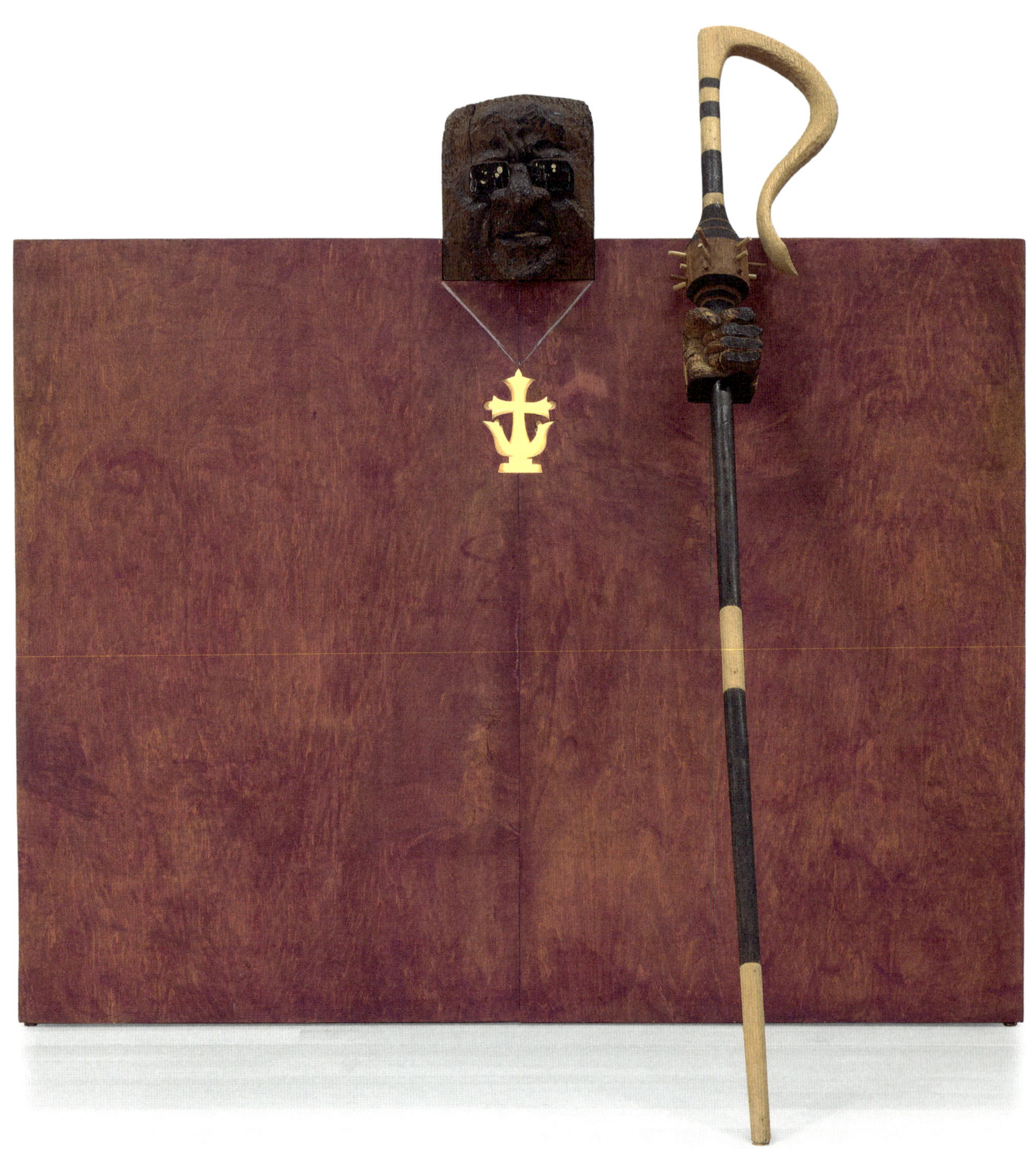

102. *Portrait of Bishop Desmond Tutu*, 1988

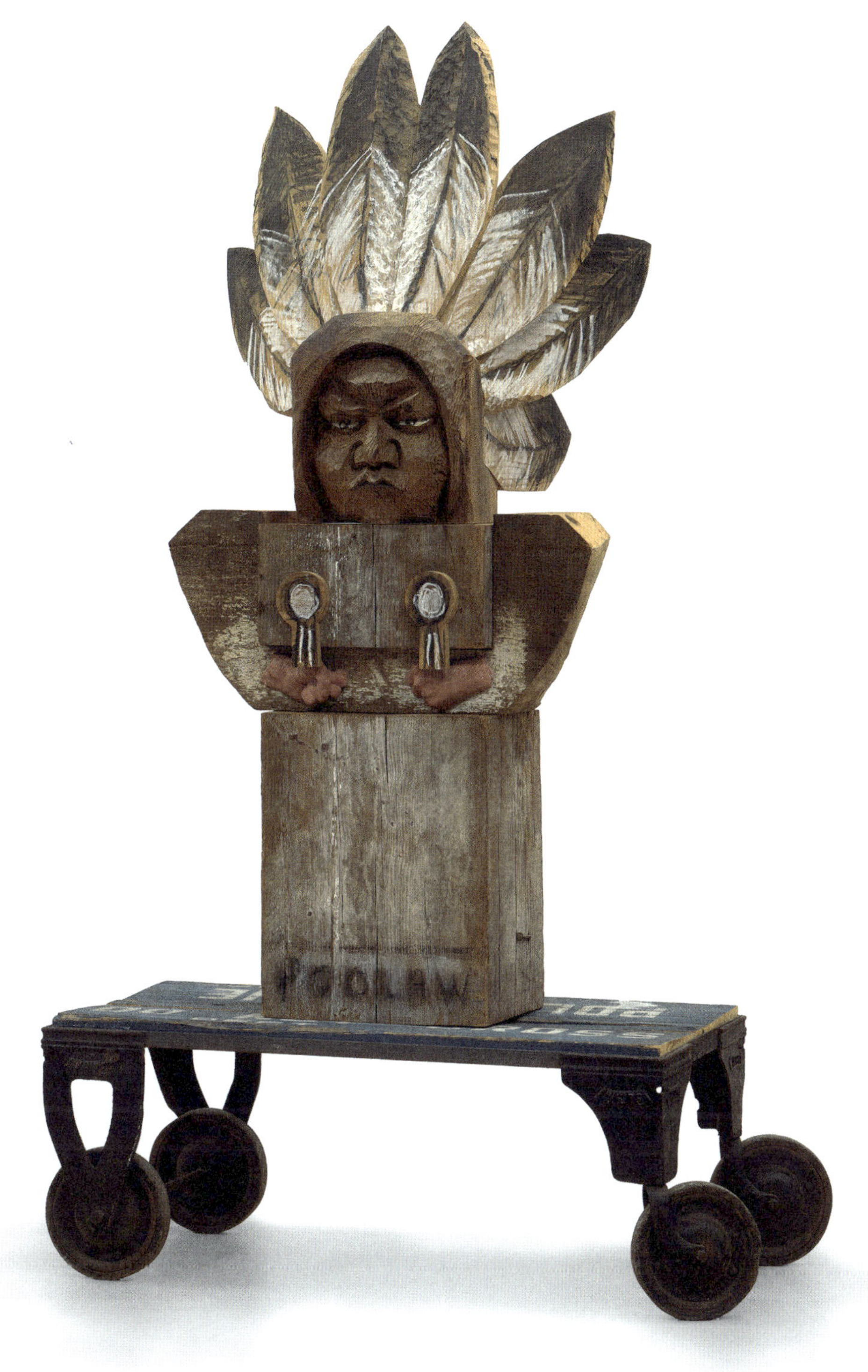

103. *Horace Poolaw*, 1993

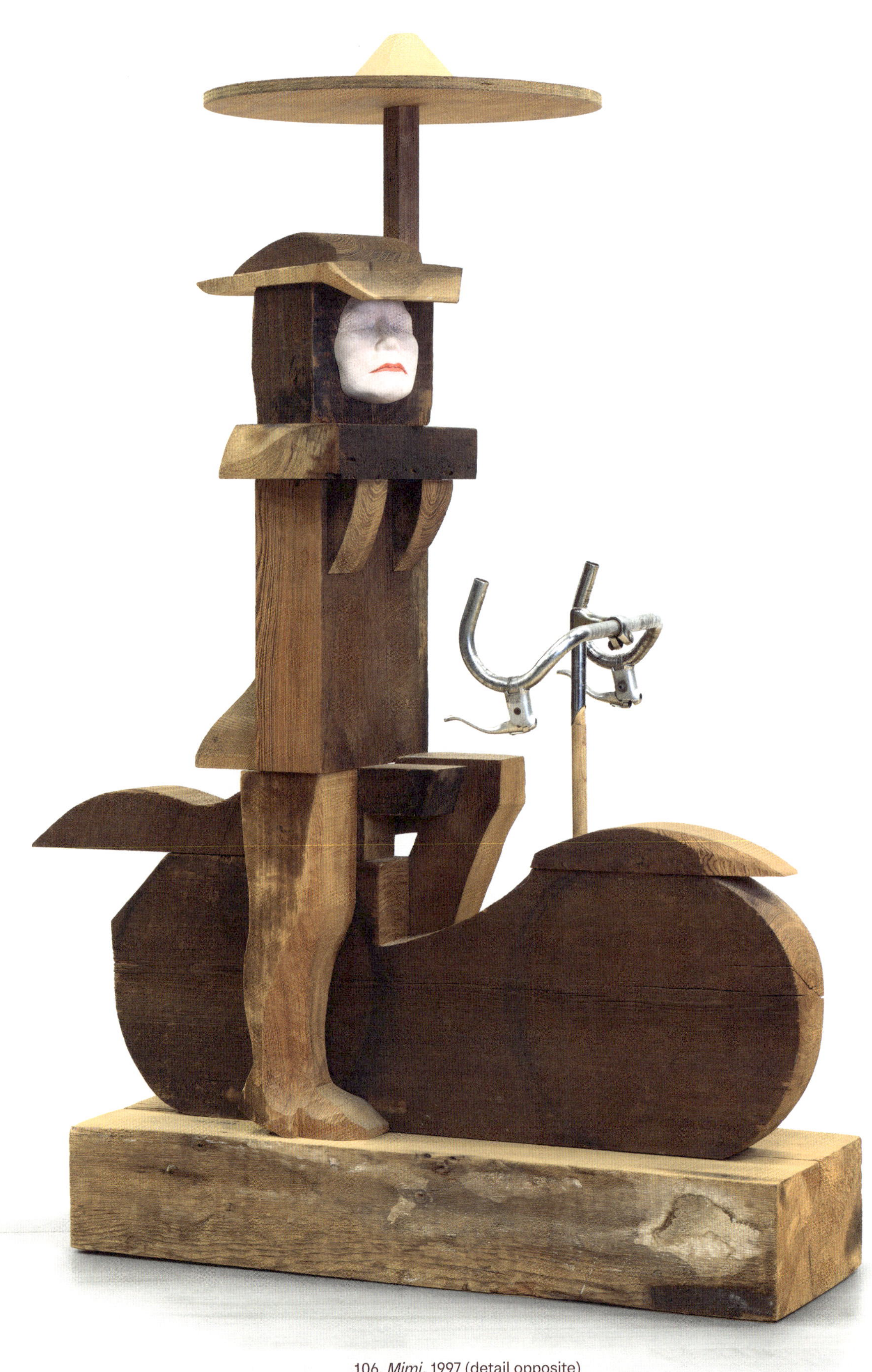

106. *Mimi*, 1997 (detail opposite)

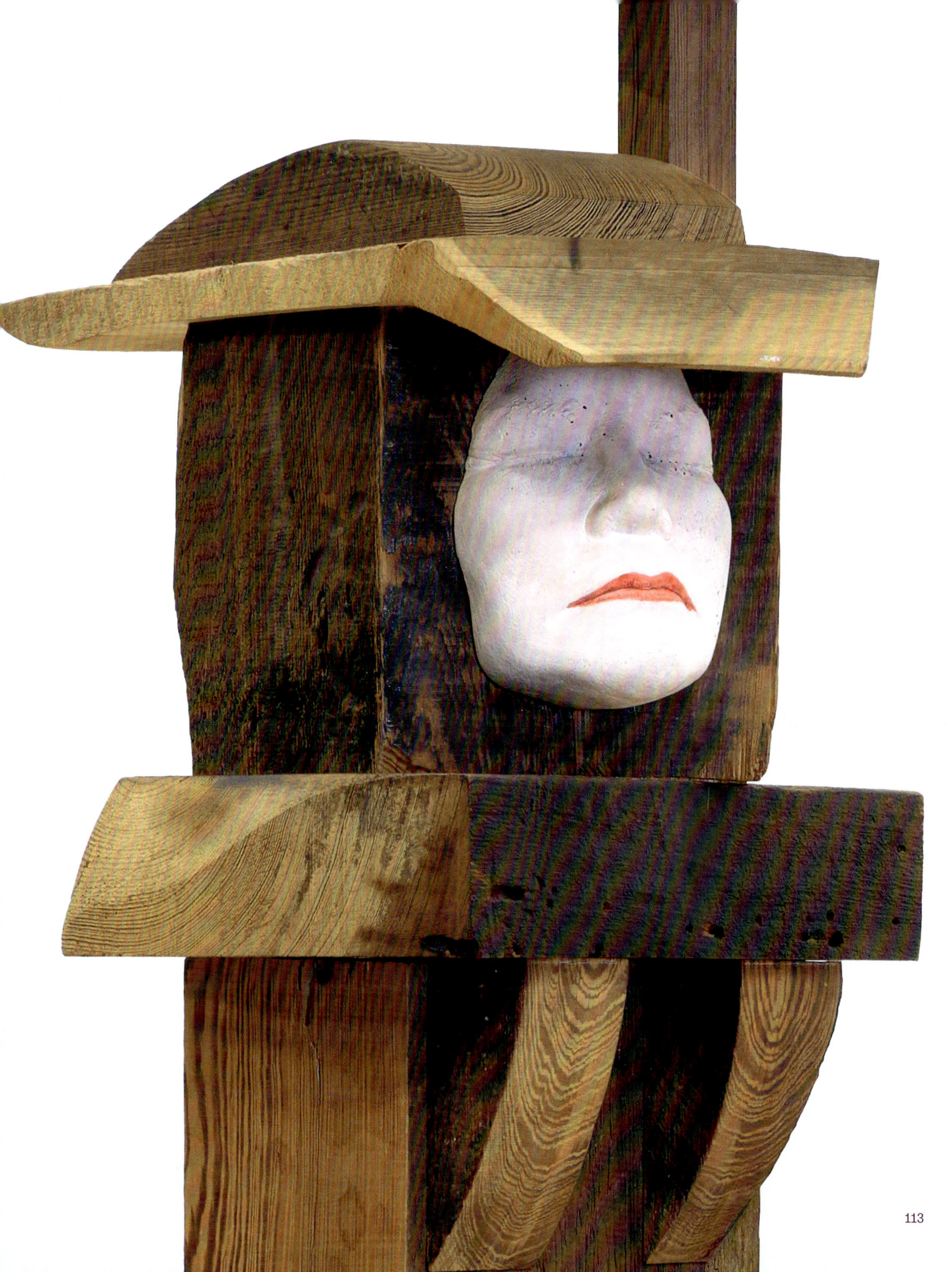

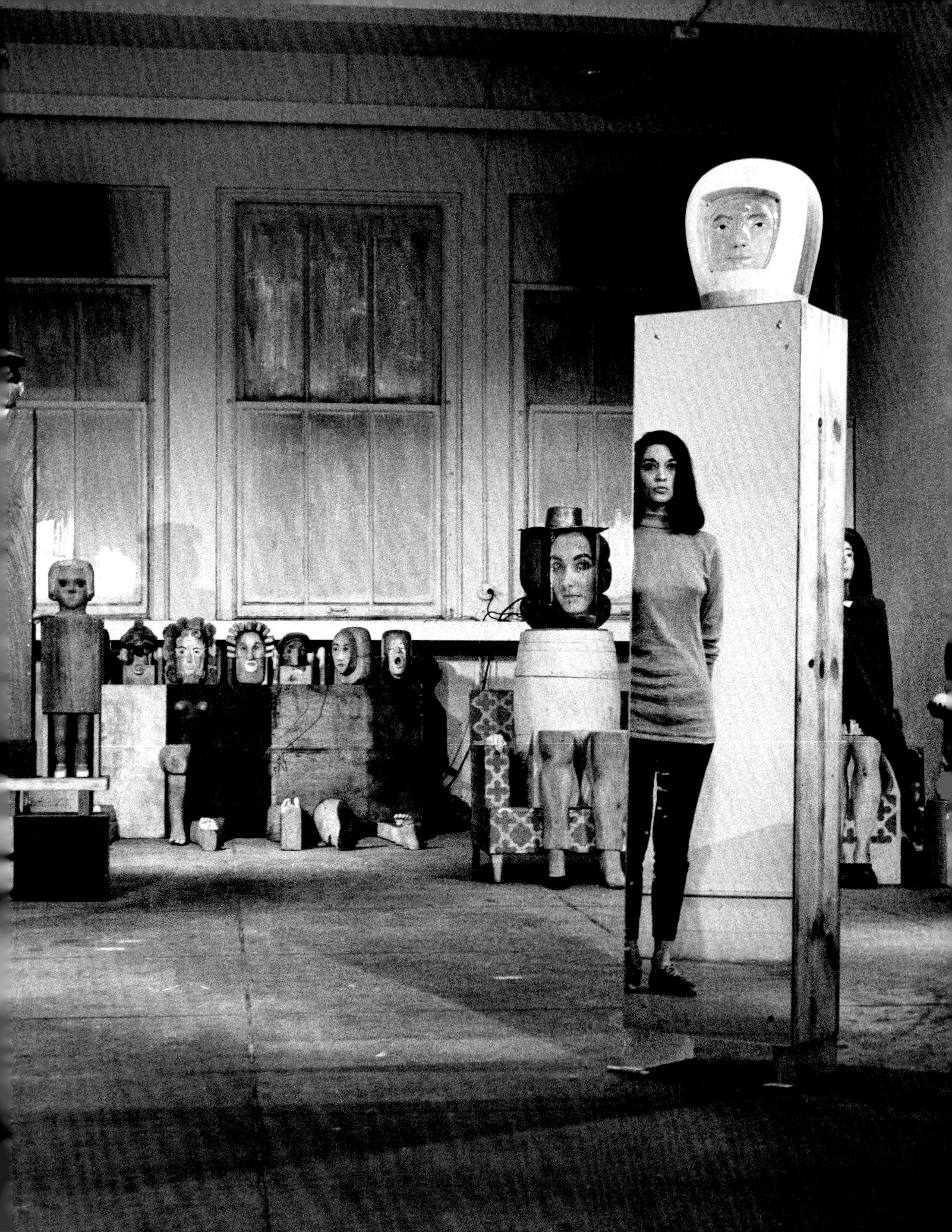

Biography

1930
Marisol is born María Sol Escobar on 22 May in Paris, the second child of Venezuelan parents. The family travelled widely as part of a nomadic Venezuelan elite. Later in life she would recall how "For the first years of my life, I thought everyone lived like this. But my only home is in art history."

c. 1935
The Escobar family returns to Venezuela from Paris. In subsequent years, they split their time between Caracas and the United States.

1941
Marisol's mother dies by suicide. Subsequently, Marisol stops speaking for several years, later observing, "I didn't want to sound the way other people did." During this period Marisol attends a French Catholic grammar school in Caracas.

1946-49
Attends high school in Los Angeles while taking night classes at the Otis Art Institute and the Jepson Art Institute.

1949
Marisol graduates high school and spends a year in Paris studying painting at the École des Beaux-Arts and the Académie Julian.

1950
Disappointed with the copy-based art training in Paris, Marisol returns to Los Angeles. She then moves to New York City where she continues her art studies with German-born American artist Hans Hofmann, among other teachers. Here and in Mexico she encounters Pre-Columbian art and becomes acquainted with American folk art.

1954
Around this time, Marisol shifts her focus from painting to sculpture, although she continues making works on paper. At the Cedar Tavern she befriends many of the first and second generation of Abstract Expressionist painters.

1955
She makes *The Hungarians* (1955), a depiction of an immigrant or refugee family arranged on

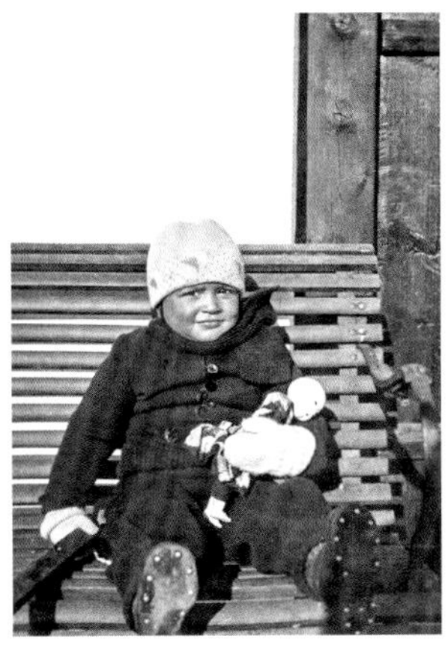

Marisol with a doll, c. 1932. Marisol Papers, Buffalo AKG Art Museum

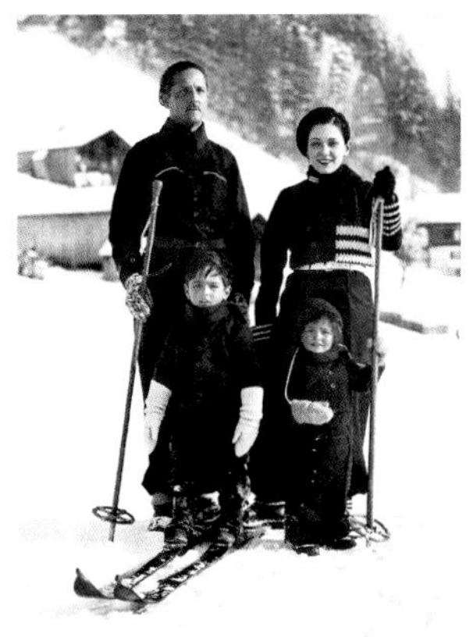

Marisol and her family skiing in Switzerland, from left: Gustavo Escobar, Josefina Hernández Escobar, Gustavo Escobar, and Marisol Escobar, c. 1933. Marisol Papers, Buffalo AKG Art Museum

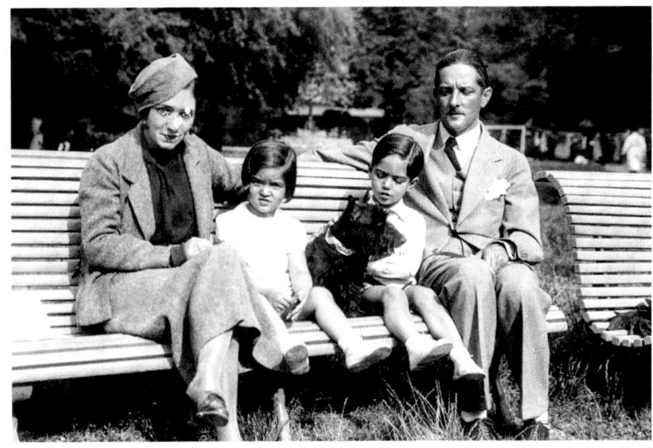

The Escobar family with pet dog, from left: Josefina Hernández Escobar, Marisol Escobar, Gustavo Escobar, and Gustavo Escobar, c. 1934. Marisol Papers, Buffalo AKG Art Museum

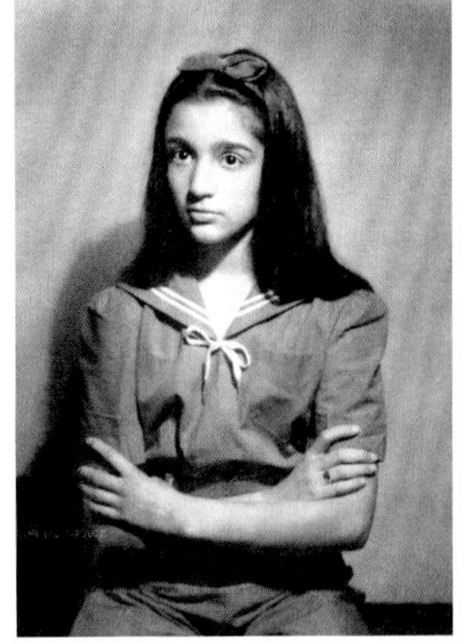

Marisol, 1943. Marisol Papers, Buffalo AKG Art Museum

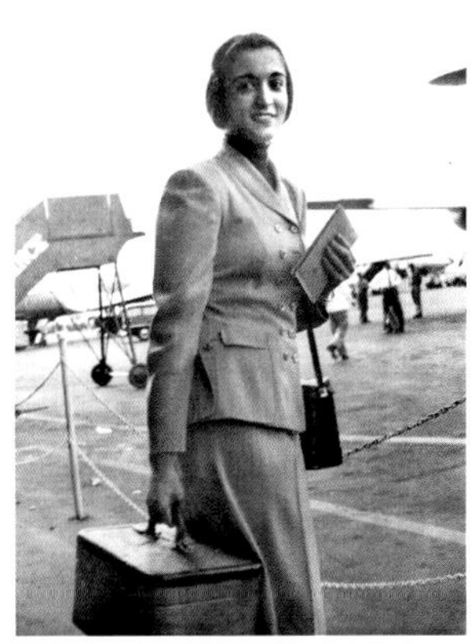

Marisol, c. early 1950s. Marisol Papers, Buffalo AKG Art Museum

Left: Marisol with her sculpture *La visita* (1964), 1964. Photo: Nancy Astor

a wooden cart with wheels. It is among her first sculptures to use found objects. Travels to Mexico and Paris.

1957
After her inclusion in several successful group exhibitions, she debuts sculptures in wood and terracotta in a well-reviewed solo exhibition at Leo Castelli Gallery, New York.

1958–59
Leaves New York for Rome and remains abroad for 18 months, where she spends time with friends, including Willem de Kooning. Having lived as an immigrant most of her life, Marisol feels she doesn't quite fit in any one place. She writes in her diary, "I am the Venezuelan, born in France, living in Italy – that has an English car with North American plates and Swiss insurance – and they want to ask me what nationality I am."

1960
Returns to New York and begins tracing her body in drawings and casting her face and other body parts for sculptures. She calls this period "the beginning of my real development".

1961
Around this time, she leaves Leo Castelli's gallery, telling him: "I want to be alone for a while and reconsider who I am and what I want to do."
In a legendary panel discussion on assemblage art held at the Artist's Club, Marisol is seated next to three male artists. She wears a mask and refuses to speak – a pointed criticism of the lack of women heard among artists leading discussions at the Club. The audience demands the mask's removal. When Marisol undid the strings, she revealed that her face was made up exactly like the mask. One of her works is shown in *The Art of Assemblage*, a landmark survey exhibition on artists' use of found objects at the Museum of Modern Art, New York.

1962
Several museums acquire works from her breakout solo exhibition at Stable Gallery, New York, which draws spectators by the thousands.

1963
Life magazine commissions Marisol to make a portrait of John Wayne. The double-page spread

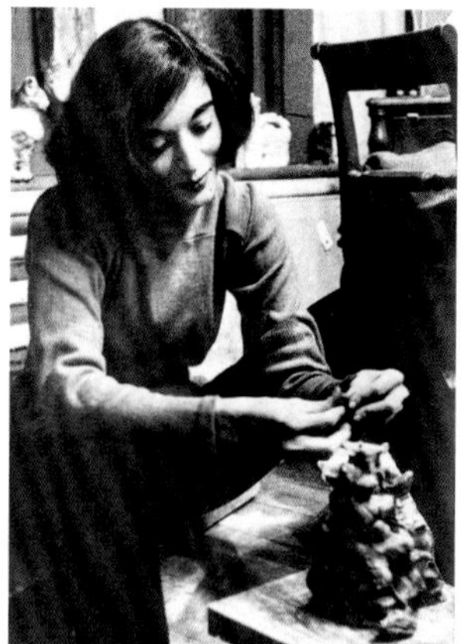

Marisol, 1957. Photo: Walter Sanders. Marisol Papers, Buffalo AKG Art Museum

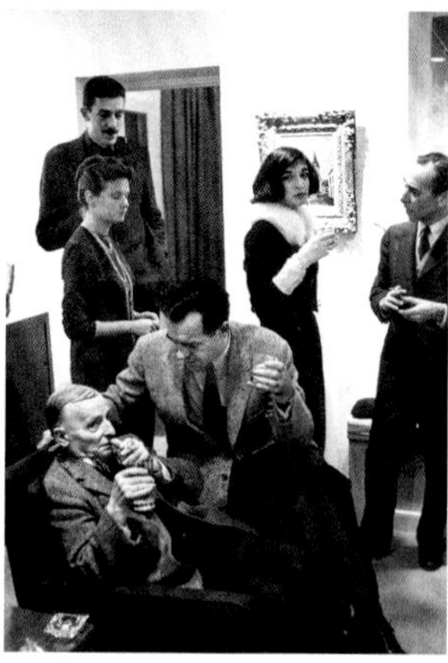

Marisol with gallerist Leo Castelli and others at unknown venue, 1957 Photo: Walter Sanders. Marisol Papers, Buffalo AKG Art Museum

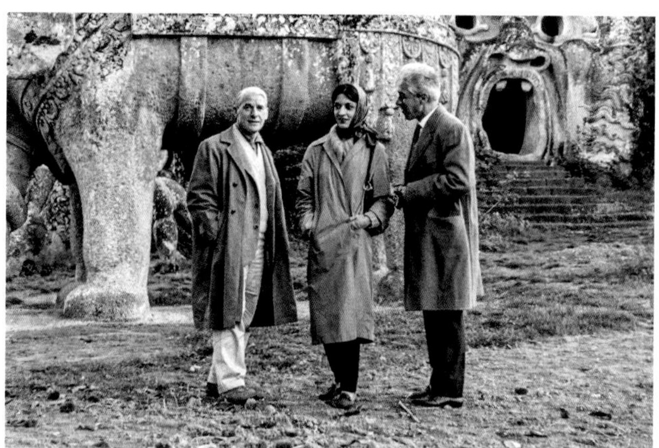

Marisol with artists Willem de Kooning (left) and Afro in the Sacro Bosco, Bomarzo, Italy, c. 1958–59. Marisol Papers, Buffalo AKG Art Museum

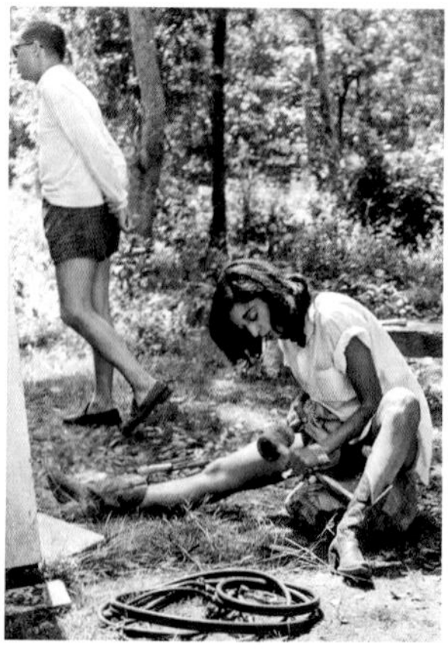

Marisol, c. early 1960s. Marisol Papers, Buffalo AKG Art Museum

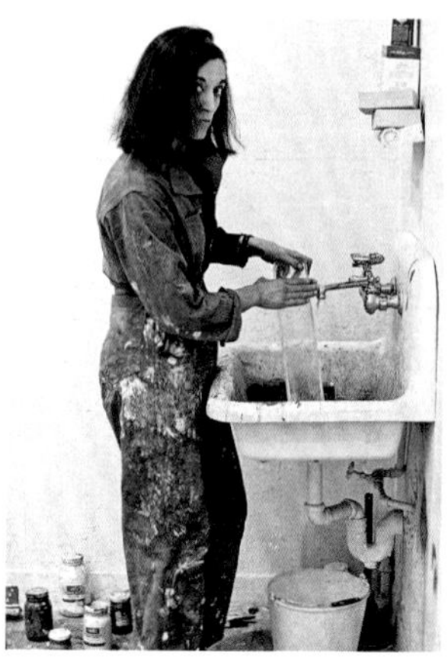

Marisol, c. 1960s. Photo: Hans Namuth. Marisol Papers, Buffalo AKG Art Museum

 Opposite: Marisol, 1964. Photo: Hans Namuth. Marisol Papers, Buffalo AKG Art Museum

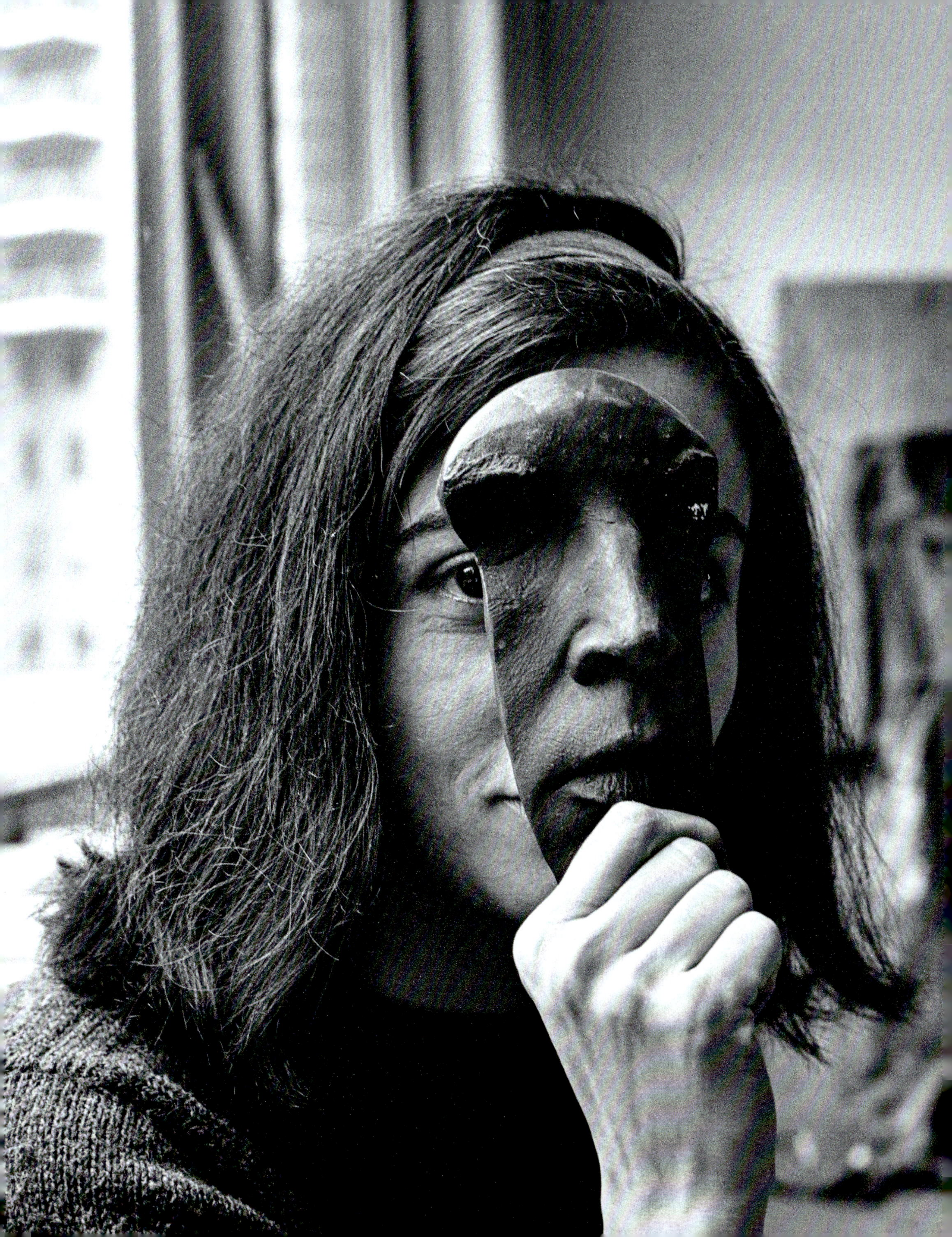

appears in the December issue. Marisol shows several works in a dedicated gallery in the group exhibition *Americans 1963* at the Museum of Modern Art, New York.

1964
Marisol meets Heinz Mack in London at the opening of *Group ZERO: Mack, Piene, Uecker*. They begin a friendship and, later, a love affair. She appears in two films by her friend Andy Warhol: *13 Most Beautiful Women* and *Kiss*. At her second solo exhibition at the Stable Gallery, half of the works are sold before the show opens. Marisol leaves the Stable Gallery to join Sidney Janis Gallery, which represents her until 1993.

1966
Shows a new body of figural sculptures in a solo exhibition at Sidney Janis Gallery, New York. Marisol has become a celebrity, with her work widely covered in both the art and fashion press. On a Saturday, three thousand people stood in line to enter the gallery.

1967
Makes the first of many public sculptures, beginning a new phase of her career as a maker of monuments, many of them in Venezuela. Marisol is commissioned by the *Daily Telegraph* to complete a portrait of the British royal family and Prime Minister Harold Wilson. She agrees, but with the stipulation that she can also include portraits of Charles de Gaulle, Francisco Franco and Lyndon B. Johnson. She travels to Europe to view her subjects and collect photographic source material.

1968
Represents Venezuela in a solo exhibition at the Venice Biennale. Much of the show travels to a solo exhibition at the Museum Boijmans Van Beuningen, Rotterdam. Marisol travels to India and Thailand, returning to New York in January 1969. Among the reasons she gives for this extended departure is a desire to escape the violence she witnessed in the suppression of antiwar rallies in the US.

1969
Learns to scuba dive over several months in Tahiti.

1970
Designs props and costumes for Louis Falco's

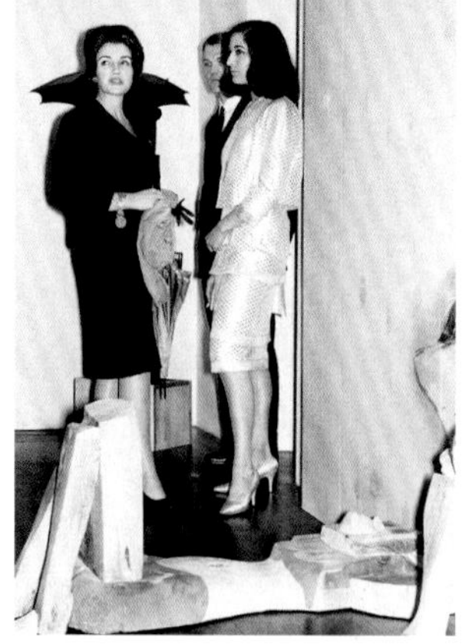

Marisol at the opening of the exhibition *Marisol*, Stable Gallery, New York City, 1962. Photo: Bela Cseh Marisol Papers, Buffalo AKG Art Museum

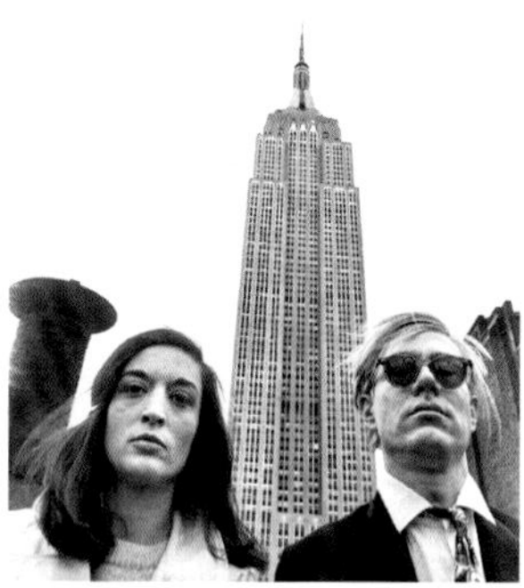

Warhol and Marisol in front of the Empire State Building, New York City, 1965 Photo: David McCabe

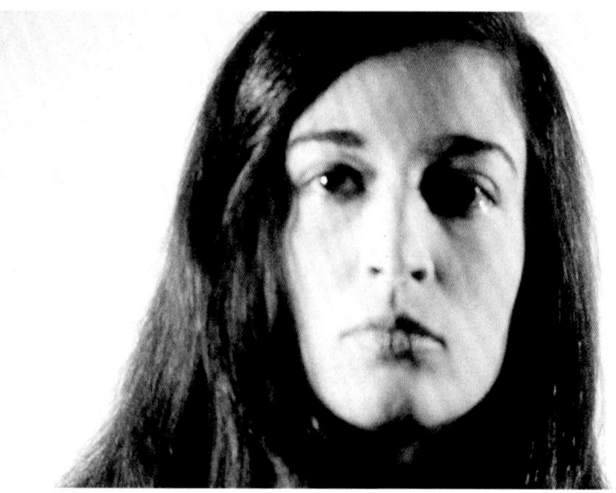

23. Andy Warhol: still from *Marisol* [ST202], 1964. Collection of The Andy Warhol Museum, Pittsburgh

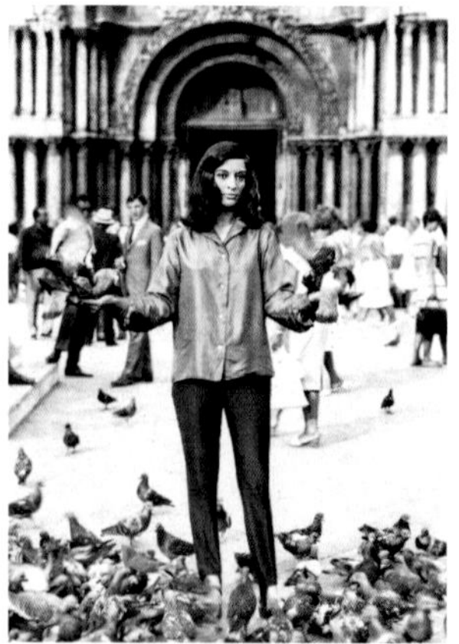

Marisol in Venice, c. 1968. Marisol Papers, Buffalo AKG Art Museum

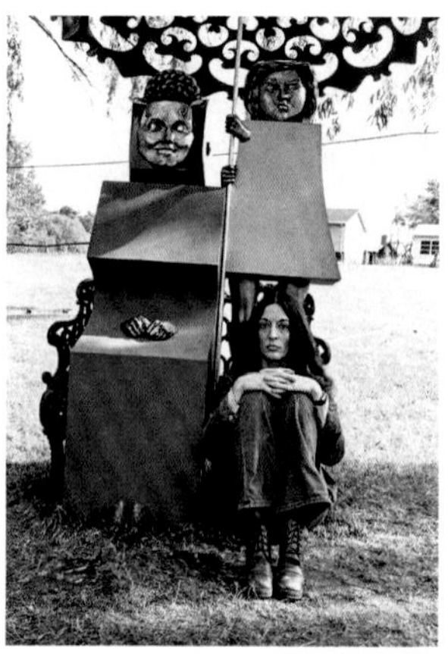

Marisol in front of *Mi Mama y Yo* (1968), 1974. Marisol Papers, Buffalo AKG Art Museum

dance *Caviar*, 1970. It is her first of many collaborations with a modern dance choreographer.

1973
Debuts ecologically conscious sculptures of anthropomorphised fish and pastel landscapes inspired by her scuba-diving in a solo exhibition at Sidney Janis Gallery. In response to an excoriating review of the exhibition, she drafts a letter to the author: "If you call my work folk art it is only because you are prejudiced about my South American background, Folk you." She has her first solo exhibition in Venezuela at Estudio Actual, Caracas.

1975
Debuts large-scale drawings and mutilated self-portrait sculptures in a solo exhibition at Sidney Janis Gallery. She laments: "Lots of people, but not selling well enough." Her set design for Martha Graham's dance *The Scarlet Letter* at Lincoln Center, New York, receives unfavourable reviews. Nevertheless, this piece marks the beginning of a years-long partnership with the Martha Graham Dance Company.

1976–79
In the latter half of the 1970s, she begins touring colleges and universities across the country, where she is a popular speaker. In 1977, Marisol produces oversized tiger costumes for Louis Falco's dance *Tiger Rag* at the Roundabout Theatre, New York.

1981
In *Artists & Artistes by Marisol*, a solo exhibition at Sidney Janis Gallery, Marisol, now 50 years old, debuts sensitive portraits of aging creative figures who inspired her, including Marcel Duchamp, Martha Graham, William Burroughs, Willem de Kooning, Louise Nevelson, Pablo Picasso and Georgia O'Keeffe.

1989
Begins exhibiting works addressing global inequities, including multifigure groups depicting impoverished families in Latin American countries.

1991
Marisol creates the *American Merchant Mariners' Memorial* at the Port of New York in Battery Park. Her solo exhibition *Magical Mixtures: Marisol*

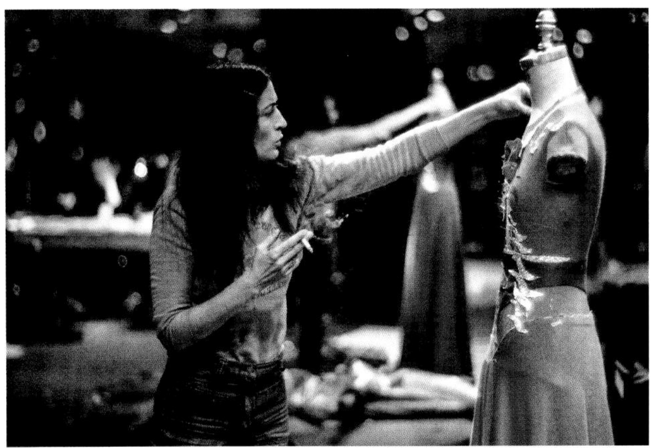

Marisol preparing costumes for *The Scarlet Letter*, 1975. Marisol Papers, Buffalo AKG Art Museum

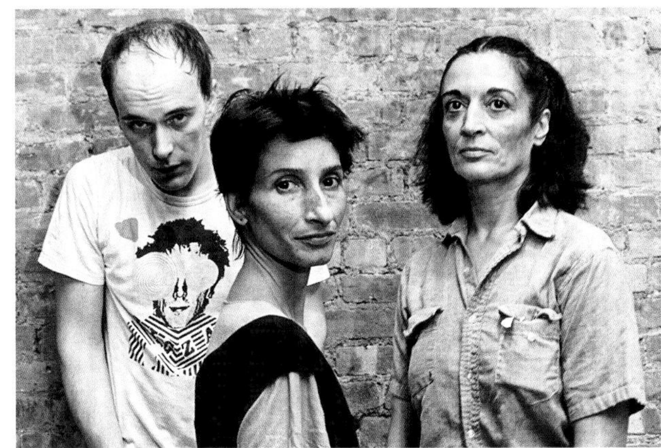

Adrian Sherwood, Elisa Monte and Marisol, 1984. Photo: Peggy Jarrell Kaplan Marisol Papers, Buffalo AKG Art Museum

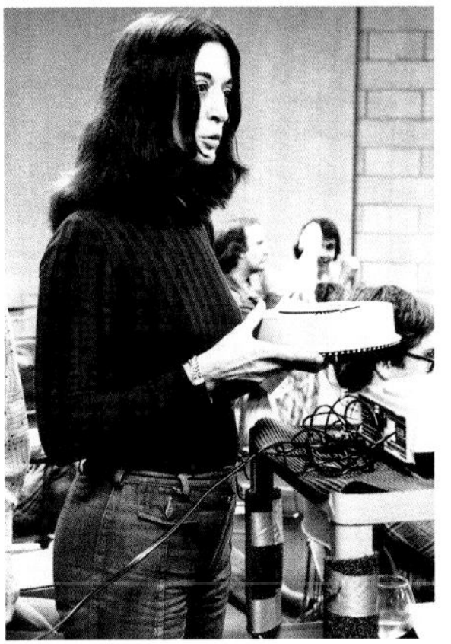

Marisol preparing for a slide lecture, c. 1976–79. Marisol Papers, Buffalo AKG Art Museum

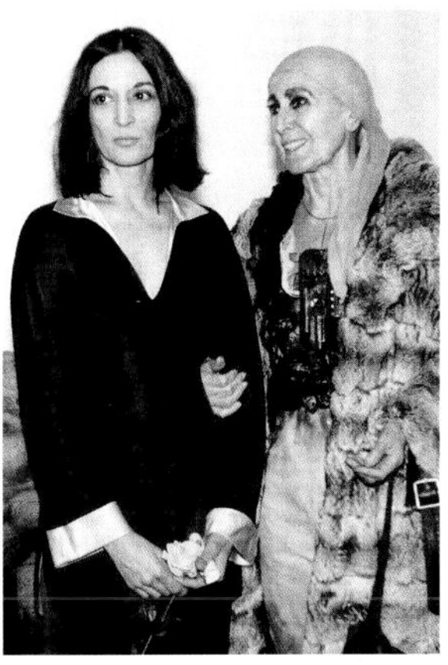

Marisol and Louise Nevelson, New York, 1981. Marisol Papers, Buffalo AKG Art Museum

Portrait Sculpture opens at the National Portrait Gallery, Smithsonian Institution, Washington, DC.

1995
Marisol is given what she recognises as her "first important retrospective in Japan" at the Hakone Open-Air Museum.

1996
Her first solo exhibition in Venezuela since 1973, at the Museo de Arte Contemporáneo de Caracas Sofía Ímber.

1998
In March, Marisol debuts portraits of Tom Thumb and René Magritte in her final solo exhibition at Marlborough Gallery, New York. She will not be represented by another gallery in her lifetime. The exhibition also includes *The Funeral* (1996), her final take on a subject from the 1960s.

2006
Around this time Marisol begins experiencing memory loss which is later diagnosed as Alzheimer's disease. Receives a Lifetime Achievement Award from the College Art Association's Women's Caucus for Art.

2014
Marisol: Sculptures and Works on Paper, the artist's last major exhibition in her lifetime, opens at the Memphis Brooks Museum of Art.

2016
On 30 April, Marisol dies of pneumonia in a hospital in New York. Tributes abound to the "Forgotten Star of Pop Art". She leaves her estate to the Albright-Knox Art Gallery (now the Buffalo AKG Art Museum), which was the first museum to acquire her work in 1962.

2023-25
Marisol: A Retrospective, the most substantial exhibition of her work ever, travels to the Montreal Museum of Fine Arts, the Toledo Museum of Art, the Buffalo AKG Art Museum and the Dallas Museum of Art. In 2025, Louisiana Museum of Modern Art presents the first major exhibition in Europe, which will later travel to Kunsthaus Zürich.

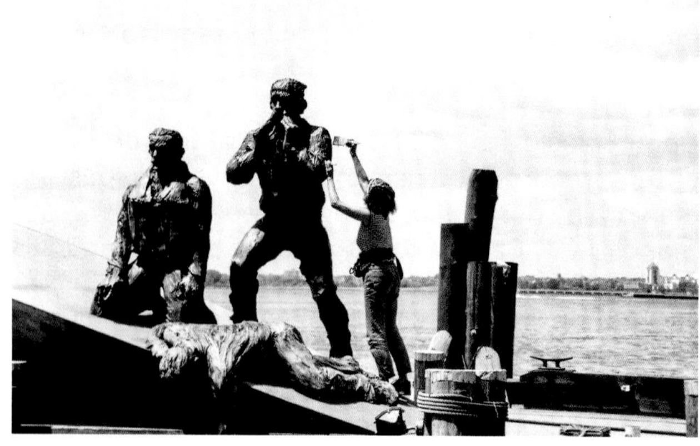

Marisol with *American Merchant Mariners' Memorial* (1991), The Battery, Manhattan, New York, 1992. Marisol Papers, Buffalo AKG Art Museum

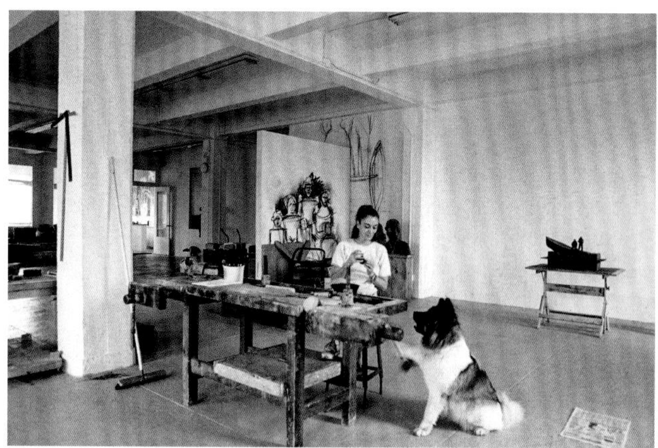

Marisol in the studio with her dog, c. 2001. Photo: Sanjiro Minamikawa Marisol Papers, Buffalo AKG Art Museum

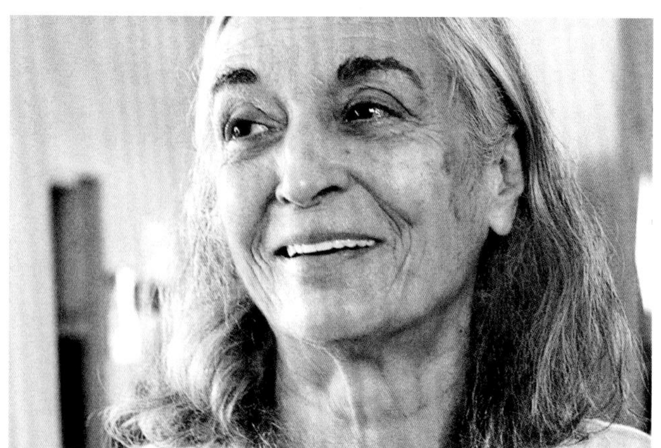

Marisol, c. 2007

This biography was adapted from the Chronology authored by Cathleen Chaffee and Julia Vazquez and published in *Marisol: A Retrospective* (Buffalo AKG Art Museum and DelMonico Books, 2023), pp. 194-212.

 Opposite: Marisol, 1989. Photo: Jack Mitchell. Marisol Papers, Buffalo AKG Art Museum

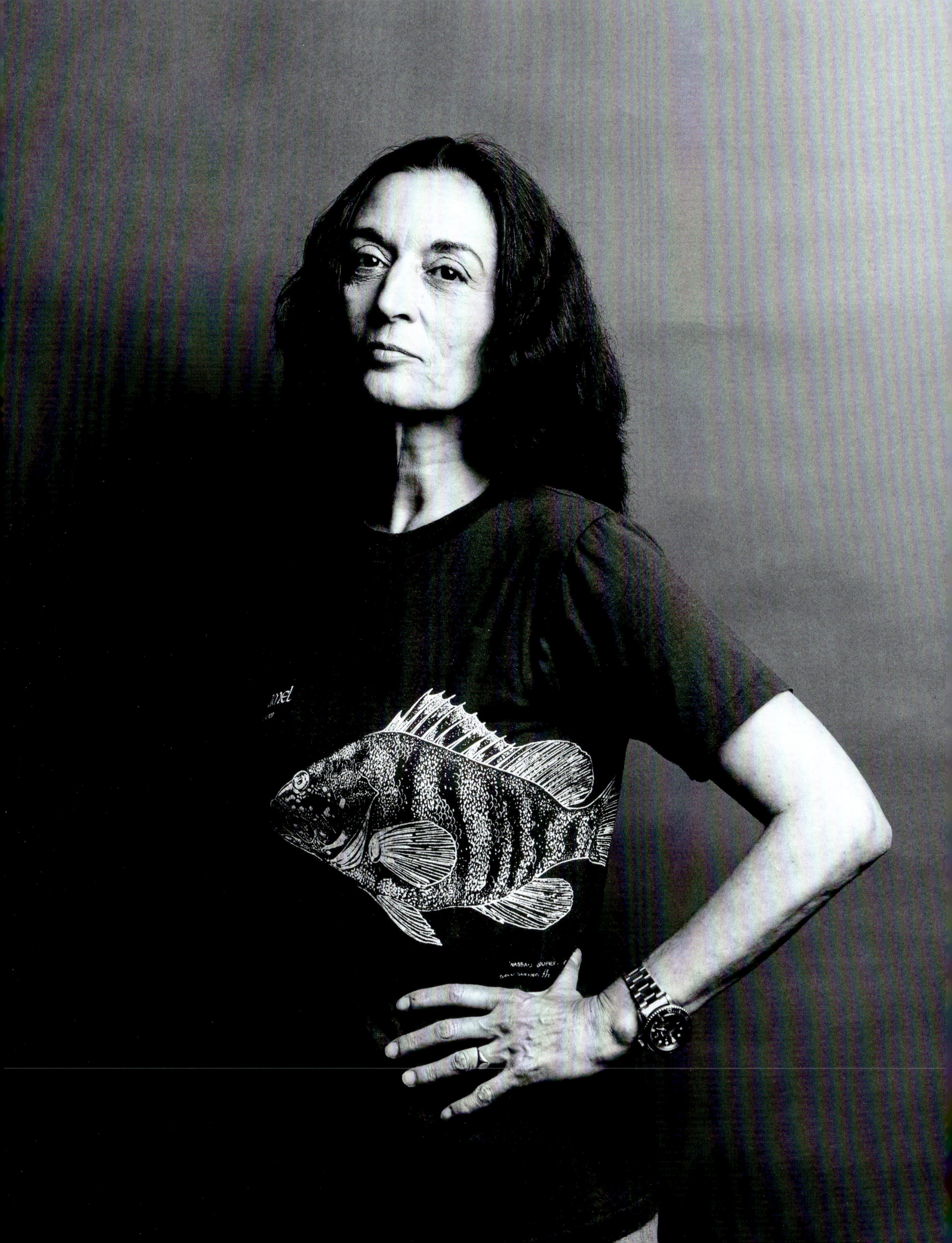

List of Works

1. **Untitled**, c. 1954-58
Ballpoint pen on paper,
40.2 × 30.2 cm
Collection Buffalo AKG Art Museum.
Bequest of Marisol, 2016 (2023:84)

2. ***The Hungarians***, 1955
Polychromed wood and metal cart,
92.7 × 68.6 × 52.1 cm
Collection Buffalo AKG Art Museum.
Bequest of Marisol, 2016 (2021:28)

3. **Untitled (Doll)**, c. 1955-63
Various fabrics, 38.1 × 15.9 × 5.1 cm
Collection Buffalo AKG Art Museum.
Bequest of Marisol, 2016 (2021:73)

4. **Untitled**, c. 1957
Coloured pencil and tape on paper,
31.8 × 22.9 cm
Collection Buffalo AKG Art Museum.
Bequest of Marisol, 2016 (2023:196)

5. **Untitled (Cat)**, 1957
Wood, stain and glass eyes,
61.6 × 25.4 × 19.1 cm
Collection Buffalo AKG Art Museum.
Bequest of Marisol, 2016 (2021:29)

6. **Untitled**, 1958
Coloured pencil, oil pastel and
ballpoint pen on paper, 22.9 × 29.8 cm
Collection Buffalo AKG Art Museum.
Bequest of Marisol, 2016 (2023:198)

7. **Untitled page from a sketchbook**,
c. 1958-60
Coloured pencil, crayon, gouache and
collage on paper, 41 × 30.5 cm
Collection Buffalo AKG Art Museum.
Bequest of Marisol, 2016 (2021:128.6)

8. **Untitled page from a sketchbook**,
c. 1958-60
Coloured pencil, crayon, gouache and
collage on paper, 41 × 30.5 cm
Collection Buffalo AKG Art Museum.
Bequest of Marisol, 2016 (2021:128.7)

9. ***My Wedding Cake***, 1959
Bronze, 50.8 × 29.2 × 23.5 cm
Collection Buffalo AKG Art Museum.
Bequest of Marisol, 2016 (2021:30)

10. ***Tea for Three***, 1960
Wood, acrylic and found objects,
162.6 × 55.9 × 68.6 cm
Collection Buffalo AKG Art Museum.
Bequest of Marisol, 2016 (2018:16a-d)

11. **Untitled**, c. 1960-65
Coloured pencil and crayon on paper,
53.7 × 37.2 cm
Collection Buffalo AKG Art Museum.
Bequest of Marisol, 2016 (2023:143)

12. ***Face Behind a Mask***, 1961
Coloured pencil on paper with
moulded plaster in wood shadowbox,
41.6 × 31.4 × 8.9 cm
Private collection, New York.
Courtesy of Craig Starr Gallery

13. ***Fingers and Faces***, 1961
Graphite on paper mounted on board,
37.2 × 26.4 cm
Collection Buffalo AKG Art Museum.
Bequest of Marisol, 2016 (2023:151)

14. ***Portrait of Betty***, 1961
Coloured pencil on cardboard with
cast plaster, 40.6 × 29.8 × 8.3 cm
The Fralin Museum of Art at the
University of Virginia. Bequest of
Buzz Miller. The Alan Groh-Buzz Miller
Collection. 1999.12.30

15. ***ABCDEFG & Hi***, 1961-62
Wood, paint, graphite, plaster,
umbrella, pearl and diamond,
193.7 × 93.3 × 93.3 cm
Collection Buffalo AKG Art Museum.
Bequest of Marisol, 2016 (2021:32a-d)

16. ***The Bathers***, 1961-62
Painted wood panel, graphite,
plaster cast and sculpted wood,
213.4 × 177.8 × 160 cm
Courtesy Crystal Bridges Museum of
American Art, Bentonville, Arkansas

17. ***Self-Portrait***, 1962
Pencil, cast plaster, fork, knife and
plate on paperboard in a painted
wood shadowbox, 83 × 49 × 10 cm
Private collection, New York.
Courtesy of Craig Starr Gallery

18. ***Baby Boy***, 1962-63
Painted wood and mixed media,
223.5 × 83.2 × 58.4 cm
Collection of Susan G. and Richard
M. Rieser, Jr., Palm Beach, Florida

19. ***Baby Girl***, 1963
Wood and mixed media,
188 × 88.9 × 119.4 cm
Collection Buffalo AKG Art Museum.
Gift of Seymour H. Knox, Jr., 1964
(K1964:8)

20. ***The Jazz Wall***, 1963
Wood, found objects, paper and paint
on wood, 241.3 × 271.8 × 35.6 cm
The Art Institute of Chicago. Gift of
The Leonard and Ruth Horwich Family
Foundation, 2016.91a-h

21. ***John Wayne***, 1963
Mixed media, 243.8 × 264.2 × 38.1 cm
Collection of the Colorado Springs
Fine Arts Center at Colorado College.
Julianne Kemper Gilliam Purchase
Fund, Debutante Ball Purchase Fund,
FA 1978.5

22. ***The Car***, 1964
Wood, plywood, paint, aluminium,
plaster, photography and sound,
120 × 307 × 91 cm
Collection Museum Boijmans Van
Beuningen, Rotterdam

23. **Andy Warhol (1928-1987)**
***Marisol* [ST202]**, 1964
16 mm film transferred to digital file,
black-and-white, silent, duration:
4:30 minutes at 16 frames per second
Collection of The Andy Warhol
Museum, Pittsburgh. Contribution
The Andy Warhol Foundation for the
Visual Arts, Inc.

24. ***La visita***, 1964
The Visit
Wood, plaster, leather and other
materials, 152.5 × 226 × 126 cm
Museum Ludwig, Cologne. Donation
Sammlung Ludwig 1976

25. ***Couple No. 1***, 1965-66
Wood, paint, fabric and electric
motor, 180.3 x 86.4 x 67.2 cm
Institute of Contemporary Art, Boston.
The Barbara Lee Collection of Art by
Women

26. ***Three Women with Umbrella***,
1965-66
Graphite and paint on wood with
plexiglass, found plastic umbrella and
stuffed bird, 205.7 × 144.8 × 83.4 cm
Collection of Betsy and Andy
Rosenfield

27. **Untitled**, c. 1966
Coloured pencil on paper,
43.2 × 35.6 cm
Collection Buffalo AKG Art Museum.
Bequest of Marisol, 2016 (2023:115)

28. ***Kiss***, 1966
Cast polyester, metal and light,
23.5 × 15.4 × 25.4 cm
Collection Buffalo AKG Art Museum.
Bequest of Marisol, 2016 (2021:34)

29. ***LBJ***, 1967
Acrylic and pencil on wood,
203.1 × 70.9 × 62.4 cm
The Museum of Modern Art, New
York. Gift of Mr. and Mrs. Lester Avnet.
1968, 776.1968.a-c.

30. ***Paris Review***, 1967
Silkscreen on paper, from an edition
of 150 plus an unknown number of
artist's proofs, 66 × 82.2 cm
Collection Buffalo AKG Art Museum.
Bequest of Marisol, 2016 (ANA290)

31. ***The Royal Family***, 1967
Mixed media, 304.8 × 198.1 × 182.9 cm
Richard and Carole Cocks Art Museum
at Miami University, Oxford, Ohio,
US. Gift of Paul and Mona Doepper.
1986.11

32. ***Self-Portrait Ring***, 1967
Gold, 3 × 3 × 3 cm
Mimi Trujillo

33. ***The Sun Bathers***, 1967
Wood, aluminium, copper and plaster
with pencil drawing, painted stands
and carpet, 230 × 145 × 160 cm
The Ella Fontanals Cisneros
Collection, Miami

34. ***Dominant Woman***, 1968
Plaster, paint, silver and glass,
15.9 × 8.9 × 7.6 cm
Collection Buffalo AKG Art Museum.
Bequest of Marisol, 2016 (2021:60)

35. ***Mi Mama y Yo***, 1968
Painted bronze and aluminium pole,
185.4 × 142.2 × 142.2 cm
Collection Buffalo AKG Art Museum.
Bequest of Marisol, 2016 (2018:15a-d)

36. **Untitled**, c. 1969
Coloured pencil on paper,
43.2 × 35.2 cm
Collection Buffalo AKG Art Museum.
Bequest of Marisol, 2016 (2023:125)

37. **Untitled**, c. 1969-72
Coloured pencil on paper,
35.6 × 27.9 cm
Collection Buffalo AKG Art Museum.
Bequest of Marisol, 2016 (2023:197)

38. ***The Death of Head and Leg***, 1969-73
Intaglio on paper, 69.9 × 102.9 cm
Louisiana Museum of Modern Art,
Humlebæk. Acquired with funding
from the sale of Louisiana Editions

39. **Untitled**, c. 1970s
Photographic print, 40.6 × 50.8 cm
Collection Buffalo AKG Art Museum.
Bequest of Marisol, 2016 (ANA407)

40. **Untitled**, c. 1970s
Felt-tip marker and coloured pencil
on paper, 47.6 × 61 cm
Collection Buffalo AKG Art Museum.
Bequest of Marisol, 2016 (2023:112)

41. ***Caviar***, 1970 (1977 revival)
Choreography by Louis Falco,
performed by the Louis Falco Dance
Company, music by Bobby Cole, décor
and costumes by Marisol
Video recording, black-and-white,
duration: 32 min.
Caviar presented courtesy of the
Louis Falco Dance Company, music
presented courtesy of the estate
of Bobby Cole and Superior Music
Publishing/Modern Works Music,
video recording courtesy of the New
York Public Library, Jerome Robbins
Dance Division

42. ***Fished***, 1970
Cast acrylic, from an edition of 75,
26.7 × 43.2 × 10.2 cm
Collection Buffalo AKG Art Museum.
Bequest of Marisol, 2016 (2021:36)

43. ***Greenfish***, 1970
Wood, varnish, plastic and plaster,
42.9 × 92.7 × 33.3 cm
Collection Buffalo AKG Art Museum.
Bequest of Marisol, 2016 (2021:33a-c)

44. ***Untitled Landscape***, 1970
Pastel on paper, 25.1 × 64.9 cm
Collection Buffalo AKG Art Museum.
Bequest of Marisol, 2016 (2025:2)

45. ***Untitled Landscape***, 1970
Pastel on paper, 27.3 × 74.9 cm
Collection Buffalo AKG Art Museum.
Bequest of Marisol, 2016 (2025:3)

46. ***Barracuda***, 1971
Wood, varnish and plastic,
55.9 × 352.4 × 14.6 cm
Collection Buffalo AKG Art Museum.
Bequest of Marisol, 2016 (2022:22a-c)

47. ***Diptych***, 1971
Lithograph on paper, 2 parts,
each 121.3 × 80.3 cm
Louisiana Museum of Modern Art,
Humlebæk. Acquired with funding
from the sale of Louisiana Editions

48. ***Five Hands and One Finger***, 1971
Lithograph on paper, 45.7 × 62.2 cm
Louisiana Museum of Modern Art,
Humlebæk. Acquired with funding
from the sale of Louisiana Editions

49. ***Needlefish I***, 1971
Wood, varnish, plastic and oil,
19.7 × 602.9 × 7.9 cm
Collection Buffalo AKG Art Museum.
Bequest of Marisol, 2016 (2022:14a-c)

50. **Untitled**, c. 1972
Coloured pencil and crayon on paper,
42.9 × 35.6 cm
Collection Buffalo AKG Art Museum.
Bequest of Marisol, 2016 (2023:123)

51. **Untitled**, c. 1972
Felt-tip marker on paper,
41.9 × 29.7 cm
Collection Buffalo AKG Art Museum.
Bequest of Marisol, 2016 (2023:70)

52. ***Saca la Lengua***, 1972
Lithograph on paper, 104.8 × 74.9 cm
Collection Buffalo AKG Art Museum.
Bequest of Marisol, 2016 (ANA363)

53. ***Triggerfish II***, 1972
Wood, varnish, plastic and oil,
104.1 × 214 × 25.4 cm
Collection Buffalo AKG Art Museum.
Bequest of Marisol, 2016 (2022:13a-b)

54. **Untitled**, 1972
Watercolour, coloured pencil and graphite on paper, 35.6 × 43.2 cm
Collection Buffalo AKG Art Museum. Bequest of Marisol, 2016 (2023:85)

55. **Untitled**, 1972
Coloured pencil on paper, 35.6 × 35.2 cm
Collection Buffalo AKG Art Museum. Bequest of Marisol, 2016 (2023:128)

56. ***Catalpa Maiden About to Touch Herself***, 1973
Lithograph on paper, 102.9 × 69.9 cm
Louisiana Museum of Modern Art, Humlebæk. Acquired with donations via louisiana.dk

57. ***Cultural Head***, 1973
Lithograph on paper, 73.7 × 55.9 cm
Louisiana Museum of Modern Art, Humlebæk. Acquired with funding from the sale of Louisiana Editions

58. ***The Fishman***, 1973
Wood, plaster, acrylic paint, resin and glass eyes, 173.4 × 71.1 × 84.5 cm
Collection Buffalo AKG Art Museum. Bequest of Marisol, 2016 (2021:37a-g)

59. ***I Hate You***, 1973
Intaglio on paper, 74.9 × 55.9 cm
Louisiana Museum of Modern Art, Humlebæk. Acquired with funding from the sale of Louisiana Editions

60. ***Needlefish III***, 1973
Wood, varnish and plastic, 21 × 750.6 × 12.4 cm
Collection Buffalo AKG Art Museum. Bequest of Marisol, 2016 (2022:16a-c)

61. ***Sexually Frustrated***, 1973
Coloured pencil on paper, 106.7 × 76.2 cm
Collection Buffalo AKG Art Museum. Bequest of Marisol, 2016 (2021:120)

62. ***All My Shoes for Ten Years***, 1974
Graphite, coloured pencil and crayon on paper, 182.9 × 237.5 cm
Collection Buffalo AKG Art Museum. Bequest of Marisol, 2016 (2025:1)

63. ***Face and Hand with Coca-Cola Bottle***, 1974
Plaster, paint and twine, 147.3 × 14 × 6.4 cm
Collection Buffalo AKG Art Museum. Bequest of Marisol, 2016 (2022:35)

64. ***Face with Rheingold Beer Can***, 1974
Plaster, paint, twine and Rheingold beer can, 165.1 × 16.5 × 6.4 cm
Collection Buffalo AKG Art Museum. Bequest of Marisol, 2016 (2022:31)

65. ***Face with Schlitz Beer Can***, 1974
Plaster, twine and Schlitz beer can, 106.7 × 15.2 × 3.8 cm
Collection Buffalo AKG Art Museum. Bequest of Marisol, 2016 (2022:29)

66. ***Gus Key (also called Face, Foot and Keys)***, 1974
Plaster, rope and metal keys, 111.8 × 15.2 × 6.4 cm
Collection Buffalo AKG Art Museum. Bequest of Marisol, 2016 (2021:38)

67. **Untitled**, 1974
Plaster, paint and twine, 25.4 × 19.1 × 8.3 cm
Collection Buffalo AKG Art Museum. Bequest of Marisol, 2016 (2022:32)

68. ***Bronze Knuckles***, 1975
Bronze, 4.9 × 14 × 5.7 cm
Collection Buffalo AKG Art Museum. Bequest of Marisol, 2016 (2021:62)

69. ***Bronze Knuckles***, 1975
Bronze, 4.1 × 17.5 × 7.9 cm
Collection Buffalo AKG Art Museum. Bequest of Marisol, 2016 (2021:61)

70. ***Coke Bottle I***, 1975
Plaster, paint, twine and Coca-Cola bottle, 133.4 × 14.6 × 6.4 cm
Collection Buffalo AKG Art Museum. Bequest of Marisol, 2016 (2022:30)

71. ***Coke Can***, 1975
Plaster, paint, Coca-Cola can and twine, 151.1 × 15.2 × 5.1 cm
Collection Buffalo AKG Art Museum. Bequest of Marisol, 2016 (2022:27)

72. ***An Elastic Skin Man***, 1975
Coloured pencil on paper, 101.6 × 76.2 cm
Collection Buffalo AKG Art Museum. Bequest of Marisol, 2016 (2021:115)

73. ***Fido's Paw***, 1975
Plaster and string, 33.7 × 14.6 × 7 cm
Collection Buffalo AKG Art Museum. Bequest of Marisol, 2016 (2022:28)

74. ***M. Marisol***, 1975
Terracotta, 22.9 × 20.3 × 8.3 cm
Collection Buffalo AKG Art Museum. Bequest of Marisol, 2016 (2021:43)

75. ***The Punch***, 1975
Plaster, paint and twine, 26.7 × 14 × 5.7 cm
Collection Buffalo AKG Art Museum. Bequest of Marisol, 2016 (2022:33)

76. ***Schaefer Can***, 1975
Plaster, paint, twine and Schaefer beer can, 165.1 × 15.2 × 5.1 cm
Collection Buffalo AKG Art Museum. Bequest of Marisol, 2016 (2022:34)

77. ***Women's Equality* from the *Kent Bicentennial Portfolio: Spirit of Independence***, 1975
Lithograph on paper, artist's proof 9 from an edition of 125 plus an unknown number of artist's proofs, 106.7 × 75.6 cm
Collection Buffalo AKG Art Museum. Bequest of Marisol, 2016 (ANA364)

78. ***The Scarlet Letter***, c. 1975-80
Pastel and coloured pencil on paper, 76.8 × 76.5 cm
Collection Buffalo AKG Art Museum. Bequest of Marisol, 2016 (2023:182)

79. **Untitled**, c. 1976
Photographic print, 20.6 × 25.7 cm
Collection Buffalo AKG Art Museum. Bequest of Marisol, 2016 (P2023:60)

80. **Untitled**, c. 1976
Photographic print, 27.9 × 35.6 cm
Collection Buffalo AKG Art Museum. Bequest of Marisol, 2016 (P2023:119)

81. **Untitled**, c. 1976
Photographic print, 50.8 × 61 cm
Collection Buffalo AKG Art Museum. Bequest of Marisol, 2016 (P2024:5)

82. **Untitled**, c. 1976
Photographic print, 50.8 × 61 cm
Collection Buffalo AKG Art Museum. Bequest of Marisol, 2016 (P2024:8)

83. **Untitled**, c. 1976
Photographic print, 40.6 × 50.8 cm
Collection Buffalo AKG Art Museum. Bequest of Marisol, 2016 (P2024:12)

84. **Untitled**, c. 1976
Photographic print, 40.6 × 50.8 cm
Collection Buffalo AKG Art Museum.
Bequest of Marisol, 2016 (P2024:15)

85. **Untitled**, c. 1970–80
Plaster, 8.9 × 12.7 × 48.3 cm
Collection Buffalo AKG Art Museum.
Bequest of Marisol, 2016 (2021:68)

86. ***Untitled***, 1976
Coloured pencil on paper,
100.3 × 69.9 cm
Collection Buffalo AKG Art Museum.
Bequest of Marisol, 2016 (2021:122)

87. ***My Father***, 1977
Wood, graphite, plaster, paint and quartz, 146.1 × 95.3 × 48.6 cm
Collection Buffalo AKG Art Museum.
Bequest of Marisol, 2016 (2021:45a-e)

88. ***Picasso***, 1977
Painted bronze, edition 3/3,
127.6 × 68.9 × 71.4 cm
Collection Buffalo AKG Art Museum.
Bequest of Marisol, 2016 (2021:46)

89. ***Portrait of Georgia O'Keeffe with Dogs***, 1977
Graphite and oil on wood,
133.7 × 134.6 × 154.3 cm
Collection Buffalo AKG Art Museum.
Bequest of Marisol, 2016 (2021:44a-i)

90. ***Thimble Thief***, 1977
Plaster, string and metal thimble,
4.5 × 26 × 10.2 cm
Collection Buffalo AKG Art Museum.
Bequest of Marisol, 2016 (2021:47)

91. ***Tiger Rag***, 1977
Choreography by Louis Falco, performed by the Louis Falco Dance Company, music by Michael Kamen, décor and costumes by Marisol and William Katz assisted by Willy Eisenhart, lighting by Richard Nelson
Digital transfer of NTSC SD video, black-and-white, duration: 30:25 min.
Tiger Rag presented courtesy of the Louis Falco Dance Company, video recording courtesy of the New York Public Library, Jerome Robbins Dance Division

92. ***Ecuatorial***, 1978
Choreography by Martha Graham, performed by the Martha Graham Dance Company, music by Edgard Varèse, capes by Marisol and executed by Halston, other costumes by Halston, set by Marisol with associate designer Karen Schulz, lighting by Gilbert V. Hemsley, Jr.
Digitization of video recording; 12 min.
Courtesy of Martha Graham Resources

93. **Underwater photograph taken Bonaire**, 1979–80
Photographic print, 40.6 × 50.5 cm
Collection Buffalo AKG Art Museum.
Bequest of Marisol, 2016 (ANA366)

94. **Untitled**, c. 1981
Watercolour on paper, 31 × 41 cm
Collection Buffalo AKG Art Museum.
Bequest of Marisol, 2016 (2023:90)

95. **Untitled**, c. 1981
Watercolour on paper, 32.5 × 41 cm
Collection Buffalo AKG Art Museum.
Bequest of Marisol, 2016 (2023:94)

96. ***Shoe***, c. 1982
Painted ceramic, 18.1 × 21.9 × 9.8 cm
Collection Buffalo AKG Art Museum.
Bequest of Marisol, 2016 (2021:74)

97. ***Lincoln***, 1984
Wood, plaster and charcoal,
254.3 × 51.1 × 52.7 cm
Collection Buffalo AKG Art Museum.
Bequest of Marisol, 2016 (2021:48a-d)

98. ***Set in Stone***, 1984
Choreography by Elisa Monte, performed by the Elisa Monte Dance Company, music by African Head Charge and produced and arranged by Adrian Maxwell Sherwood, décor and costumes by Marisol, lighting by Craig Miller
Digital transfer from NTSC SD video, colour, 23 min. 5 sec.
Set in Stone presented courtesy of Elisa Monte, music presented courtesy of Adrian Sherwood, video recording courtesy BAM Hamm Archives

99. ***Hand Holding Hand***, c. 1985
Bronze, 22.9 × 15.9 × 10.2 cm
Collection Buffalo AKG Art Museum.
Bequest of Marisol, 2016 (2021:70)

100. ***Querube's hands***, 1987
Plaster, 19.1 × 11.4 × 10.8 cm
Collection Buffalo AKG Art Museum.
Bequest of Marisol, 2016 (2022:26)

101. **Untitled**, 1987
Plaster, 20.3 × 10.2 × 8.3 cm
Collection Buffalo AKG Art Museum.
Bequest of Marisol, 2016 (2021:66)

102. ***Portrait of Bishop Desmond Tutu***, 1988
Wood, stain and fluorescent light,
195.6 × 201.9 × 139.4 cm
Collection Buffalo AKG Art Museum.
Bequest of Marisol, 2016 (2021:49a-c)

103. ***Horace Poolaw***, 1993
Wood, paint, graphite, plaster and metal wheeled base,
198.1 × 117.8 × 77.5 cm
Collection Buffalo AKG Art Museum.
Bequest of Marisol, 2016 (2022:21a-d)

104. ***The Funeral***, 1996
Paint, crayon and oil on wood,
142.9 × 319.4 × 85.7 cm
Collection Buffalo AKG Art Museum.
Bequest of Marisol 2016, (2021:54a-v)

105. ***Magritte***, 1997
Oil, charcoal, wood, plaster and umbrella, 139.1 × 65.4 × 71.8 cm
Collection Buffalo AKG Art Museum.
Bequest of Marisol, 2016 (2021:56a-d)

106. ***Mimi***, 1997
Wood, metal, plaster, charcoal and paint, 176.5 × 127 × 66 cm
Collection Buffalo AKG Art Museum.
Bequest of Marisol, 2016 (2023:1a-d)

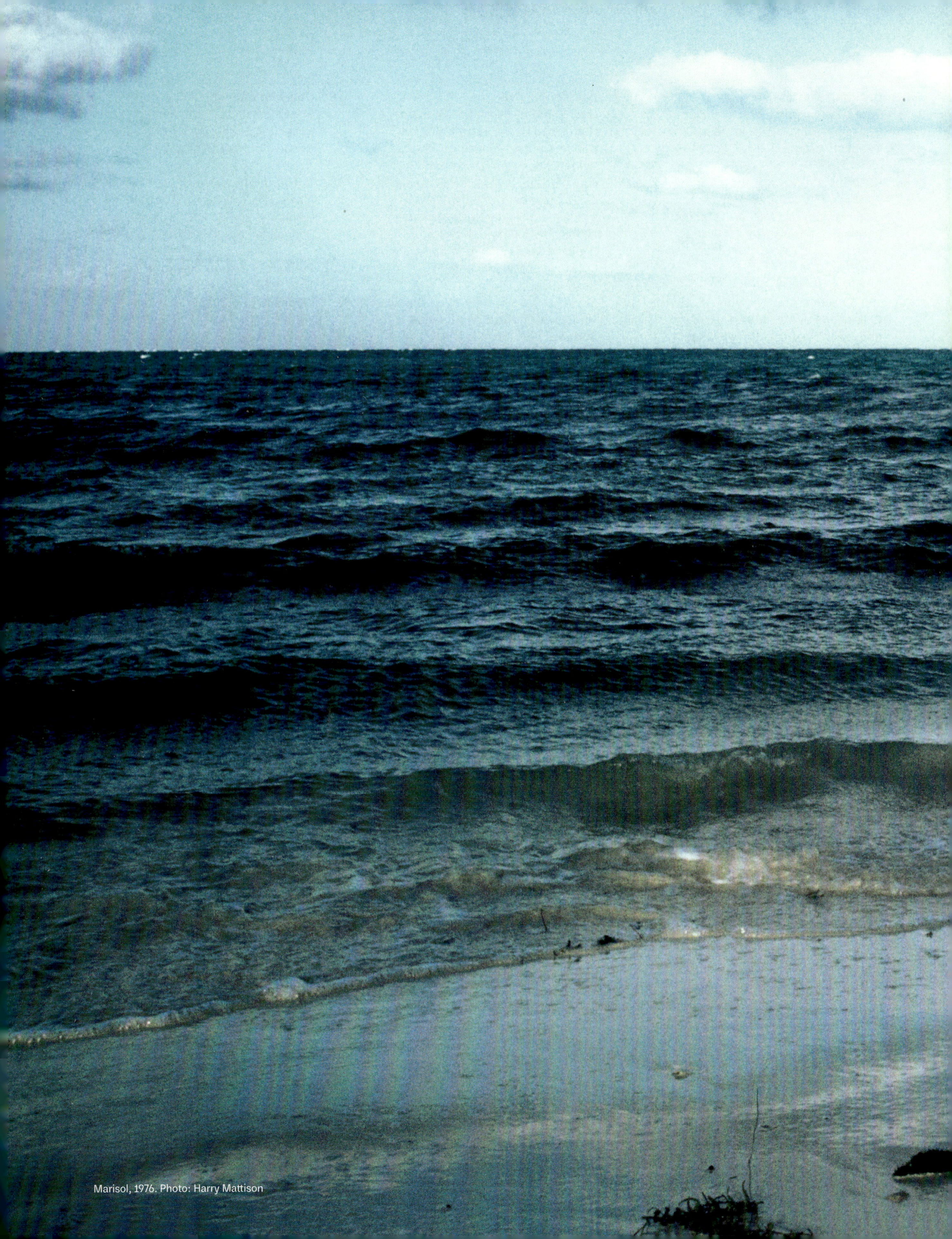

Marisol, 1976. Photo: Harry Mattison

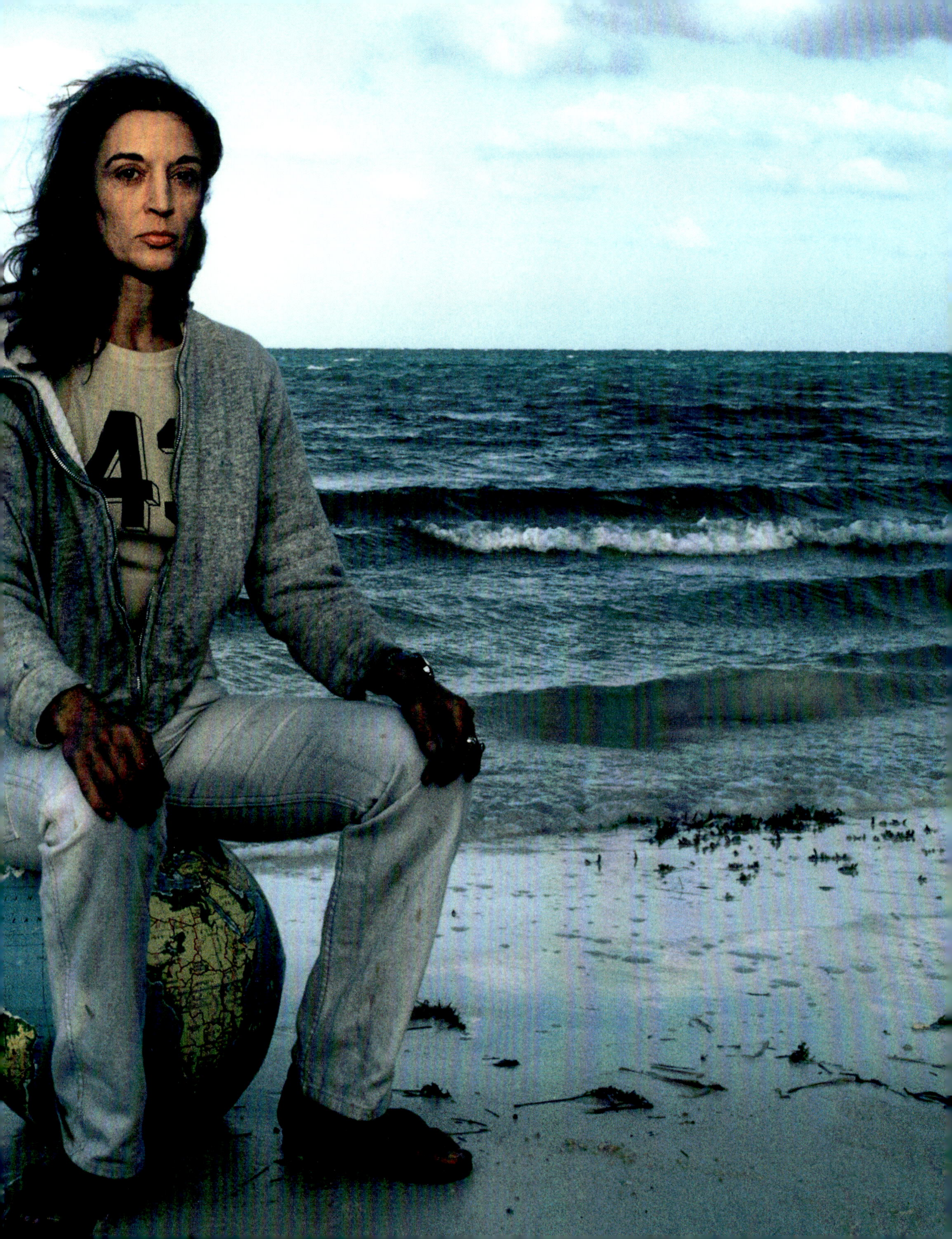

Marisol
© Louisiana Museum of Modern Art & the contributors

Edited by Lærke Rydal Jørgensen and Kirsten Degel
Graphic Design: Marie Lübecker
Translations: Glen Garner (foreword)
Proofreading: Henry Broome and Thomas Balfe
Photo Editors: Camilla Stephan and Grethe Røndal Christensen
Cover, front: Marisol, detail of *La visita,* 1964
Wood, plaster, leather and other materials, 152.5 × 226 × 126 cm
Museum Ludwig, Cologne. Donation Sammlung Ludwig 1976
Photo: © Rheinisches Bildarchiv, rba_202
Cover, back: Marisol with *La visita*, 1964
Photo: Nancy Astor. Marisol Papers Collection, Buffalo AKG Art Museum. Digital image: Amanda Smith, Buffalo AKG Art Museum
Endpapers: Marisol's studio in New York City, 2017. Buffalo AKG Art Museum Digital Assets Collection
Photo: Jason Mandella
Texts by Nicole Rudick, David J. Getsy and Delia Solomons have been peer-reviewed

Litho/Print: Narayana Press
ISBN: 978-87-93659-92-6
Printed in Denmark 2025
www.louisiana.dk

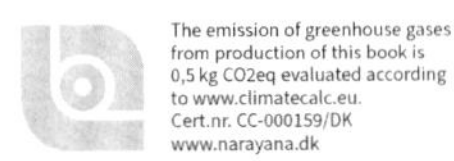

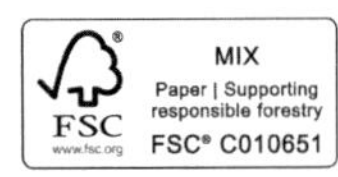

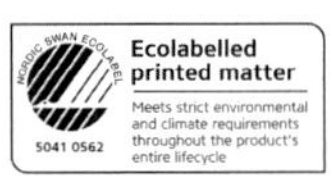

Photo
p. 3: © The Robert Mapplethorpe Foundation, Inc. Brenda Bieger, Buffalo AKG Art Museum; pp. 6, 7, 8, 9, 10, 11, 12, 13, 14 right, 16, 17, 18, 19, 22, 24, 25, 27, 28, 29, 30, 31, 32 bottom, 33 bottom, 34, 46, 64, 59, 60, 65, 71 bottom, 74, 75, 76, 77, 78, 79, 80, 82, 83 bottom, 84 bottom, 85, 86, 87, 90-91, 92, 93, 98-99, 100, 101, 102, 103, 104-105, 106, 107, 108, 109, 110, 111, 112, 113, 119 top: Brenda Bieger, Buffalo AKG Art Museum; p. 14 left: Archive Heinz Mack; p. 15: Bob Adelman © Bob Adelman Estate; pp. 20, 71 top: Thomas Barratt Photography; pp. 21, 23, 70: Courtesy of The Fralin Museum of Art at the University of Virginia; p. 31 top: Life magazine, 14 July 1958, Volume 45, No. 2.; pp. 32 top, 42-43: Collection of the Colorado Springs Fine Arts Center at Colorado College; pp. 33 top, 38-39: Jannes Linders; pp. 36, 37, 79 top: Brad Flowers; pp. 40-41: © Rheinisches Bildarchiv, rba_2024; p. 45: Edward C. Robison III; pp. 47, 94, 95, 96, 97: Courtesy Universal Limited Art Editions; pp. 48, 49 top: John D. Schiff; p. 49 bottom: Geoffrey Clements through Carroll Janis; pp. 50, 67 bottom: Digital image: Whitney Museum of American Art / Licensed by Scala; p. 51 top: Albin Dahlstrøm / Moderna Museet; pp. 51 bottom, 52 bottom: Louisiana Museum of Modern Art; pp. 52 top, 81, 84 top, 115, 116 middle, 116 bottom left, 118 bottom, 119 bottom left and right, 120 top: Marisol Papers, Buffalo AKG Art Museum. Digital Image: Amanda Smith, Buffalo AKG Art Museum; pp. 54-55, 69 bottom: © 2025 The Art Institute of Chicago / Art Resource, NY/ Scala, Florence; p. 57: Digital Image © The Museum of Modern Art/Licensed by SCALA / Art Resource, NY; p. 59 Miami University; pp. 60, 68 bottom, 69 top: Cisneros Fontanals Art Foundation CIFO; pp. 61, 66: Institute of Contemporary Art/Boston/ ARS, NY / VISDA; p. 67 top: Courtesy Sotheby's, New York; p. 68 top: Jack Mitchell/Getty Images; p. 114: Nancy Astor; p. 116 top left and right: Walter Sanders; pp. 116 bottom right, 117: © 1991 Hans Namuth Estate, Center for Creative Photography, University of Arizona; p. 118 top left: Bela Cseh; p. 118 middle: The Andy Warhol Museum (film clip); p. 118 top right: David McCabe; p. 119 middle: Peggy Jarrell Kaplan; p. 120 middle: Sanjiro Minamikawa; p. 120 bottom: Neuhoff Edelman Gallery, unknown photographer; p. 121: Jack Mitchell; pp. 126-127: Courtesy of Bill Katz/Harry Mattison

The catalogue is published on the occasion of the exhibition *Marisol*
Louisiana Museum of Modern Art, Humlebæk: 1 October 2025 – 22 February 2026
Kunsthaus Zürich: 17 April – 23 August 2026
Marisol is co-produced by Louisiana Museum of Modern Art, Humlebæk and Kunsthaus Zürich, and created in collaboration with the Buffalo AKG Art Museum

Curators: Kirsten Degel (Louisiana) and Sandra Gianfredda (Kunsthaus Zürich)
Consultant Curator: Cathleen Chaffee, Charles Balbach Chief Curator, Buffalo AKG Art Museum
Curatorial Coordinator/Registrar: Marianne Ahrensberg
Conservator/Exhibition Producer: Jesper Lund Madsen
Exhibition Architect: Gudrun Krabbe
Graphic Design: Marie Lübecker, Maria Hviid Bengtson and Thomas Joakim Winther

The exhibition at Louisiana Museum of Modern Art is supported by:

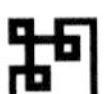
C.L. DAVIDS FOND OG SAMLING